A Treasury for All Seasons
Cookbook

Book I	Grill & Barbecue Cooking
Book II	Old-Fashioned Family Cookbook By Clarice L. Moon
Book III	Light Menus By Louise Mariano
Book IV	All Holidays Menus By Barbara Grunes

Ideals Publishing Corporation
Nashville, Tennessee

Book I
Grill & Barbecue
Cooking

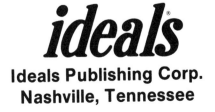

Ideals Publishing Corp.
Nashville, Tennessee

Contents

A very special thank you to the following for their cooperation and help in supplying selected recipes from their test kitchens and files:

American Dairy Association; American Meat Industry/National Livestock & Meat Board; American Spice Trade Association; 1980 Beef Industry Council; California Olive Industry; Florida Department of Natural Resources/Bureau of Marketing & Extension Services; Kohl's Food Stores; National Pork Producers Council; Ocean Spray; Reynolds Aluminum; Weber-Stephen Products Co.

Published by Ideals Publishing Corporation
Nashville, Tennessee 37214
Published simultaneously in Canada

Photo opposite:
Summer Fruit Basket, page 41
Grilled Steaks
Baked Potatoes
Lemonade

Cover recipe:
Orange and Beer Chicken, page 22

Barbecue Basics

Basic Types of Barbecues

There is a wide variety of barbecue grills, from the tabletop hibachi to crowd-size pit barbecues. Generally speaking, the principle of barbecue cooking, no matter what the size of the equipment, is application of even heat to the food to be cooked. The most commonly used barbecues are the round covered kettle, the rectangular firebox with a hinged lid, and the open brazier. For year-round use, gas and electric grills and charcoal cooking kettles are excellent.

Tools and Accessories

A wide range of gadgets and gizmos is readily available for making outdoor grilling easier, but only a few tools are really needed. You'll need long, sturdy tongs for moving hot coals and turning food, a long-handled fork and spatula, and insulated gloves and potholders. For brushing on sauces and marinades, use a nylon brush with a long handle. And, for greater accuracy when timing doneness, a meat thermometer is ideal.

When cooking large cuts of meat that require long cooking or meat with a large amount of fat, an aluminum drip pan is needed. This will catch the fat that would otherwise drip onto the coals and cause flare-ups. Drip pans can be purchased or you can make your own by following the easy instructions below:

How to Make a Drip Pan

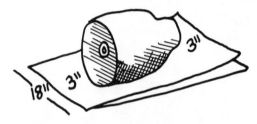

1. Tear off an 18-inch-wide piece of heavy-duty aluminum foil that is at least 3 inches longer than the food to be grilled. Fold to make a double thickness.

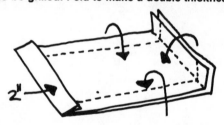

2. Fold all sides in about 2 inches. Press to flatten foil.

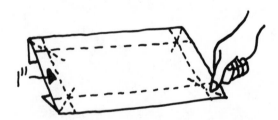

3. Turn foil over. Using your fingernail, score foil about 1 inch from edge. At corners, score diagonally to edge.

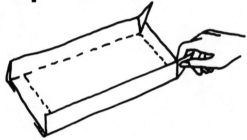

4. Fold edges up and pinch corners.

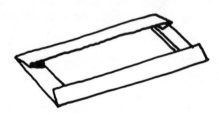

5. Fold corners flat against sides.

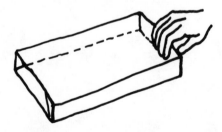

6. Bring all sides up to form pan. Place pan in center of firebox.

Spit Roasting Equipment

Most large grills are made so that spit roasting equipment can be added. Simply stated, this equipment consists of a support, motor, and a pair of forks that slide onto the spit rod at each end to hold the food in place. Before you buy any equipment, be certain that it will fit your barbecue model and that it is well built with a heavy-duty motor.

Cooking Methods

There are four cooking methods that cover the entire range of barbecue cooking. Choose whichever method is appropriate for the type of food you plan to cook.

Grill Cooking — Open Grill

Braziers, hibachies, and built-in brick barbecues are designed for open-grill cooking. Although most manufacturers of covered grills recommend cooking with the lid on, these grills can be used for open-grill cooking too.

Good candidates for open-grill cooking are hamburgers, hot dogs, and steaks. If the food to be cooked is thicker than two inches, cover it loosely with an aluminum foil tent to capture some of the heat. If possible, the grill should be about 6 inches above the heat source.

Cooking — Covered Grill

Most larger barbecue equipment is equipped with a lid which makes it possible to cook even on cold or windy days. The primary function of the cover is to make an oven to trap heat for even cooking. Air flow can be adjusted by opening or closing dampers located on the lid or under the firebox.

Covered grill cooking is especially suited to large food such as roasts or whole poultry. Cooking by this method reduces or eliminates a large amount of the flare-up problem that is often experienced in open-grill cooking, since the air flow is easily adjusted.

Spit Roasting

Nothing beats the succulent juiciness of spit-roasted roasts or poultry. Spit roasting attachments for braziers operate by adjusting the spit up or down in the slots in the hood. On covered, rectangular barbecue grills, the spit is stationary and the firebed is moved up or down as necessary. *(For more information, see page 24.)*

Skewer Cooking

This cooking method is appropriate for any type of food, be it meat, fish, fowl, or vegetables. Skewer cooking can be used with any type of grill and requires only the purchase of long skewers onto which the food is threaded.

Here are several things to remember when skewer cooking:

- Grill kebabs over a solid bed of coals just slightly larger than the area occupied by the filled skewers.
- When threading skewers, leave a little space between chunks of food for more even cooking.
- When cooking kebabs over charcoal, place skewers on the grill about 4 inches above coals.
- To prevent flare-ups from dripping sauces and marinades, remove skewers from the grill before basting.
- For even cooking, turn skewers frequently.

Starting a Charcoal Fire

About 30 to 40 minutes before you intend to cook, prepare the firebox and start the fire. First, line the grill box with heavy-duty aluminum foil to aid in clean up. Place the grill away from shrubs, dry wood, and buildings. The fire can be started with a liquid, a solid, or an electric starter. If using a liquid starter, pile the number of briquets needed in a pyramid in the center of the firebox. The number of briquets needed will depend on the type of equipment you are using and the food you plan to cook. Generally speaking, to prepare a solid bed of coals in an 18- to 22-inch barbecue grill, you will need 25 to 35 briquets. (If you are making a divided bed of coals, add 5 to 10 briquets.) Use liquid starter according to label directions. Ignite briquets. Do not add fire starter after the fire has started.

If using an electric starter, be sure to remove it from the firebox after 8 to 10 minutes to prevent damage to the heating element.

For using grills other than charcoal burning, follow manufacturers' instructions.

Shape of the Fire

Coals can be arranged in a single layer in the firebox for uniform direct heat or they can be arranged on either side of the firebox for indirect heating.

Barbecue Basics

The choice of direct or indirect cooking is usually made based on the food to be cooked. Fast-cooking meat, flat meat, and poultry are usually grilled over direct heat; large cuts of meat and fatty foods are cooked over indirect heat with a drip pan dividing the coal bed. *(See page 4 for directions on how to make your own drip pan.)*

For spit roasting, coals are arranged in a solid, rectangular bed about 6 inches across and extending 3 to 4 inches beyond the food to be spit roasted. When spit roasting, add 5 or 6 briquets every ½ hour to maintain temperature level.

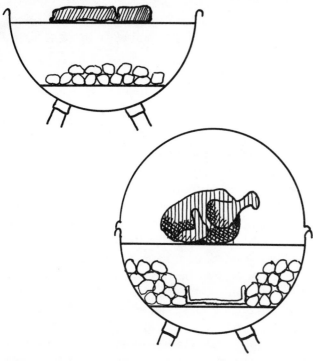

Ready — Start — Glow

Recipes in this book call for a cooking temperature of hot, medium-hot, or low. To determine the temperature of your fire, use the following tests:

HOT — Coals are lightly covered with gray ash. Temperature reading on a thermometer is about 400° F. To test by hand, hold your hand over the grill and near the fire. If you can hold it only 2 to 3 seconds, coals are hot.

MEDIUM-HOT — Coals are partially covered with ash as the fire begins to cool down. Temperature is about 350° F. Test by hand: 3 to 4 seconds.

LOW — Coals are completely covered with thick, gray ash. Temperature is about 300° F. Test by hand: 4 to 5 seconds.

Grilling Timetable

The time required for grilling will vary depending on the type of barbecue equipment, temperature of the coals, and distance from the heat source. *For more information, see individual recipes.*

Beef Cuts		
1 inch thick		
Rare	8 to 12 minutes	
Medium	12 to 15 minutes	
Well-done	15 to 20 minutes	
1½ inches thick		
Rare	10 to 15 minutes	
Medium	14 to 18 minutes	
Well-done	18 to 25 minutes	
2 inches thick		
Rare	18 to 20 minutes	
Medium	25 to 30 minutes	
Well-done	45 to 60 minutes	
2½ inches thick		
Rare	20 to 30 minutes	
Medium	35 to 45 minutes	
Well-done	60 to 75 minutes	

Ground Beef		
Hamburgers		
Rare	10 to 12 minutes	
Medium	14 to 15 minutes	
Well-done	18 to 20 minutes	

Lamb Chops and Steaks		
1 inch thick		
Medium-rare	8 to 16 minutes	
Well-done	18 to 25 minutes	
1½ inches thick		
Medium-rare	8 to 16 minutes	
Well-done	20 to 30 minutes	

Chicken		
Split or Cut-up		
25 to 45 minutes		

Ham Steaks		
1 inch thick		
30 to 35 minutes		
1½ inches thick		
35 to 45 minutes		

Fish Steaks		
1 inch thick		
6 to 9 minutes		
1½ inches thick		
8 to 12 minutes		

Beef

Marinated Beef Kebabs

Makes 6 servings

- ¼ cup vegetable oil
- 2 tablespoons cider vinegar
- 1 teaspoon celery salt
- 1 teaspoon onion salt
- ¾ teaspoon garlic salt
- ½ teaspoon salt
- ¾ teaspoon crushed leaf oregano
- ½ teaspoon black pepper
- 1 boneless beef shoulder *or* top round roast (about 2 pounds), cut in 1-inch cubes
- 6 medium mushroom caps
- 2 small zucchini, cut in ½-inch pieces

In a small saucepan, combine oil, vinegar, all salts, oregano, and pepper. Bring to boiling; remove from heat; let stand until cool. Place meat in a shallow pan or in a double plastic bag. Add mushrooms and zucchini. Pour marinade over meat and vegetables. Cover or seal. Refrigerate 4 to 6 hours, turning occasionally. Alternately thread meat and vegetables on 6 skewers. Grill over hot coals 10 to 15 minutes or until desired doneness, basting often with marinade.

Barbecued Short Ribs

Makes 4 servings

- 4 pounds beef short ribs
- 2 teaspoons salt
- ¼ teaspoon black pepper
- 1 can (8 ounces) tomato sauce
- ¼ cup catsup
- ⅓ cup packed brown sugar
- ¼ cup vinegar
- 2 tablespoons prepared mustard
- ½ cup chopped onion
- 1 clove garlic, minced
- 1 tablespoon chili powder

Place short ribs in a covered skillet. Grill slowly over low heat 1½ hours, turning occasionally. Season with salt and pepper. In a small saucepan, combine tomato sauce, catsup, brown sugar, vinegar, mustard, onion, garlic, and chili powder. Bring to boiling over medium heat, stirring frequently. Reduce heat; simmer 5 minutes. Dip ribs in sauce, coating all sides. Grill over low heat 20 to 30 minutes or until done, turning and brushing with sauce occasionally.

Spanish Olive Steak

Makes 4 servings

- 1 beef blade chuck steak (about 1½ inches thick, 3 to 3½ pounds)
- ½ cup sliced pimiento-stuffed olives
- 2 cloves garlic, sliced
- ⅓ cup lemon juice
- 3 tablespoons olive *or* vegetable oil
  Instant meat tenderizer
- 1 can (2 ounces) anchovy fillets, drained, optional
  Olive slices

Place steak in a shallow pan or in a double plastic bag. Top with olives. In a small bowl, combine garlic, lemon juice, and oil; pour over steak. Cover or seal. Refrigerate at least 8 hours, turning steak once. Drain marinade from steak; reserve marinade. Sprinkle on meat tenderizer following label directions. Grill about 4 inches from medium-hot coals 10 to 15 minutes on each side or until desired doneness. While steak is grilling, marinate anchovies in remaining olive oil marinade. Place steak on a heated serving platter. If desired, arrange anchovies in a criss-cross pattern over steak. Garnish with olive slices. Slice across the grain and serve.

Steak with Country Sauce

Makes 5 to 6 servings

- 1 teaspoon garlic salt
  Dash black pepper
- 1 beef flank steak (about 2 pounds)
- 2 slices bacon, diced
- 1 medium onion, chopped
- 1 tablespoon cider vinegar
- ½ cup grape jelly
- ½ cup catsup

Sprinkle garlic salt and pepper on both sides of steak. Place steak in a shallow pan or double plastic bag; set aside. In a large skillet, fry bacon until crisp; push to one side. Add onion; sauté until onion is golden. Add remaining ingredients; simmer until jelly melts and mixture is smooth, stirring occasionally. Pour sauce over steak. Cover or seal. Let stand 1 hour, turning steak once. Drain sauce from steak. Grill until desired doneness, brushing several times with sauce. Heat remaining sauce and serve with sliced steak.

Mustard Buttered Steaks

Makes 4 servings

    2 tablespoons butter, softened
    2 tablespoons prepared mustard
    4 T-bone steaks (about 1½ inches thick)

In a small dish, blend butter and mustard; set aside. Slash fat on edges of steaks to keep from curling. Grill over medium-hot coals 6 to 7 minutes on each side. Spread mustard butter over steak; grill 1 to 2 minutes. Turn steaks and spread the other side with mustard butter. Grill until desired doneness.

Tendered Beef

Makes 8 servings

    Instant meat tenderizer
    1 beef round or chuck roast (about 2 inches thick, 3 pounds)
    1 bottle (5 ounces) soy sauce
    ¼ cup packed brown sugar
    1 tablespoon lemon juice
    ¼ cup bourbon or brandy
    1 teaspoon Worcestershire sauce
    1½ cups water

Sprinkle meat tenderizer over roast following label directions. Place in a shallow pan or in a double plastic bag. In a small bowl, combine remaining ingredients; pour marinade over. Cover or seal. Refrigerate at least 6 hours, turning once. Drain marinade from roast; reserve marinade. Grill over hot coals 20 to 30 minutes or until desired doneness, turning and basting with marinade every 8 minutes.

Barbecued Top Sirloin Steak

Makes 4 servings

    1 beef top sirloin steak (1½ inches thick, 3 pounds)
    2 cups Burgundy wine
    1 teaspoon onion powder
    ¼ teaspoon garlic powder
    ¼ teaspoon black pepper

Place steak in a shallow pan or in a double plastic bag. Pour wine over steak; sprinkle on seasonings. Cover or seal. Refrigerate overnight, turning once. Drain marinade from steak; reserve marinade. Grill over medium-hot coals until desired doneness, basting occasionally with marinade.

Herb and Wine Barbecued Roast

Makes 8 servings

    1 beef round or shoulder roast (about 2½ inches thick, 3 pounds)
    2 cups dry red wine
    ½ cup vegetable oil
    2 tablespoons instant minced onion
    1½ tablespoons crushed leaf marjoram
    1 tablespoon salt
    ½ teaspoon minced garlic
    ¼ teaspoon black pepper

Place roast in a shallow pan or in a double plastic bag. In a small bowl, combine remaining ingredients; pour over meat. Cover or seal. Refrigerate about 24 hours, turning 2 or 3 times. Drain marinade from roast; reserve marinade. Grill over hot coals 20 to 30 minutes or until desired doneness, turning and basting with marinade every 8 minutes.

Mushroom Bacon Burgers

Makes 8 servings

    2 pounds lean ground beef
    1 can (8 ounces) mushroom stems and pieces, drained
    ¼ cup minced onion
    1 teaspoon salt
    ¼ teaspoon black pepper
    8 slices bacon, crisp-cooked and crumbled
    Butter Sauce, optional (recipe follows)
    8 hamburger rolls, split

In a large bowl, combine ground beef, mushrooms, onion, seasonings and bacon; blend well. Shape mixture into 8 patties. Chill 1 hour. Grill over medium-hot coals until desired doneness, brushing often with Butter Sauce, if desired. Serve on hamburger rolls.

Butter Sauce

Makes 1 cup

    ½ cup butter
    ½ cup chopped onion
    ½ cup catsup
    ¼ cup packed brown sugar
    1½ teaspoons chili powder
    1 teaspoon salt
    ⅛ teaspoon black pepper
    3 tablespoons Worcestershire sauce
    Dash hot pepper sauce

In a small saucepan, melt butter. Sauté onion until tender. Stir in catsup, brown sugar, chili powder, salt, pepper, and Worcestershire and hot pepper sauces. Simmer 5 minutes, stirring often.

Chuckwagon Steak

Makes 4 servings

    1 beef flank steak (about 1 pound)
    1 can (15 ounces) tomato sauce
    ¼ cup vegetable oil
    1 small onion, chopped
    2 tablespoons red wine vinegar
    1 teaspoon brown sugar
    1 teaspoon crushed red pepper flakes

Score both sides of steak with a sharp knife. In a small bowl, combine tomato sauce, oil, onion, vinegar, brown sugar, and red pepper flakes; blend well. Place steak in a shallow pan or in a double plastic bag. Pour sauce over steak. Cover or seal. Refrigerate at least 2 hours. Drain sauce from steak; reserve sauce. Grill over hot coals until desired doneness, turning and basting after 10 minutes. To serve, cut crosswise into thin slices. Heat remaining sauce and serve with steak.

Teriyaki Steak Sandwiches

Makes 12 servings

    Easy Hard Rolls (recipe follows) or 12
    French baguettes
    1 cup soy sauce
    ¾ cup vegetable oil
    3 tablespoons chopped onion
    1 clove garlic, crushed
    3 tablespoons brown sugar
    6 pounds beef skirt steaks

Prepare Easy Hard Rolls; set aside. In a large, flat baking dish or plastic container, combine soy sauce, vegetable oil, onion, garlic, and brown sugar; stir to dissolve sugar. Add steaks to marinade; turn to coat well. Refrigerate at least 2 hours. Drain marinade from steaks; reserve marinade. Grill steaks over hot coals 6 to 7 minutes on each side for medium well done. Cut into pieces and serve on sliced hard rolls or baguettes.

Easy Hard Rolls

Makes 12 rolls

    1 package (¼ ounce) active dry yeast
    1 cup warm water (110 to 115° F.)
    2 tablespoons vegetable shortening
    3 cups flour
    2 tablespoons sugar
    1¼ teaspoons salt
    1 egg white mixed with 1 tablespoon water

In a small bowl, sprinkle yeast over water; set aside to soften. In a large mixing bowl, cut shortening into flour, sugar, and salt until consistency of fine crumbs. Add yeast; stir until a soft dough forms. Cover and let rise in a warm, draft-free place for 20 minutes. Divide dough into 12 portions. Flatten each portion into a 4 x 3-inch rectangle. Roll up from long side; pinch edges to seal. Preheat oven to 375° F. Place rolls about 3 inches apart on a greased baking sheet. Brush with egg white. Cover and let rise for 1 hour. Bake 25 to 30 minutes or until golden. Cool on a wire rack. Split each roll lengthwise.

Wine Marinated Blade Steak

Makes 3 to 4 servings

    ½ cup red wine vinegar
    ½ cup water
    1 medium onion, chopped
    1½ teaspoons sugar
    1 teaspoon salt
    ½ teaspoon crushed leaf basil
    ¼ teaspoon celery seed
    ⅛ teaspoon black pepper
    1 beef chuck blade steak (¾ to 1 inch thick, 2 pounds)

In a small saucepan, combine vinegar, water, onion, sugar, salt, basil, celery seed, and pepper; blend well. Simmer 10 minutes, stirring occasionally; cool. Place steak in a shallow pan or in a double plastic bag. Pour marinade over steak. Cover or seal. Refrigerate 6 to 8 hours, turning once. Drain marinade from steak; reserve marinade. Grill steak over hot coals until desired doneness, basting often.

Italian Hamburger Kebabs

Makes 6 servings

    1½ pounds lean ground beef
    1 cup soft bread crumbs
    1 egg, lightly beaten
    2 tablespoons grated Parmesan cheese
    1¼ teaspoons salt
    1 teaspoon Italian seasoning
    1 can (8 ounces) whole mushrooms, drained
    Vegetable oil
    Sliced Italian bread, optional

In a small bowl, combine all ingredients, except mushrooms, oil, and bread; blend well. Shape into 1½-inch balls. Alternately thread meatballs and mushrooms on skewers. Brush on oil. Grill over hot coals 6 to 10 minutes, turning to cook all sides. Serve on sliced Italian bread, if desired.

Teriyaki Steak Sandwiches
Fire and Ice Tomatoes, 43

Beef

Hawaiian Burgers

Makes 8 servings

- 2 pounds lean ground beef
- ½ cup minced onion
- 2 teaspoons salt
- ¼ teaspoon black pepper
- 2 eggs
- 3 tablespoons prepared mustard
- 3 tablespoons catsup
- 1½ tablespoons soy sauce
- 8 pineapple slices, drained and heated

In a large bowl, combine ground beef, onion, salt, pepper, and eggs; blend well. Shape into 8 large patties; set aside. In a small bowl, combine mustard, catsup, and soy sauce; blend well. Brush mustard mixture over hamburger patties. Grill over low heat until desired doneness. Serve each topped with a pineapple slice.

Stuffing Stuffed Burgers

Makes 6 servings

- 1½ pounds lean ground beef
- 1½ teaspoons salt
- 1 cup seasoned stuffing mix
- 1 medium onion, grated
- ¼ cup butter or margarine
- 2 tablespoons lemon juice
- ¼ teaspoon black pepper
  Dash cayenne pepper

In a medium bowl, combine ground beef and salt; blend well. Divide into 12 equal portions. Flatten each portion between pieces of waxed paper into 5-inch patties. Do not remove patties from waxed paper. In a small bowl, combine remaining ingredients; blend well. Divide stuffing mixture among 6 of the hamburger patties. Top each with a second patty; press edges together to seal. Remove from waxed paper. Grill over medium-hot coals until desired doneness.

Cookout Burgers

Makes 6 servings

- 1½ pounds lean ground beef
- 1 cup instant nonfat dry milk
- 1 teaspoon salt
- 1 egg
- 1 tablespoon instant minced onion
- 6 hamburger rolls

In a large bowl, combine all ingredients, except rolls; blend well. Shape into 6 large, flat patties.

Grill patties over medium-hot coals until desired doneness. Serve on hamburger rolls.

Variation

Shape beef mixture into 18 balls. Alternately thread meatballs on a skewer along with tomato and green pepper wedges, mushrooms, and onions. Grill over medium-hot coals or hot coals, wrapped in heavy-duty aluminum foil, until desired doneness.

Grill Top Pizza

Makes 4 servings

- 1 pound lean ground beef
- 1 teaspoon salt
- 1 can (8 ounces) refrigerated crescent rolls, separated
- 1 jar (8 ounces) pizza sauce
- 1 medium onion, sliced
- 1 can (4 ounces) mushroom stems and pieces, drained
- ⅓ cup pitted ripe olives, sliced
- 4 ounces mozzarella cheese, shredded (1 cup)

Brown ground beef in a skillet on the grill; drain on paper towels. Sprinkle on salt. In the same skillet, arrange crescent roll dough in a circle; press edges together to form a crust. Spread half of the pizza sauce over the dough. Spoon ground beef over pizza sauce. Top with onion, mushrooms, and olives. Pour remaining sauce over all. Sprinkle on cheese. Cover tightly with aluminum foil. Grill over medium-hot coals 20 to 30 minutes or until crust is golden brown.

Pizza Patties

Makes 4 servings

- 1 pound lean ground beef
- ¾ cup cracker crumbs
- ½ cup grated mozzarella cheese
- 1 small onion, minced
- 1 clove garlic, minced
- ¼ teaspoon crushed leaf oregano
  Salt and pepper
- 1 egg, lightly beaten
- ¼ cup tomato paste
- ¼ cup red wine
- 4 hamburger rolls

In a large bowl, combine all ingredients, except rolls; blend well. Shape into 4 patties. Grill over hot coals until desired doneness. Serve on hamburger rolls.

Bean and Pepper Enchiladas

Makes 8 servings

    2 pounds lean ground beef
    1 medium onion, chopped
    2 teaspoons salt
    2 cans (16 ounces each) kidney beans, drained;
        reserve ½ cup liquid
    2 ounces Cheddar cheese, shredded (½ cup)
    1 clove garlic, minced
    1 can (16 ounces) tomatoes, undrained
    1 can (15 ounces) tomato sauce
    1 can (4 ounces) chopped green chilies, drained
    1 package (10 ounces) corn tortillas

Brown ground beef and onion in a large saucepan or Dutch oven directly on grill, if desired; drain fat. Sprinkle on salt; set aside. In a small saucepan, combine beans and ½ cup reserved bean liquid; mash with a fork; heat through. Add cheese and garlic to beans; blend well. Add remaining bean liquid, tomatoes, tomato sauce, and chilies to ground beef. Cover and cook 30 minutes. Dip 2 or 3 tortillas at a time into meat mixture to soften. Remove to waxed paper. Spoon about 3 tablespoons bean mixture down center of each tortilla; fold 2 sides in, overlapping in center and enclosing bean mixture. Tear off a piece of heavy-duty aluminum foil 2 inches longer than diameter of skillet; pierce several times with a fork. Place foil over meat mixture in skillet. Place filled tortillas on foil; cover and cook over low heat 15 to 20 minutes. Remove tortillas and foil. Serve with hot beef mixture.

Teriyaki Hamburger Steak

Makes 8 servings

    2 pounds lean ground beef
    1 teaspoon salt
    ¼ teaspoon black pepper
    2 tablespoons minced parsley
      Bottled teriyaki sauce
      Green onions, sliced diagonally
    8 hamburger rolls

In a large bowl, combine ground beef, salt, pepper, parsley, and 2 tablespoons teriyaki sauce; mix lightly. Shape into 8 1¼-inch-thick oval patties. Brush on teriyaki sauce. Grill over medium-hot coals until desired doneness, brushing occasionally with teriyaki sauce. Carefully remove steaks from grill with two spatulas. Serve on hamburger rolls topped with sliced green onions.

Vegetable Stuffed Burgers

Makes 4 servings

    8 ground steak patties, about ¼ inch thick
    8 green pepper strips
    4 onion rings
    4 slices tomato
    4 slices American cheese
      Salt and pepper
      Prepared mustard
    4 hamburger rolls

On a large square of heavy-duty aluminum foil, place 1 ground steak patty. Top with 2 green pepper strips, 1 onion ring, 1 tomato slice, and 1 cheese slice. Season to taste with salt, pepper, and mustard. Top with a second patty; press edges together to seal. Repeat for remaining steak patties. Wrap each securely in foil. Grill over low heat 10 minutes on each side. Serve on hamburger rolls.

Stuffed Green Peppers

Makes 6 servings

    1½ pounds lean ground beef
    2 tablespoons minced onion
    2 tablespoons minced green pepper
    1 can (15 ounces) tomato sauce
    ½ cup uncooked instant quick-cooking rice
    4 small tomatoes, peeled and quartered
    1 cup water
      Salt and pepper
    6 medium green peppers, tops removed, seeded
      Tomato sauce

Brown ground beef and onion in a skillet on the grill; drain fat. Add minced green pepper, tomato sauce, rice, tomatoes, water, and salt and pepper to taste; blend well. Simmer 15 minutes, stirring occasionally. Stuff peppers with beef mixture. Place filled peppers in a large baking pan. Top each with a spoonful of tomato sauce. Cover pan with aluminum foil. Grill over indirect heat 40 to 50 minutes or until peppers are tender.

Pork and Lamb

Barbecued Pork Loin Roast

Makes 6 to 8 servings

   1 boneless pork loin roast (3 to 4 pounds)
     Salt and pepper
 ¼ cup sugar
 ⅓ cup catsup
   3 tablespoons vinegar
   1 tablespoon prepared mustard
   1 tablespoon vegetable oil

Season roast with salt and pepper to taste. Cover loosely with a piece of heavy-duty aluminum foil. Grill over medium-hot coals for 1 hour. While roast is grilling, combine remaining ingredients in a small saucepan. Bring to boiling; reduce heat. Simmer 5 minutes, stirring often. After 1 hour, baste roast with barbecue sauce; continue basting every 15 minutes until roast is done, about 1½ to 2 hours (170° F. on a meat thermometer inserted in the thickest part of the roast).

Lamb and Vegetable Kebabs

Makes 6 servings

   1 carton (8 ounces) dairy sour cream *or* plain yogurt
   2 tablespoons lemon juice
   1 teaspoon olive *or* vegetable oil
   1 large onion, minced
 ½ cup snipped mint leaves *or* 4 teaspoons dried mint
   2 tablespoons chopped parsley
 ¼ teaspoon cayenne pepper
     Salt and pepper
   2 pounds boneless leg of lamb, cubed
 18 cherry tomatoes
   2 green peppers, cut in chunks
 18 pearl onions, peeled
 18 medium mushrooms
     Fluffy hot rice

In a small bowl, combine sour cream, lemon juice, oil, onion, mint, parsley, cayenne, and salt and pepper to taste; blend well. Place cubed lamb in a shallow pan or in a double plastic bag. Pour sauce over lamb. Cover or seal. Refrigerate at least 4 hours, turning occasionally. Remove from refrigerator 2 hours before grilling. Remove lamb cubes from sauce. Alternately thread lamb, tomatoes, peppers, onions, and mushrooms on skewers. Grill over hot coals about 5 minutes on each side or until lamb is desired doneness. Serve with rice.

Grilled Ham Steaks with Honey Glaze

Makes 4 to 6 servings

   3 tablespoons honey
   1 tablespoon Worcestershire sauce
   1 tablespoon dry mustard
 ¾ teaspoon ground ginger
     Dash black pepper
   1 center-cut ham slice (1 inch thick, about 2 pounds)

In a small bowl, combine honey, Worcestershire sauce, dry mustard, ginger, and pepper; blend well; set aside. Grease grill lightly. Place ham on grill 4 to 6 inches over low heat. Grill about 20 minutes, or until browned, turning and basting with honey glaze.

Variation

Brown Sugar Glaze: Combine 1 cup ginger ale and ½ cup brown sugar. Top ham with pineapple rings and cherries, if desired.

Orange Barbecued Ribs

Makes 3 to 4 servings

   3 pounds country-style pork spareribs
     Salt and pepper
 ⅓ cup orange marmalade
 ¼ cup lemon juice
 ¼ cup soy sauce
   1 clove garlic, minced
   2 teaspoons cornstarch
   2 tablespoons water

On a large double thickness of heavy-duty aluminum foil, arrange the spareribs in a single layer. Season lightly with salt and pepper. Fold foil up and over ribs; seal edge and ends with a double fold. Place on grill about 4 inches from coals. Grill about 45 minutes over medium-hot coals, turning once. While ribs are grilling, combine orange marmalade, lemon juice, soy sauce, and garlic in a small saucepan. Dissolve cornstarch in water; add to marmalade mixture. Cook over medium heat until thickened, stirring constantly. Remove ribs and foil from grill; discard foil. Dip ribs in sauce to coat well. Grill 5 minutes on each side directly on grill.

Pork/Lamb

Grilled Precooked Whole Ham

1 precooked whole ham (Allow ¾ pound per person)
Pineapple rings, optional
Maraschino cherry halves, optional

Remove any rind from outside and score fat in a diamond pattern, using a sharp knife. Grill over indirect heat 9 minutes per pound or until heated through. For best results, use a meat thermometer. After the first ½ hour, baste with Honey or Brown Sugar Glaze (recipes on page 15) or use your favorite glaze. If desired, garnish with pineapple rings and cherries about 15 minutes before the end of cooking time and brush with glaze.

Note: If using a partially cooked ham, such as smoked or cured, heat to an internal temperature of 160° F.

Western Barbecued Ribs

Makes 4 to 5 servings

4 pounds country-style pork spareribs, cut in serving pieces
1 teaspoon salt
¼ teaspoon black pepper
⅔ cup catsup
3 tablespoons cider vinegar
1 tablespoon soy sauce
2 tablespoons instant minced onion
1 tablespoon chili powder
¼ teaspoon garlic powder

Sprinkle both sides of ribs with salt and pepper. Fold foil up and over ribs; seal edge and ends with a double fold. Place on grill about 4 inches from coals. Grill about 45 minutes over medium-hot coals, turning once. While ribs are grilling, combine remaining ingredients in a small bowl; blend well. Brush generously over ribs. Grill over hot coals 5 minutes on each side.

Grilled Smoked Ham Steak

Makes 3 to 4 servings

2 uncooked smoked ham steaks, 1 inch thick
1 cup apple cider
3 tablespoons brown sugar
1 tablespoon dry mustard
3 whole cloves, crushed

Trim fat from ham. Score edges at 1-inch intervals. Place ham in a large skillet. Cover with boiling water. Bring to a boil; parboil 5 minutes; drain. In a small bowl, combine remaining ingredients; blend well. Pour over ham steaks in skillet; let stand 15 minutes. Drain marinade from steaks; reserve marinade. Grease grill with fat trimmings. Grill over medium-hot coals until browned on both sides, turning and basting often with marinade until done (160° F. on a meat thermometer).

Pork Sausage and Chili Scrambled Eggs

Makes 3 to 4 servings

6 eggs
¼ cup half-and-half *or* milk
1 teaspoon salt
¼ teaspoon chili powder
Dash black pepper
3 tablespoons butter *or* margarine
6 to 8 precooked sausage links

In a medium bowl, combine eggs, half-and-half, salt, chili powder, pepper, and butter; beat lightly until blended. Pour into a greased aluminum foil pan. Place pan on grill along with sausage links. Grill over low heat 10 to 15 minutes, turning sausages and stirring eggs frequently.

Pineapple Glazed Spareribs

Makes 6 servings

4 to 5 pounds country-style spareribs
1½ teaspoons salt
½ teaspoon garlic salt
½ cup apple *or* currant jelly
1 can (29 ounces) sliced pineapple, drained; reserve liquid
⅓ cup honey
1 tablespoon soy sauce
½ teaspoon ground ginger
¼ teaspoon red food coloring, optional

On a large double thickness of heavy-duty aluminum foil, arrange the spareribs in a single layer. Combine salts in a small dish; sprinkle evenly over ribs. Fold foil up and over ribs; seal edge and ends with a double fold. Place on grill about 4 inches from coals. Grill about 1 hour, turning once. While ribs are grilling, combine jelly and reserved pineapple liquid, honey, soy sauce, ginger, and food coloring, if desired, in a medium saucepan. Bring to boiling over low heat; stirring frequently. Simmer 5 minutes, stirring often. Remove ribs and foil from grill; discard foil. Dip ribs in sauce to coat well. Place ribs directly on grill. Grill 5 minutes and serve.

Lemon Marinated Kebabs

Makes 8 servings

- ¼ cup olive or vegetable oil
- ⅓ cup lemon juice
- 2 teaspoons salt
- 1 teaspoon black pepper
- 2 cloves garlic, minced
- 1 teaspoon crushed rosemary leaves
- 1 boneless leg or shoulder of lamb (2 to 2½ pounds) cut in 1-inch cubes
- 1 large onion, cut in chunks
- 2 large green peppers, cut in chunks
- 16 whole cherry tomatoes
- 32 pitted ripe olives

In a small bowl, combine olive oil, lemon juice, salt, pepper, garlic, and rosemary; blend well. Place lamb cubes, onion, and green pepper in a pan just large enough to hold all or in a double plastic bag. Pour marinade over meat and vegetables; toss lightly to coat. Cover or seal. Refrigerate at least 4 hours, turning occasionally. Drain marinade from meat and vegetables; reserve marinade. Alternately thread meat, onion, green peppers, tomatoes, and ripe olives on 16 skewers. Grill over hot coals, turning and basting often with marinade, until meat is no longer pink inside.

Leg of Lamb

Makes 6 servings

- 1 leg of lamb (about 8 pounds)
  Salt and pepper
- 2 cloves garlic, cut in slivers

Season leg of lamb with salt and pepper to taste. Make several slits in lamb with a sharp knife. Insert a garlic sliver in each slit. Place lamb in center of grill over indirect heat. Cook about 2 hours or until for well done (180° F. on a meat thermometer inserted in the thickest portion).

Orange Marmalade Leg of Lamb

Makes 6 to 8 servings

- 3 tablespoons teriyaki sauce
- ⅔ cup orange juice
- 1 clove garlic, minced
- 1 leg of lamb (about 8 pounds), butterflied
- ½ cup orange marmalade

In a small bowl, combine teriyaki sauce, orange juice, and garlic; blend well. Place lamb in a shallow pan or in a double plastic bag. Pour sauce over lamb. Cover or seal. Refrigerate at least 4 hours, basting occasionally with sauce. Grill lamb over hot coals about 1¼ hours or until desired doneness, basting occasionally with marinade. During the last half hour of cooking, stir marmalade into marinade and continue basting.

Ground Lamb Kebabs

Makes 6 servings

- ¾ cup instant minced onion, rehydrated; divided
- ¾ cup water
- 2 tablespoons butter or margarine
- 2 pounds lean ground lamb
- 1 egg, lightly beaten
- 2 tablespoons parsley flakes
- 1¾ teaspoons salt
- ¾ teaspoon ground cumin
- ⅛ teaspoon black pepper
- 12 whole cherry tomatoes
  Rice Pilaf (recipe on page 40), optional

Rehydrate onion in water 10 minutes. In a small skillet, melt butter. Add half of the onion; sauté 4 minutes. In a large mixing bowl, combine sautéed onion, lamb, egg, parsley flakes, salt, cumin, and pepper; blend just until mixed. Shape meat mixture into 2 x ¾-inch oval patties. Alternately thread meat and tomatoes on 6 skewers. Grill over hot coals 10 to 12 minutes or until desired doneness, turning often. Sprinkle kebabs with remaining onion. Serve with Rice Pilaf, if desired.

Scalloped Potatoes and Ham

Makes 8 servings

- 6 medium potatoes, peeled and sliced
- ¼ cup chopped onion
- 1 cup diced ham
- 1 can (10¾ ounces) cream of mushroom soup, undiluted
- ½ cup milk
- 1 teaspoon salt
- ⅛ teaspoon black pepper

Grease an 11 x 7-inch aluminum foil pan; set aside. In a bowl, combine sliced potatoes, onion, and ham; mix lightly. In a small bowl, combine soup, milk, salt, and pepper; blend well. Blend into potato mixture. Transfer to prepared pan. Grill, uncovered, over medium-hot coals about 1 hour or until potatoes are tender.

Variety Meats

Stuffed Frankfurters

Makes 4 servings

- 4 frankfurters
  Mustard
- 1 slice American cheese, cut in 4 strips
- 8 tablespoons sauerkraut
- 4 strips bacon
- 4 frankfurter rolls

Slit frankfurters lengthwise to make a pocket. Brush with mustard. Place a strip of cheese and 2 tablespoons sauerkraut in each slit. Wrap a strip of bacon spiral-fashion around each hot dog; fasten with toothpicks. Grill over hot coals until bacon is crisp. Serve on frankfurter rolls.

Franks with Pepper Relish

Makes 8 to 10 servings

- 2 tablespoons vegetable oil
- 2 medium onions, sliced
- 1 large green pepper, cut in thin strips
- 1 large red pepper, cut in thin strips
- ¼ cup water
- 1 teaspoon salt
- ¼ teaspoon Italian seasoning
- 1 pound frankfurters (8 to 10 per pound)
- 8 to 10 5-inch pieces French bread

In a large skillet heat oil; sauté onions until tender. Add green and red pepper strips; cook slowly for 15 minutes, stirring frequently. Add water, salt, and Italian seasoning. Bring to boiling; reduce heat. Cover and simmer 10 minutes. While relish is cooking, grill frankfurters over hot coals 8 to 10 minutes, turning occasionally. Cut through centers of bread to open but not separate. Place frankfurters on bread and top with pepper relish.

Grilled Hot Dogs

Makes 8 to 10 servings

- 1 pound frankfurters
- 8 to 10 frankfurter buns
  Catsup, mustard, relish, etc.

Grill frankfurters over medium-hot coals 12 to 15 minutes or until heated through. Top with your favorite condiments. Serve on frankfurter buns.

Brats 'n Kraut

Makes 4 servings

- 1 cup beer
- 4 bratwursts
- 1 can (16 ounces) sauerkraut
- 4 brat buns or hard rolls, split

Pour beer into an 11 x 7-inch pan. Place pan in center of grill. Brown bratwursts on side of grill over hot coals, turning with tongs until light brown. Place brats in beer. Cover and cook 25 minutes or until brats are done. About 15 minutes before end of cooking time, empty sauerkraut into a small pan. Place pan on grill and heat sauerkraut through, about 15 minutes. Serve bratwursts on buns or hard rolls topped with sauerkraut.

Sausage Italiano

Makes 4 servings

- 1½ tablespoons vegetable oil
- 2 large green peppers, cut in 1½-inch strips
- ¼ cup boiling water
- ½ teaspoon salt
- 4 Italian sausages
- 2 teaspoons vegetable oil
- 1 medium onion, chopped
- 1 clove garlic, minced
- 1 cup diced fresh tomatoes or 1 cup canned tomatoes
- 1 teaspoon sugar
- 1 teaspoon salt
- ¼ teaspoon black pepper
- ¼ teaspoon crushed leaf basil
- 4 hard rolls, split

In a large skillet, heat 1½ tablespoons oil. Add green peppers; sauté until tender-crisp. Add boiling water and salt. Cover and simmer 20 minutes or until tender; drain peppers; set aside. Grill sausages over direct heat 10 minutes or until lightly browned, turning to brown evenly on all sides. Move sausages to center of grill directly over drip pan. Cover and cook 25 to 30 minutes or until done. While sausages are grilling, heat 2 teaspoons oil in a medium saucepan; sauté onion and garlic until tender. Add tomatoes, sugar, salt, pepper, and basil. Bring to boiling. Simmer, uncovered, 25 minutes or until thickened. Add drained green peppers; blend well. Place sausages in hard rolls. Top with green pepper-tomato sauce and serve.

Grilled Hot Dogs
German Potato Salad, 44

Variety Meats

German Bratwurst

Makes 4 servings

- 2 tablespoons vegetable oil
- 4 bratwursts
- 1½ cups chopped onions
- 1 can (12 ounces) beer
- 2 tablespoons butter *or* margarine
- ½ teaspoon onion salt
- 4 bratwurst *or* frankfurter rolls
- ½ cup grated sharp Cheddar cheese
- 4 slices bacon, crisp-fried and crumbled

In a skillet, heat oil. Brown bratwursts on all sides. Add onions and beer. Simmer, uncovered, 20 to 30 minutes. In a small bowl, combine butter and onion salt; blend well. Spread onion butter on rolls. Slit each bratwurst lengthwise to within ½ inch of each end. Place bratwursts in rolls. Top with onion, cheese, and bacon bits. Place each on a piece of heavy-duty aluminum foil. Bring foil up and over sandwich; seal tightly. Grill 3 to 5 minutes or until cheese melts.

Knackwurst Bavarian

Makes 4 servings

- 4 slices bacon, crisp-cooked and crumbled; reserve drippings
- ½ cup chopped onion
- 4 cups shredded red cabbage
- 1 tart apple, peeled, cored, and chopped
- 1 tablespoon sugar
- ½ teaspoon salt
- ⅛ teaspoon black pepper
- ¼ teaspoon caraway seed
- 3 tablespoons cider vinegar
- 4 knackwursts

In a large skillet, heat reserved bacon drippings. Add onion; sauté until onion is tender. Add cabbage, apple, sugar, salt, pepper, and caraway seed; blend well. Cover and simmer 10 minutes. Add vinegar; blend well; set aside. Brown knackwursts on grill on all sides. Place in an 11 x 7-inch aluminum pan. Top with cabbage mixture. Cover and place on grill. Grill 15 to 20 minutes or until knackwursts are done and cabbage is tender. Top with bacon and serve.

Chicken Livers and Mushrooms

Makes 4 servings

- 1 pound chicken livers, rinsed and halved
- 2 tablespoons butter *or* margarine, melted
- ¼ cup dry white wine
- ½ cup dry bread crumbs
- ¼ teaspoon onion salt
- 4 large mushrooms, quartered
- 2 large tomatoes, cut in wedges
- ½ cup French dressing

In a medium bowl, combine livers, butter, and wine; stir lightly. Cover and refrigerate 30 minutes. In a small bowl, combine bread crumbs and onion salt. Drain liquid from livers. Roll in crumb mixture to coat well. Alternately thread livers, mushrooms, and tomato wedges on four 10-inch skewers. Brush with French dressing. Grill over medium coals 15 minutes or until livers are just browned, turning and basting once. Be careful not to burn livers.

Texas Liver and Onion Kebabs

Makes 4 servings

- Texas Barbecue Sauce (recipe follows)
- 1 pound beef, lamb, or calf's liver, thinly sliced
- 4 slices bacon
- 1 sweet red pepper, seeded and cubed
- 1 sweet green pepper, seeded and cubed
- 8 small white onions, peeled and parboiled

Prepare Texas Barbecue Sauce; set aside. Cut liver into 1-inch strips. Place bacon on a flat surface; top each piece with 1 or 2 strips liver. Alternately thread liver and bacon accordian-style onto skewers along with peppers and onions. Brush with barbecue sauce. Grill over hot coals 15 minutes or just until bacon is crisp, turning and brushing often with sauce. Do not overcook.

Texas Barbecue Sauce

Makes about 1½ cups

- ½ cup cold coffee
- ½ cup Worcestershire sauce
- ½ cup catsup
- ¼ cup cider vinegar
- ¼ cup packed brown sugar
- 1 tablespoon chili powder
- 1½ teaspoons salt
- ½ cup chopped onion
- 2 teaspoons minced jalapeno peppers
- ½ teaspoon garlic powder

In a saucepan, combine all ingredients. Simmer, uncovered, 30 minutes, stirring frequently.

Chicken Kebabs with Pineapple

Makes 3 to 4 servings

    1 can (16 ounces) pineapple chunks, drained;
      reserve juice
    4 teaspoons soy sauce
    ½ teaspoon grated fresh gingerroot
    2 green peppers, cut in chunks
    4 whole chicken breasts, skinned and boned

In a small bowl, combine reserved pineapple juice, soy sauce, and gingerroot; blend well. Cut chicken breasts into large chunks. Alternately thread chicken, peppers, and pineapple chunks onto skewers. Place skewers in a shallow pan. Pour marinade over skewers. Let stand 1 hour. Drain marinade from kebabs; reserve marinade. Grill kebabs over medium-hot coals about 20 minutes or until chicken is tender, turning and basting often.

Stuffed Chicken Breasts

Makes 8 servings

    8 whole chicken breasts, boned
      Salt and pepper
    1 package (8 ounces) seasoned croutons
    1 can (10¾ ounces) cream of mushroom soup,
      undiluted, divided
    1 can (7 ounces) crab meat, drained and flaked
    ¼ cup chopped green pepper
    1 egg, lightly beaten
    1 tablespoon lemon juice
    2 teaspoons Worcestershire sauce
    1 teaspoon prepared mustard
    ¼ teaspoon salt
    ¼ cup vegetable oil
    ¼ teaspoon onion juice
    1 teaspoon Kitchen Bouquet

Sprinkle inside of chicken breasts with salt and pepper to taste. In a bowl, combine croutons, ½ can of the soup, crab meat, green pepper, egg, lemon juice, Worcestershire sauce, mustard, and ¼ teaspoon salt; blend well. Divide stuffing among chicken breasts. Roll breasts up; secure with skewers. Grill stuffed breasts over medium-hot coals 30 minutes. While breasts are cooking, combine remaining ½ can soup, oil, onion juice, Kitchen Bouquet, and a dash of pepper in a small bowl; blend well. Baste chicken with sauce. Grill 15 minutes, turning and basting frequently.

Onion Barbecue Chicken

Makes 8 servings

    1 can (10¾ ounces) onion soup, undiluted
    ½ cup catsup
    ¼ cup vegetable oil
    ¼ cup vinegar
    2 tablespoons brown sugar
    1 tablespoon Worcestershire sauce
    ⅛ teaspoon hot pepper sauce
    2 cloves garlic, minced
    2 broiler-fryer chickens (2½ to 3 pounds each), cut up

In a medium saucepan, combine soup, catsup, oil, vinegar, brown sugar, and Worcestershire and hot pepper sauces. Cook over medium heat until hot, stirring often. Place chicken in a shallow pan or in a double plastic bag. Pour sauce over chicken. Cover or seal. Refrigerate several hours or overnight. Drain sauce from chicken; reserve sauce. Grill chicken over hot coals about 15 minutes, turning to brown both sides. Brush with sauce. Grill 30 minutes or until chicken is tender, turning and basting often.

Orange Teriyaki Chicken

Makes 8 servings

    1 can (6 ounces) frozen orange juice concentrate,
      thawed
    ¼ cup soy sauce
    2 tablespoons chopped onion
    1 tablespoon vegetable oil
    ½ teaspoon ground ginger
    ½ teaspoon hot pepper sauce
    2 broiler-fryer chickens (2½ to 3 pounds each), cut up

In a small bowl, combine orange juice concentrate, soy sauce, onion, oil, ginger, and hot pepper sauce; blend well. Place chicken in a shallow pan or in a double plastic bag. Pour marinade over chicken. Cover or seal. Refrigerate at least 2 hours, turning once. Drain marinade from chicken; reserve marinade. Grill chicken over medium-hot coals about 45 minutes or until tender, turning and basting often.

Poultry

Orange and Beer Chicken

Makes 6 to 8 servings

- 1 can (12 ounces) beer
- 1 teaspoon salt
- ¼ teaspoon seasoned pepper
- 2 tablespoons lemon juice
- Generous dash hot pepper sauce
- ½ teaspoon orange extract
- 1 teaspoon grated orange peel
- 1 tablespoon brown sugar
- 1 tablespoon dark molasses
- 2 broiler-fryer chickens (2½ to 3 pounds each), halved

In a small bowl, combine beer, salt, pepper, lemon juice, hot pepper sauce, orange extract and peel, brown sugar, and molasses; blend well. Place chicken in a shallow pan or in a double plastic bag. Pour marinade over chicken. Cover or seal. Refrigerate several hours or overnight. Drain marinade from chicken; reserve marinade. Grill chicken over hot coals about 45 minutes or until tender, turning and basting often.

Grilled Lemon Chicken

Makes 4 to 6 servings

- ½ cup lemon or lime juice
- ½ cup butter or margarine, melted
- 1 teaspoon crushed leaf thyme
- ¼ teaspoon hot pepper sauce
- Salt and pepper
- 2 broiler-fryer chickens (2½ to 3 pounds each), quartered

In a small bowl, combine lemon juice, butter, thyme, and hot pepper sauce; blend well. Sprinkle salt and pepper to taste on chickens. Grill chickens over hot coals about 45 minutes or until tender, turning and basting often. Serve with remaining lemon butter.

Golden Glazed Chicken

Makes 4 servings

- ¼ cup butter or margarine
- 1 can (30 ounces) spiced peaches, drained; reserve syrup
- 2 tablespoons vinegar
- 1 teaspoon soy sauce
- 2 tablespoons prepared mustard
- 2 tablespoons minced onion
- 1 teaspoon salt
- 1 broiler-fryer chicken (2½ to 3 pounds), quartered

In a small saucepan, combine butter, 1½ cups reserved peach syrup, vinegar, soy sauce, mustard, onion, and salt. Bring to boiling, stirring often. Place chicken in a shallow pan. Pour peach mixture over chicken. Let stand 30 to 40 minutes. Drain marinade from chicken; reserve marinade. Grill chicken over hot coals about 45 minutes or until tender, turning and basting often. Serve with warmed spiced peaches.

Cranberry Barbecued Chicken

Makes 8 servings

- 1 can (8 ounces) jellied cranberry sauce
- 4 teaspoons soy sauce
- 2 teaspoons lemon juice
- ½ teaspoon ground ginger
- 16 chicken legs or thighs

In a saucepan, combine cranberry sauce, soy sauce, lemon juice, and ginger; blend well. Cook over medium heat 10 minutes, stirring occasionally. Arrange chicken on a large double thickness of heavy-duty aluminum foil. Grill over hot coals about 15 minutes, turning often. Baste with cranberry mixture. Grill 30 to 35 minutes or until tender, turning and basting often.

Island Broiled Chicken

Makes 6 to 8 servings

- ½ cup soy sauce
- ¼ cup water
- ⅓ cup vegetable oil
- 2 tablespoons instant minced onion
- 2 tablespoons sesame seed
- 1 tablespoon sugar
- 1 teaspoon ground ginger
- ¾ teaspoon salt
- ½ teaspoon instant minced garlic
- ⅛ teaspoon cayenne pepper
- 2 broiler-fryer chickens (2½ to 3 pounds each), quartered

In a small bowl, combine soy sauce, water, oil, onion, sesame seed, sugar, ginger, salt, garlic, and pepper; blend well. Place chicken in a shallow pan or in a double plastic bag. Pour marinade over chicken. Cover or seal. Refrigerate 8 hours or overnight, turning occasionally. Drain marinade from chicken; reserve marinade. Grill chicken over hot coals 45 minutes or until tender, turning and basting.

Poultry

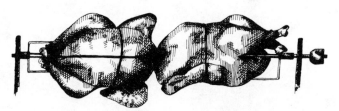

Soy Glazed Cornish Hens

Makes 4 servings

    4 Cornish game hens (1 to 1½ pounds each)
      Salt and pepper
    ½ cup soy sauce
    ½ cup dry sherry
    1 tablespoon lemon juice
    ¼ cup vegetable oil
    1 clove garlic, crushed

Sprinkle cavities of hens with salt and pepper. Secure neck skin to backs of chickens with skewers. Press wings over breasts and tie with heavy string. Tie legs together; tie legs to tail. Insert spit rod crosswise through each hen just below the breastbone, leaving about 1 inch between hens. Secure with holding forks. Test balance; attach to spit. Turn on motor. Grill over drip pan surrounded by medium-hot coals about 45 minutes. In a bowl, combine soy sauce, sherry, lemon juice, oil, and garlic. Brush on hens. Grill 15 minutes or until leg joints move easily, basting often with sauce.

Stuffed Chicken

Makes 4 servings

    4 tablespoons butter *or* margarine, divided
    ½ cup shredded zucchini
    ¾ cup water
    ½ package (6½ ounces) stuffing mix with rice
    ½ cup shredded mozzarella cheese
    1 teaspoon grated lemon peel
    2 tablespoons lemon juice
    ½ teaspoon crushed leaf basil
    1 roasting chicken (4 to 4½ pounds)
    1 teaspoon salt

In a large saucepan, melt 1 tablespoon butter. Sauté zucchini until tender. Stir in water and seasonings from stuffing mix. Bring to boiling; remove from heat. Add stuffing mix; toss lightly with a fork until moistened. Let stand 15 minutes

to cool slightly. Stir in cheese. In a small saucepan, melt remaining 3 tablespoons butter. Stir in lemon peel, lemon juice, and basil; set aside. Rinse chicken; pat dry with paper towels. Sprinkle cavity with salt. Stuff cavity and neck lightly. Secure neck skin to back of chicken with skewers. Press wings over breast and tie with heavy string. Tie legs together; tie legs to tail. Insert spit rod under legs and through center of bird. Secure with holding fork. Test balance; attach to spit. Turn on motor. Grill over drip pan surrounded by medium-hot coals 1½ to 2 hours or until tender, basting often with lemon-butter mixture.

Spit Roasted Whole Chicken

Makes 4 servings

    1 broiler-fryer chicken (2½ to 3 pounds)
      Salt
      Honey Glaze (recipe follows)

Sprinkle cavity of chicken with salt. Secure neck skin to back of chicken with skewers. Press wings over breast and tie with heavy string. Tie legs together; tie legs to tail. Insert spit rod under legs and through center of bird. Secure with holding forks. Test balance; attach to spit. Turn on motor. Grill over drip pan surrounded by medium-hot coals 1½ to 2 hours or until tender, basting with Honey Glaze the last 20 minutes of cooking time.

Honey Glaze

Makes about 1 cup

    ½ cup honey
    ½ cup soy sauce
    2 cloves garlic, minced
    3 tablespoons catsup

In a small bowl, combine all ingredients; blend well.

Stuffed Turkey

Makes 10 to 12 servings

- 1 frozen turkey (8 to 15 pounds), thawed
- 8 ounces bulk pork sausage
- 1 cup chopped celery
- 1 cup chopped onions
- 8 ounces mushrooms, sliced
- 1 bag (16 ounces) seasoned stuffing mix
- 1 loaf white *or* whole wheat bread, torn into
  pieces and dried
  Boiling water
- 3 eggs, lightly beaten
  Melted butter

Remove neck and giblets. Rinse turkey; pat dry. In a skillet, brown sausage. Push sausage to side of pan. Add celery, onions, and mushrooms. Sauté until tender-crisp; drain fat; set aside. In a large bowl, combine stuffing mix and dried bread. Cut butter into pieces; add to bread. Pour enough boiling water over bread to moisten as desired. Add sausage and vegetables; blend well. Add eggs; blend well. Fill neck and body cavity lightly with stuffing. Truss. (For best results, insert a meat thermometer between the leg and thigh without touching bone.) Place turkey on grill over drip pan. Grill over medium coals 13 minutes per pound with the lid on and dampers adjusted according to manufacturer's instructions. Add coals to each side of drip pan every hour. Baste often with melted butter during the last 1½ hours cooking time. Let stand 15 minutes before carving.

Lemon Duckling

Makes 2 servings

- 1 frozen duckling (about 5 pounds), thawed
- 1 can (6 ounces) frozen lemon concentrate, thawed
  Grated peel from ½ lemon
- 1 tablespoon cider vinegar

Pierce duck with a sharp fork in several places. Place on a rack in a roasting pan. Bake at 400° F. 1 hour. In a small bowl, combine lemonade concentrate, lemon peel, and vinegar; blend well. Secure neck skin to back of duckling with skewers. Press wings over breast and tie with heavy string. Tie legs together; tie legs to tail. Insert spit rod under legs and through center of bird. Secure with holding forks. Test balance; attach to spit. Turn on motor. Grill over drip pans surrounded by medium-hot coals for 30 minutes or until tender, basting often with lemon marinade.

Orange Smoked Turkey

Makes 10 to 12 servings

- 1 thawed frozen turkey (8 to 10 pounds), giblets
  and neck removed from cavity and rinsed
- 2 oranges, cut in halves
- 1 teaspoon poultry seasoning
- 1 small onion, quartered
- 1 rib celery, cut in pieces

Prepare grill for smoking. (See page 29.) Rub turkey with 2 of the orange halves. Rub poultry seasoning on outside and inside of turkey. Place oranges, onion, and celery in cavity. Secure neck skin to back of turkey with skewers. Press wings over breast and tie with heavy string. Tie legs together; tie legs to tail. (For best results, insert a meat thermometer between leg and thigh without touching bone.) Place a pan of water under center of grill. Place turkey about 6 inches above low coals and smoking chips and over pan of water. Smoke 7 to 8 hours, adding water to pan and smoking chips and hot coals to firebed every hour. Let stand 20 minutes before carving.

Tex-Mex Chicken

Makes 4 servings

- 1 broiler-fryer chicken (2½ to 3 pounds), halved
- 1 lemon, cut in half
- 6 cloves garlic, minced
- 1 tablespoon cayenne pepper
- 2 tablespoons paprika
  Salt

Rub chicken with lemon halves. Sprinkle with garlic, cayenne, paprika, and salt to taste; rub into skin. Refrigerate overnight. Grill over medium-hot coals 45 minutes or until tender, turning often.

Minted Chicken

Makes 6 servings

- ½ cup honey
- ¼ cup vegetable oil
- 2 tablespoons snipped mint leaves *or* mint flakes
  Salt
- 2 pounds chicken thighs

In a small bowl, combine honey, oil, mint, and salt to taste; blend well. Grill thighs over low coals about 15 minutes, turning once. Baste with honey glaze and grill 20 minutes, turning and basting often.

Fish and Shellfish

Soy Barbecued Shrimp

Makes 4 servings

 2 pounds raw fresh *or* thawed frozen shrimp
 2 cloves garlic, mashed
 ½ teaspoon salt
 ½ cup soy sauce
 ½ cup lemon *or* lime juice
 3 tablespoons finely chopped parsley
 2 teaspoons onion flakes
 ½ teaspoon black pepper

Shell and devein shrimp, leaving tails intact. Arrange shrimp in a shallow 1½-quart baking dish. In a small bowl, combine garlic and salt. Stir in remaining ingredients. Pour marinade over shrimp. Refrigerate 1 hour. Drain marinade from shrimp; reserve marinade. Thread shrimp on skewers. Place skewers in a well-greased hinged wire grill 4 inches above medium-hot coals. Grill 3 minutes, basting with marinade. Turn. Grill 5 minutes, basting several times with marinade. Serve remaining marinade as a dip.

Shrimp Scampi

Makes 6 servings

 ¾ cup butter *or* margarine
 2 cloves garlic, minced
 ½ teaspoon crushed leaf tarragon
 ½ teaspoon crushed leaf rosemary
 ½ teaspoon crushed leaf thyme
 3 tablespoons lemon juice
 2 pounds raw fresh *or* thawed frozen uncooked
   large shrimp (15 to 20 per pound), shelled
   and deveined
   Salt and pepper
 1 loaf French bread, wrapped in aluminum foil

In a small saucepan, combine butter, garlic, tarragon, rosemary, and thyme. Melt over low heat; let stand 3 to 4 minutes to blend flavors. Add lemon juice. Tear off six 12-inch pieces of heavy-duty aluminum foil. Arrange 4 or 5 shrimp on each piece of foil. Pour garlic-butter mixture over shrimp. Season each serving with salt and pepper to taste. Bring foil up and over shrimp; seal tightly. Grill over medium-hot coals 10 to 20 minutes or until shrimp is tender. Place French bread on grill the last 5 minutes of cooking time. Cook 5 minutes, turning once. Serve with shrimp.

Bacon and Onion Grilled Fish

Makes 4 servings

 2 pounds pan-dressed fresh *or* thawed frozen fish
 ¾ cup margarine *or* butter, melted
 1 envelope (1½ ounces) onion soup mix
 ¼ teaspoon black pepper
 ⅓ pound sliced bacon

Rinse and pat fish dry. In a small bowl, combine margarine, soup mix, and pepper; blend well. Brush fish inside and outside with butter mixture. Wrap a bacon slice around each fish. Place fish in a well-greased hinged wire grill about 5 inches above medium-hot coals. Grill 10 to 15 minutes. Baste with butter mixture; turn. Grill 10 to 15 minutes or until fish flakes easily when tested with a fork.

Grilled Fish with Orange Barbecue Sauce

Makes 4 servings

 1½ pounds fresh *or* thawed frozen fish fillets
 ¾ teaspoon salt
 ¼ teaspoon black pepper
   Orange Barbecue Sauce (recipe follows)
   Orange slices, optional

Skin fillets and cut in serving portions. Sprinkle on salt and pepper. Brush both sides with Orange Barbecue Sauce. Place fillets in a well-greased hinged wire grill about 4 inches above medium-hot coals. Grill 5 to 8 minutes; baste with sauce. Turn and grill 5 to 8 minutes or until fish flakes easily when tested with a fork. Garnish with orange slices, if desired.

Orange Barbecue Sauce

Makes about 1 cup

 ½ cup orange juice
 ⅓ cup catsup
 3 tablespoons brown sugar
 2 tablespoons lemon juice
 1 tablespoon instant minced onion
 1 tablespoon soy sauce
 ¼ teaspoon salt

In a small saucepan, combine all ingredients. Cook over low heat until heated through, stirring often.

Fish/Shellfish

Oyster Supreme

Makes 4 servings

24 shell oysters
⅓ cup butter or **margarine, melted**
3 tablespoons chopped onion
2 tablespoons chopped drained pimiento
1 tablespoon chopped parsley
¼ teaspoon salt
¼ teaspoon hot pepper sauce
¼ teaspoon Worcestershire sauce
¼ teaspoon dry mustard

Shuck and drain oysters. Place oysters on deep half of shells. In a skillet, melt butter. Add onion; sauté until onion is tender but not brown. Add remaining ingredients. Spoon sauce over oysters. Place oysters on grill over medium-hot coals. Grill 20 to 25 minutes or until edges begin to curl.

Zesty Shrimp

Makes 4 servings

1½ pounds raw jumbo fresh or **thawed frozen shrimp**
1 bottle (8 ounces) zesty Italian dressing
½ teaspoon salt

Peel and devein shrimp. In a 2-quart bowl, combine Italian dressing and salt; blend well. Add shrimp; stir to coat with dressing. Refrigerate 30 minutes, stirring occasionally. Drain shrimp from dressing; reserve dressing. Place shrimp in a well-greased, hinged wire grill 4 inches above medium-hot coals. Grill 4 to 6 minutes; baste with dressing. Turn and grill 6 to 8 minutes or until shrimp are tender.

Backyard Scallops

Makes 4 servings

1 pound fresh or **thawed frozen bay scallops**
¼ cup vegetable oil
¼ cup lemon juice
1 teaspoon salt
⅛ teaspoon hickory liquid smoke
1 package (8 ounces) sliced bacon, partially cooked and cut in thirds
½ cup sesame seed

Rinse scallops in cold water to remove any shell. In a 2-quart bowl, combine oil, lemon juice, salt, and liquid smoke. Add scallops; toss lightly to coat. Cover and refrigerate 30 minutes, stirring occasionally. Remove scallops from marinade. Wrap a bacon piece around each scallop; fasten with a wooden pick. Roll scallops in sesame seed. Place in a well-greased hinged wire grill, about 4 inches above medium-hot coals. Grill 2 to 4 minutes or until sesame seed browns. Turn and grill 2 to 4 minutes or until tender.

Oyster Kebabs

Makes 4 servings

⅓ cup olive or **vegetable oil**
2 tablespoons dry vermouth
1 teaspoon chopped parsley
¼ teaspoon crushed leaf marjoram
¼ teaspoon crushed leaf thyme
⅛ teaspoon black pepper
⅛ teaspoon garlic salt
1 can (15½ ounces) select oysters, rinsed and drained
1 large green pepper, cut in 1-inch pieces
½ pound fresh mushrooms
10 slices bacon, cut in thirds

In a small bowl, combine oil, vermouth, parsley, and herbs and spices; blend well. Add oysters, green pepper, and mushrooms to marinade. Cover and refrigerate 1 hour. Drain marinade from oysters; reserve marinade. Wrap a piece of bacon around each oyster. Thread oysters and vegetables on four 12-inch skewers. Place skewers in a well-greased hinged wire grill 4 inches above medium-hot coals. Grill 5 to 7 minutes; baste with sauce. Turn and grill until bacon is crisp.

Backyard Patio Fish Supreme

Makes 4 servings

1½ pounds fresh or **thawed frozen thick fish fillets**
½ cup vegetable oil
½ cup sesame seed
⅓ cup brandy
⅓ cup lemon juice
3 tablespoons soy sauce
1 teaspoon salt
1 large clove garlic, crushed

Cut fish in serving portions. Place fish in a single layer in a 12 x 8-inch baking pan. In a small bowl, combine remaining ingredients. Pour marinade over fish. Cover and refrigerate 30 minutes, turning once. Drain marinade from fish; reserve marinade. Place fish in a well-greased hinged wire grill about 4 inches above medium-hot coals. Grill 8 minutes; baste with marinade. Turn and grill 7 to 10 minutes or until fish flakes easily when tested with a fork.

Smoking Fish

Smoked fish, meat, and poultry can be successfully produced in hooded or covered electric, gas or charcoal grills. Cooking times for smoke cooking will vary according to the type of equipment being used, the heat of the fire, and the distance the fish is from the heat source. Temperatures should be adjusted according to the recipe used, and for best results, use an oven thermometer if using a charcoal grill.

The best choices for smoking are fat fish, such as mullet, mackerel, blue fish, or salmon. Good results can also be obtained using lean fish, such as trout, catfish, and carp if they are basted frequently with cooking oil during the smoking process. Fat fish should be basted only near the end of cooking time.

To smoke fish, soak 1 pound of hardwood chips (hickory, apple, oak or cherry) in 2 quarts of water for several hours or overnight. Spread about one-third of the chips over coals or ceramic briquets. Add the remaining chips as needed while the fish is being smoked.

For stronger flavor, low temperatures (150° to 175° F.) are required. Good results can be obtained, however, in temperatures up to 300° F., which will reduce cooking time.

The same procedure for smoking is used regardless of the type of grill being used.

Smoked fish will keep 3 days if wrapped loosely and refrigerated.

To freeze smoked fish, wrap loosely and refrigerate until chilled. Rewrap in moisture-vapor-proof freezer wrap and place in the freezer. Smoked fish can be frozen up to 3 months. To use, remove freezer paper, wrap in aluminum foil, and heat 20 to 30 minutes in a 300° F. oven.

Seafood Smoking Chart

Size 'n' shape	How much to serve 4	How long to marinate in brine*	Cook at one of these temperatures	How long
Butterfly fillets (including bone, 1 pound each)	4 pounds	30 minutes	150°-175°F. / 200°F. / 250°F.	1 hr. + 30 min. / 45 min. / 30 min.
Fillets or steaks (½ inch thick)	1½ pounds	30 minutes	150°-175°F. / 200°F. / 250°F.	1 hr. / 30 min. / 20 min.
Fillets or steaks (¾ inch thick)	1½ pounds	45 minutes	150°-175°F. / 200°F. / 250°F.	1 hr. + 30 min. / 30-45 min. / 30 min.
Fillets or steaks (1 inch thick)	1½ pounds	45 minutes	150°-175°F. / 200°F. / 250°F.	1 hr. + 45 min. / 30-45 min. / 30 min.
Fillets or steaks (1½ inches thick)	1½ pounds	1 hour	150°-175°F. / 200°F. / 250°F.	2 hours / 1 hr. + 15 min. / 45-50 min.
Pan-dressed	2½ pounds	30 minutes	150°-175°F. / 200°F. / 250°F.	2 hours / 1 hr. + 15 min. / 45-50 min.

*To Brine Fish: Thaw fish if frozen. Combine 1 gallon cold water and 1 cup salt; stir until dissolved. Marinate fish in brine in refrigerator for 30 minutes before smoking. Rinse fish thoroughly in cold water and dry carefully after brining.

Plain Delicious Smoked Fish

Makes 6 servings

- 4 pounds fresh *or* thawed frozen fish fillets
- 1 cup salt
- 1 gallon water
- 1 box (3 ounces) crab boil (in pouch)
- Vegetable oil

Prepare the grill for smoking. (See page 29.) Clean and rinse fish fillets in cold water. In a 2-gallon bowl, combine salt and 1 gallon water. Add pouch of crab boil. Add fish; refrigerate 30 minutes, stirring occasionally. Remove fish from brine; rinse well and pat dry. Place fish fillets, skin side down, on a well-greased grill 4 to 6 inches above smoking chips in smoke oven. Close hood on grill; open vent slightly to keep smoke and air circulating. Smoke fish about 1 hour at 150° to 175° F. or 30 to 45 minutes at 200° F. Baste fish with vegetable oil near end of cooking time. Fish is done when the cut surface is golden brown and flesh flakes easily when tested with a fork.

Smokehouse Oysters

Makes 4 servings

- 12 shell oysters, shucked and drained
- 1/8 teaspoon salt
- 1/8 teaspoon black pepper
- 1/4 cup butter *or* margarine, softened
- 2 tablespoons chopped green onion
- 2 tablespoons chopped parsley
- 1/4 cup cornflake crumbs
- 1/4 cup grated Parmesan cheese
- Rock salt
- Chopped parsley

Prepare the grill for smoking. (See page 29.) Place oysters on deep half of shell. Sprinkle on salt and pepper. In a small bowl, combine butter, onion, and parsley; blend well. Dot oysters with butter mixture. In a small bowl, combine cornflake crumbs and cheese; blend well. Sprinkle over oysters. In a shallow 9 x 11-inch aluminum foil pan, place a layer of rock salt 1 inch deep. Place oyster shells on top of the rock salt. Place pan on grill about 4 inches above hot coals and smoking chips in smoke oven. Smoke 15 to 20 minutes or until tops are brown and edges of oysters curl. Garnish with chopped parsley.

Note: Rock salt is used to hold shells upright and to keep the oysters hot.

Smoked Fish with Ginger Sauce

Makes 4 servings

- Ginger Sauce (recipe follows)
- 1½ pounds fresh *or* thawed frozen fish fillets
- ¾ teaspoon salt
- ¼ teaspoon black pepper

Prepare the grill for smoking. (See page 29.) Prepare Ginger Sauce; set aside. Cut fish fillets into serving portions. Season with salt and pepper. Brush both sides with Ginger Sauce. Place fillets on a well-greased grill about 4 inches above medium-hot coals and smoking chips in smoke oven. Smoke 10 to 15 minutes; baste with sauce. Smoke 10 to 15 minutes or until fish flakes easily when tested with a fork.

Ginger Sauce

Makes about 1 cup

- ½ cup catsup
- ¼ cup chicken broth
- 2 tablespoons soy sauce
- 1 tablespoon honey
- 2 teaspoons grated fresh gingerroot

In a small bowl, combine all ingredients; blend well.

Smoked Scallop Kebabs

Makes 4 servings

- ½ pound fresh *or* thawed frozen bay *or* calico scallops
- 12 lime slices
- 4 slices Canadian bacon, cut in half
- ¼ cup lime juice
- ¼ cup butter *or* margarine, melted
- ¼ cup grated Parmesan cheese
- ½ teaspoon salt
- ¼ cup chopped parsley

Prepare the grill for smoking. (See page 29.) Rinse scallops in cold water to remove any shell. Alternately thread scallops, lime slices, and Canadian bacon on four 10-inch skewers. In a small bowl, combine lime juice and butter; blend well. Baste scallops with marinade. In a small bowl, combine cheese, salt, and parsley; blend well. Sprinkle on scallops. Place skewers on a well greased grill about 4 inches above medium-hot coals and smoking chips in smoke oven. Smoke 4 to 6 minutes. Turn and smoke 4 to 6 minutes or until scallops are tender.

Packet Meals

Foods that are irregular in shape or contain a lot of moisture are made easily and deliciously when wrapped in individual packets and grilled. Following are instructions for two methods of wrapping foil packets. Use whichever method you feel is best for your recipe.

Drugstore Wrap

Place the food in the center of an oblong piece of heavy-duty aluminum foil, being certain that the foil is large enough to fold at the top and sides. (Fig. A)

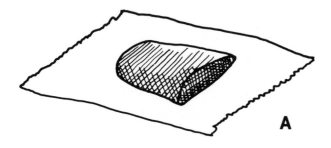

A

Bring two sides together above the food, then fold down loosely in a series of locked folds allowing for heat circulation and expansion. (Fig. B)

B

Fold the short ends up and over again and crimp edges to seal. The ends can be rolled or twisted to close the packet or the fold can be made on the side of the packet. Foods tend to cook more evenly with the thick fold at the side. (Fig. C)

C

Bundle Wrap

Tear off a piece of heavy-duty aluminum foil large enough to allow adequate folding and wrapping. Place food in the center of the foil. (Fig. A)

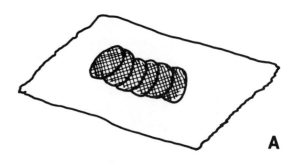

A

Bring four corners up and into the center. (Fig. B)

B

Fold the openings together loosely to allow for heat circulation and expansion. (Fig. C)

C

Seal by folding over ends and pressing to the package (Fig. D)

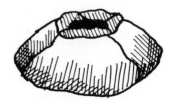

D

Parmesan Potatoes

Makes 4 servings

- **4 large baking potatoes**
- **Onion salt**
- **Celery salt**
- **Black pepper**
- **½ cup grated Parmesan cheese**
- **½ cup butter** or **margarine**

Scrub potatoes; do not peel. Cut lengthwise into ¼-inch-thick slices. Spread on a 20-inch length of heavy-duty aluminum foil. Sprinkle on onion and celery salts and pepper. Sprinkle on Parmesan cheese. Arrange potato slices in center of foil. Dot with butter. Bring foil up and over potatoes; seal tightly. Grill over medium-hot coals 30 to 45 minutes or until tender, turning several times.

Chutney Shrimp

Makes 4 servings

- **1 pound raw fresh** or **thawed frozen shrimp, peeled and deveined**
- **1 medium onion, sliced**
- **1 medium green pepper, cut in rings**
- **2 medium carrots, cut in 3-inch sticks**
- **1 jar (9 ounces) chutney**
- **Chopped parsley**

Tear off 4 large pieces of heavy-duty aluminum foil; grease lightly. Divide shrimp, onion, green pepper, and carrots among pieces of foil. Spoon 1 tablespoon chutney over shrimp. Bring foil up and over shrimp; seal tightly. Grill about 4 inches above medium-hot coals 10 to 15 minutes or until shrimp is tender. Heat remaining chutney and serve with shrimp. Garnish with parsley.

Chicken Packets

Makes 4 servings

- **1 broiler-fryer chicken (3 to 3½ pounds), quartered**
- **¼ cup butter** or **margarine**
- **1 envelope (1½ ounces) onion soup mix**
- **1 teaspoon paprika**
- **1 can (4 ounces) mushroom stems and pieces, drained**
- **½ cup half-and-half**

Rinse chicken, pat dry, and remove any small protruding bones. Tear off 4 pieces of heavy-duty aluminum foil. On each piece of foil, place 1 teaspoon butter, 1 tablespoon soup mix, and ½ teaspoon paprika. Place a chicken quarter in center of foil. Sprinkle on remaining soup mix and butter. Divide mushrooms among packets. Spoon 2 tablespoons half-and-half over each chicken packet. Bring foil up and over chicken; seal tightly. Grill over medium-hot coals about 45 minutes or until tender, turning chicken packets every 10 minutes.

Garden Pot Roast

Makes 6 to 8 servings

- **1 package (½ ounce) Italian salad dressing mix**
- **¼ cup flour**
- **1 teaspoon salt**
- **½ teaspoon paprika**
- **⅛ teaspoon black pepper**
- **1 beef blade roast (3 to 4 pounds)**
- **2 cups thinly sliced carrots**
- **2 cups sliced zucchini (¾-inch slices)**

In a small bowl, combine salad dressing mix, flour, salt, paprika, and pepper; blend well. Place roast in the center of a double thickness piece of heavy-duty aluminum foil. Coat both sides of roast with flour mixture. Bring foil up and over meat; seal tightly. Grill over medium-hot coals 1½ hours, turning after 1 hour. Remove foil packet from grill; open carefully. Place carrots and zucchini on roast. Reseal packet. Grill over medium-hot coals about 30 minutes or until vegetables and meat are tender. Do not turn packet.

Stuffed Chicken Breasts

Makes 6 servings

- **1 package (10 ounces) frozen chopped spinach, thawed and drained**
- **1 cup seasoned stuffing mix**
- **1 can (7½ ounces) ready-to-serve cream of mushroom soup**
- **¾ cup grated Cheddar cheese**
- **2 teaspoons minced onion**
- **6 whole chicken breasts, skinned, boned, and split**
- **Salt**
- **Paprika**

Tear off 6 pieces of heavy-duty aluminum foil. In a medium bowl, combine spinach, stuffing mix, soup, cheese, and onion; blend well. Place about ½ cup spinach mixture in center of each piece of foil. Place chicken breast on spinach mixture; fold sides under. Season with salt and paprika to taste. Bring foil up and over chicken; seal tightly. Grill over medium-hot coals about 40 minutes or until chicken is tender, turning once.

Packet Meals

Fish Banquet

Makes 2 servings

> 1 fish (1 pound)
> 2 slices bacon
> 2 potatoes, peeled and quartered
> 1 onion, sliced
> Salt and pepper

Tear off a large double thickness of heavy-duty aluminum foil. Place 1 slice bacon on foil. Place fish on top of bacon. Top with remaining bacon slice. Arrange potatoes and onion on top of fish. Season with salt and pepper to taste. Bring foil up and over fish; seal tightly. Grill over indirect heat 15 to 20 minutes on each side or until fish flakes easily with a fork. Serve directly from packet.

Grilled Fish in a Packet

> 1 fish, scaled and cleaned, whole or cut in steaks
> Vegetable oil or melted butter
> Salt and pepper
> Lemon juice
> 2 tablespoons chopped tomato
> Lemon slices

Tear off a large sheet of heavy-duty aluminum foil. Place fish on foil. Brush fish with oil. Season with salt and pepper, and lemon juice to taste. Top with chopped tomato. Garnish with lemon slices. Bring foil up and over fish; seal tightly. Grill over medium-hot coals 10 minutes on each side for a 1 to 1½-pound fish; 20 minutes per side for 4 to 5-pound fish. Fish is done when it flakes easily with a fork.

Fresh Vegetable Packets

Makes 4 servings

> 2 medium tomatoes, sliced ½ inch thick
> 2 medium onions, sliced
> 2 medium green peppers, cut in rings
> 12 mushrooms, halved
> Salt and pepper
> 4 teaspoons butter

Tear off 4 large pieces of heavy-duty aluminum foil. Divide tomatoes, onions, and green peppers among foil, overlapping pieces in rows. Top with mushrooms. Season with salt and pepper to taste. Dot each with 1 teaspoon butter. Bring foil up and over vegetables; seal tightly. Grill over medium-hot coals 15 minutes.

Backyard Clambake

Makes 4 servings

> Seaweed, optional
> 12 steamer clams, scrubbed
> 1 fresh or thawed frozen lobster (about 1 pound), rinsed and split
> ½ small broiler-fryer chicken (about 1½ pounds), cut in serving pieces and sharp bones removed
> 1 ear corn, husked and quartered
> 1 small onion, quartered
> 1 potato, cut lengthwise in eighths
> Salt and pepper
> Melted butter

Tear off 4 large pieces of heavy-duty aluminum foil. Cover each with a piece of cheesecloth cut to fit. If you are using seaweed, place a handful on the cheesecloth. Top with clams, lobster, and chicken. Tuck in corn, onion, and potato wherever there is room. Season with salt and pepper to taste. (If you are not using seaweed, add ¼ cup water to each packet.) Tie cheesecloth up and over food. Bring foil up and over food; seal tightly. Grill over medium-hot coals 45 minutes to 1 hour or until chicken is tender. Open a packet after 35 minutes to test chicken for doneness. If it is not tender, close packet and return to grill. Serve with individual bowls of melted butter for dipping.

Beef and Vegetables Packet

Makes 6 servings

> 1 beef chuck steak (about 2 pounds), cut in 1-inch cubes
> 6 medium potatoes, peeled and diced
> 6 tablespoons chopped onion
> 6 carrots, peeled and sliced
> ½ cup chopped parsley
> 2 cans (10¾ ounces each) cream of mushroom soup, undiluted
> 6 tablespoons water
> Salt and pepper
> Hot pepper sauce

Tear off 6 large pieces of heavy-duty aluminum foil. Divide all ingredients into six portions and place on foil pieces. Add 1 tablespoon water to each portion. Season with salt and pepper to taste. Sprinkle on hot pepper sauce to taste. Bring foil up and over food; seal tightly. Grill over hot coals 1 hour or until beef is done and potatoes are tender.

Breads and Sandwiches

Hard Rolls with Lemon Butter

Makes 12 servings

- ½ cup butter *or* margarine
- 2 tablespoons chopped parsley
- 1 tablespoon lemon juice
- 12 hard rolls, split

In a small bowl, combine butter, parsley, and lemon juice; blend well. Spread rolls with lemon butter. Wrap each roll in sheet of heavy-duty aluminum foil. Grill 10 to 15 minutes or until heated through, turning occasionally.

Herb Bread

Makes 12 servings

- 1 cup butter *or* margarine
- ¾ cup minced chives
- ¾ cup chopped parsley
- 2 tablespoons minced basil
  Garlic salt
- 1 loaf French bread

In a small bowl, combine butter, chives, parsley, basil, and garlic salt to taste; blend well. Slice bread diagonally about ¾ inch apart without cutting through bottom crust. Spread herb butter between slices and on top of bread. Wrap loaf in a sheet of heavy-duty aluminum foil. Grill about 15 minutes or until heated through, turning occasionally.

Blue Cheese and Herb Bread

Makes 12 servings

- 1 cup butter, softened
- 4 ounces crumbled blue cheese
- 2 teaspoons minced onion
- 1 teaspoon crushed leaf rosemary
- 1 teaspoon crushed leaf basil
- 2 tablespoons chopped parsley
- 1 loaf French bread

In a small bowl, combine all ingredients, except bread; blend well. Slice bread diagonally about ¾ inch apart without cutting through bottom crust. Spread herb and cheese mixture between slices and on top of bread. Wrap loaf in a sheet of heavy-duty aluminum foil. Grill about 15 minutes or until heated through, turning occasionally.

Quick Garlic Bread

Makes 12 servings

- ½ cup butter *or* margarine, softened
- 1 clove garlic, minced *or* ⅛ teaspoon garlic powder
- 1 loaf French bread

In a small bowl, combine butter and garlic; blend well. Slice bread diagonally about ¾ inch apart without cutting through bottom crust. Spread garlic butter between slices and on top of bread. Wrap loaf in a sheet of heavy-duty aluminum foil. Grill about 15 minutes or until heated through, turning occasionally.

French Bread with Cheese

Makes 12 to 14 servings

- ½ cup butter *or* margarine
- ½ cup grated Swiss cheese
- ¼ cup crumbled cooked bacon
- 1 tablespoon minced chives
- 2 teaspoons poppy seed
- 1 tablespoon prepared mustard
- ½ teaspoon grated lemon peel
- 1½ teaspoons lemon juice
  Dash pepper
- 1 loaf French bread

In a small bowl, combine all ingredients, except bread; blend well. Slice bread diagonally about ¾ inch apart without cutting through bottom crust. Spread cheese mixture between slices and on top of bread. Wrap loaf in a sheet of heavy-duty aluminum foil. Grill about 20 minutes or until heated through and cheese is melted, turning occasionally.

Onion Bread

Makes 12 servings

- 1 cup butter *or* margarine
- 1 tablespoon chopped parsley
- 1 envelope (1½ ounces) onion soup mix
- 2 loaves brown-and-serve French bread

In a small bowl, combine butter, parsley, and onion soup mix; blend well. Slice bread diagonally about ¾ inch apart without cutting through bottom crust. Spread onion butter between slices and on top of bread. Make an aluminum foil pan to fit each loaf. Place loaves on grill. Grill about 15 minutes or until hot and lightly browned.

Grilled Parmesan Toast

Makes 8 servings

  ½ cup butter *or* margarine, softened
  ¼ cup grated Parmesan cheese
  2 tablespoons chopped parsley
  1 loaf Italian bread

In a small bowl, combine butter, cheese, and parsley; blend well. Slice bread about 1½ inches apart; split lengthwise cutting through bottom crust. Spread cheese butter between slices. Toast about 5 minutes on each side or until golden brown.

Smoked Fish and Olive Sandwiches

Makes 4 servings

  1 cup flaked smoked fish
  1 tablespoon minced pimiento-stuffed green olives
  1 cup grated sharp Cheddar cheese
  ⅓ cup mayonnaise *or* salad dressing
  ¼ teaspoon Worcestershire sauce
  ¼ teaspoon garlic salt
  ⅛ teaspoon black pepper
  4 onion rolls, split
  Whole pimiento-stuffed green olives, optional

In a medium bowl, combine all ingredients, except onion rolls and whole olives. Place about ⅓ cup fish mixture on bottom half of each roll. Cover with top of roll. Wrap each sandwich in a piece of heavy-duty aluminum foil. Grill over medium-hot coals 10 to 15 minutes or until cheese melts. Garnish with olives on a wooden pick, if desired.

Hot Ham and Cheese Rolls

Makes 8 to 12 servings

  ½ pound boiled ham, cut in ½-inch pieces
  ½ pound processed sharp cheese, cut in ½-inch cubes
  ¼ cup chopped onion
  ½ cup pimiento-stuffed olives, sliced
  2 hard-cooked eggs, coarsely chopped
  2 tablespoons mayonnaise
  ½ cup tomato paste
  8 to 12 frankfurter rolls, split

In a small bowl, combine ham, cheese, onion, olives, and eggs. Add mayonnaise and tomato paste; blend well. Divide among frankfurter rolls, spreading evenly. Wrap each sandwich in a piece of heavy-duty aluminum foil; twist ends tightly to seal. Grill over hot coals until heated through.

Taco Franks

Makes 8 servings

  ½ cup chili sauce
  Dash hot pepper sauce
  1 teaspoon chili powder
  8 frankfurter rolls, split
  4 slices American cheese, cut in half
  8 frankfurters
  1 cup shredded lettuce
  1 cup chopped tomatoes

In a small bowl, combine chili and hot pepper sauces, and chili powder; blend well. Spread each frankfurter roll with chili sauce mixture. Place a piece of cheese in each roll. Add frankfurters. Top with lettuce and tomatoes. Wrap each sandwich in a piece of heavy-duty aluminum foil. Grill over low heat 15 minutes or until frankfurters are hot and cheese is melted, turning occasionally.

Beef and Cheese Sandwiches

Makes 6 servings

  1 pound lean ground beef
  1 tablespoon minced onion
  ½ cup tomato sauce
  ½ cup catsup
  2 tablespoons grated Parmesan cheese
  ½ teaspoon garlic powder
  ¼ teaspoon fennel seed
  ⅛ teaspoon ground oregano
  6 Kaiser rolls, split
  Garlic Butter (recipe follows)
  6 slices mozzarella cheese

In a large skillet, brown ground beef and onion, stirring to break up meat; drain fat. Stir in tomato sauce, catsup, Parmesan cheese, garlic powder, fennel seed, and oregano. Simmer 20 minutes, stirring occasionally. Spread rolls with Garlic Butter. Divide meat mixture among rolls. Top each with a slice of cheese. Wrap each sandwich in a piece of heavy-duty aluminum foil; twist ends tightly to seal. Grill over hot coals about 15 minutes or until cheese melts.

Garlic Butter

  2 tablespoons butter, softened
  ¼ teaspoon garlic powder
  ½ teaspoon paprika

In a small bowl, combine all ingredients; blend well.

Vegetables and Rice

Broccoli and Cheese Casserole

Makes 4 to 6 servings

   6 tablespoons butter *or* margarine, divided
   ¼ cup minced onion
   2 tablespoons flour
   ½ cup water
   1 jar (8 ounces) processed cheese spread
   2 packages (10 ounces each) frozen chopped
      broccoli, thawed and drained
   3 eggs, well beaten
   ½ cup soft bread crumbs

In a skillet, melt 4 tablespoons butter. Add onion; sauté until onion is tender. Stir in flour; blend well. Gradually stir in water. Cook over low heat until thickened, stirring constantly. Blend in cheese. In an 11 x 7-inch aluminum foil pan, combine sauce, broccoli, and eggs; stir carefully to blend. Sprinkle crumbs over top. Dot with remaining 2 tablespoons butter. Grill over medium-hot coals about 30 minutes or until heated through.

Baked Bean Pot

Makes 6 to 8 servings

   1 pound dried beans (kidney, navy, lima, or
      combination)
   1 large onion, chopped
   1 green pepper, chopped
   2 tablespoons vegetable oil
   ¼ pound bacon, cut in pieces
   2 teaspoons salt
   1 can (16 ounces) tomatoes, undrained
   2 tablespoons brown sugar
   2 teaspoons prepared mustard
   ½ teaspoon hot pepper sauce
   ½ teaspoon Worcestershire sauce

Place beans in a large saucepan; cover with water. Bring to boiling; reduce heat. Cover and simmer about 1 hour. While beans are cooking, sauté onion and green pepper in oil 5 minutes or until tender. Add onion-green pepper mixture to beans along with remaining ingredients. Cover and simmer 1 hour, stirring occasionally. Add water, if necessary, to keep beans covered. Can be made ahead and reheated on the grill.

Baked Potatoes

Makes 4 servings

   4 medium baking potatoes
      Vegetable oil
      Salt and pepper
      Baked Potato Toppings

Scrub and rinse potatoes. Brush with oil. Place each potato on a piece of heavy-duty aluminum foil. Bring foil up and over potatoes; seal tightly. Grill over medium-hot coals 45 to 60 minutes, turning occasionally. Open foil. Slit each potato down center; fluff with a fork. Sprinkle on salt and pepper to taste. Top with your favorite topping.

Baked Potato Toppings

   Sour cream and chopped chives *or* parsley
   Cream cheese and chopped onion
   Chopped olives and sour cream
   Crumbled crisp bacon
   Sautéed sliced mushrooms
   Shredded Cheddar cheese
   Chopped green pepper
   Lemon-butter sauce
   Plain yogurt

Garden Casserole

Makes 6 to 8 servings

   3 small carrots, peeled and sliced
   ½ pound green beans, trimmed and sliced
   1 small yellow squash, sliced
   1 small zucchini, sliced
   ½ head cauliflower, broken into flowerets
   ¼ cup butter, divided
   1 clove garlic, minced
   1 cup chicken broth
   1 teaspoon salt
   ½ teaspoon white pepper

In a buttered 2-quart casserole, arrange all vegetables. In a small saucepan, melt 2 tablespoons butter. Add garlic; cook and stir until garlic is fragrant. Stir in broth, salt, and pepper. Pour broth over vegetables. Dot with remaining butter. Cover and bake at 350° F. 30 minutes or until all vegetables are tender.

Note: To cook on grill-top, use an aluminum pan and cover with foil.

Vegetables and Rice

Sherried Rice

Makes 4 to 6 servings

- 1 tablespoon butter *or* margarine
- ½ cup sliced green onions
- 1 can (4 ounces) mushroom stems and pieces, drained
- 1 cup fresh *or* thawed frozen peas
- 1 can (15 ounces) chicken broth
- ¾ cup dry sherry
- 1 teaspoon salt
- ½ teaspoon white pepper
- 1½ cups long-grain rice

Butter an 11 x 7-inch aluminum foil pan; set aside. In a saucepan, melt butter. Add onions; sauté until onions are tender. Add mushrooms, peas, broth, sherry, salt, and pepper. Stir in rice. Pour into prepared pan. Cover tightly with aluminum foil. Grill over medium-hot coals about 15 minutes or until rice is tender. Fluff with a fork and serve.

Grilled Onions

Makes 4 servings

- 4 medium onions
- Salt and pepper
- 4 tablespoons butter
- 4 slices bacon, cut in half

Clean onions; remove a thin slice from top and bottom of each. Make a criss-cross cut from top ¾ of the way through onions. Sprinkle on salt and pepper to taste. Place 1 tablespoon butter in center of each onion. Lay 2 pieces bacon across top. Wrap each onion in a piece of heavy-duty aluminum foil. Grill over medium-hot coals 45 minutes or until onions are tender. To serve, place bacon under onion and pull sides down to form a flower.

French Fries in a Poke

Makes 4 servings

- 1 bag (16 ounces) frozen French fries, partially thawed
- Salt and pepper

Tear off a large piece of heavy-duty aluminum foil. Place fries on foil. Season with salt and pepper to taste. Gather foil up and over French fries; seal tightly. Grill over medium-hot coals 15 minutes or until hot, shaking package occasionally.

Rice Pilaf

Makes 6 servings

- 1½ cups long-grain rice
- 3 cups water
- 1 teaspoon salt
- ⅓ cup butter *or* margarine
- 1 chicken bouillon cube
- ¼ teaspoon crushed leaf rosemary
- 1 can (4 ounces) mushroom stems and pieces, drained

In a large saucepan, combine rice, water, salt, butter, bouillon, and rosemary. Bring to boiling; reduce heat. Cover and simmer 15 minutes. Let stand 5 minutes. Stir in mushrooms; let stand 2 to 3 minutes to heat through. Fluff with a fork and serve.

Parmesan Corn

Makes 8 servings

- ½ cup grated Parmesan cheese
- ½ cup butter *or* margarine, softened
- 1 tablespoon chopped parsley
- ½ teaspoon salt
- 8 ears corn, husked

In a small bowl, combine cheese, butter, parsley, and salt; blend well. Place each ear of corn on a piece of heavy-duty aluminum foil. Spread 1 tablespoon of butter mixture on each ear. Wrap corn tightly. Grill over medium-low coals 20 to 30 minutes or until corn is tender, turning once.

Crumb Topped Tomatoes

Makes 6 to 8 servings

- ½ cup soft bread crumbs
- 2 tablespoons grated Parmesan cheese
- Dash salt
- ⅛ teaspoon black pepper
- 6 medium tomatoes, halved
- 2 tablespoons butter, melted

In a small bowl, combine bread crumbs, cheese, salt, and pepper; blend well. Top each tomato half with a spoonful of crumb mixture. Drizzle melted butter over each. Place each tomato, cut side up, on a piece of heavy-duty aluminum foil. Grill over medium-low coals 10 minutes or until heated through.

Salads and Relishes

Garden Tomato and Avocado Salad

Makes 4 servings

> Herbed French Dressing (recipe follows)
> ½ head lettuce *or* 1 bunch escarole
> Lemon juice
> 2 ripe avocados, peeled and sliced
> 4 large tomatoes, peeled and cut in wedges

Prepare Herbed French Dressing; chill. Wash, drain, and chill lettuce or escarole. Sprinkle lemon juice on avocados to keep from turning brown. Refrigerate about 1 hour. Arrange greens, tomatoes, and avocados in a salad bowl. Drizzle dressing over salad. Separate with a fork to coat with dressing but do not toss.

Herbed French Dressing

Makes about 1 cup

> ¾ cup olive *or* vegetable oil
> ¼ cup lemon juice
> 2 tablespoons minced chives
> 1 tablespoon minced fresh tarragon *or* 1 teaspoon crushed leaf tarragon
> 1 tablespoon minced dillweed *or* 1 teaspoon dried dillweed
> 2 teaspoons salt
> Dash pepper

In a small bowl, combine all ingredients; blend well. Refrigerate at least 30 minutes. Mix with a fork before using.

Quick Fruit Salad

Makes 8 to 10 servings

> 1 cantaloupe, cut in chunks
> 1 small jar (10 ounces) maraschino cherries, drained and halved
> 1 cup pineapple chunks, drained
> 1 cup mandarin orange segments, drained
> 1 banana, sliced
> 1 can (21 ounces) peach pie filling

In a medium bowl, combine all fruit. Stir in peach pie filling; blend well. Chill at least 1 hour before serving.

Note: Proportions of fruit can be varied without adding additional pie filling.

Macaroni Fruit Salad with Orange Dressing

Makes 6 to 8 servings

> 1 package (7 ounces) elbow macaroni, cooked according to package directions and drained
> ½ cup wheat germ
> 1 can (13¼ ounces) pineapple tidbits, drained; reserve juice
> 1 cup cantaloupe balls
> 1 can (4 ounces) mandarin orange segments, drained
> 1 cup seedless grape halves
> 1 carton (8 ounces) mandarin-orange-flavored yogurt
> 2 tablespoons honey
> Salad greens, optional

In a large bowl, place macaroni. Reserve 2 tablespoons wheat germ. Sprinkle remaining wheat germ over macaroni; blend well. Add pineapple, cantaloupe, oranges, and grapes; toss lightly to blend. In a small bowl, combine 2 tablespoons of the reserved pineapple juice, yogurt, and honey; blend well. Pour yogurt dressing over fruit and macaroni; blend well. Sprinkle reserved wheat germ over top of salad. Refrigerate until chilled, about 2 hours. Serve on crisp salad greens, if desired.

Summer Fruit Basket

Makes 8 to 10 servings

> ½ watermelon (slice lengthwise)
> 1 cantaloupe
> 1 quart strawberries
> 1 quart blueberries
> 1 quart cherries
> 1 fresh pineapple *or* 1 can (16 ounces) pineapple chunks, drained
> 3 limes, cut in wedges, optional
> Mint sprigs, optional

Use a melon scoop to make balls from watermelon and cantaloupe. Refrigerate melons while preparing basket. Hollow out watermelon shell. Use a sharp knife to make a scalloped or sawtooth edge on the watermelon. Combine melon balls, strawberries, blueberries, cherries, and pineapple in watermelon basket. Garnish with lime wedges and mint sprigs, if desired. Chill well before serving.

Note: Any fresh fruit can be substituted if some of those listed are not available.

Fire and Ice Tomatoes

Makes 6 to 8 servings

>   Mustard Ring Mold (recipe follows)
> 6 large tomatoes, thickly sliced
> ¼ cup minced onion
> 2 teaspoons crushed leaf basil
> 2 teaspoons salt, divided
> ¼ cup wine vinegar
> ¾ cup olive *or* vegetable oil
> 1 clove garlic, minced
> 1 teaspoon Worcestershire sauce
> ½ teaspoon black pepper
> ½ teaspoon sugar

Prepare Mustard Ring Mold. Line the bottom of a large serving bowl with tomato slices. In a separate bowl, combine onion, basil, and 1 teaspoon of the salt. Sprinkle some of the onion mixture over tomatoes in bowl. Layer remaining tomato slices, sprinkling onion mixture over each layer. In a stoppered jar or cruet, combine wine vinegar, olive oil, garlic, Worcestershire sauce, remaining 1 teaspoon salt, pepper, and sugar; shake to blend well. Pour dressing over tomatoes. Cover and refrigerate until well chilled. To serve, carefully tip bowl to drain excess liquid or transfer to Mustard Ring Mold with a slotted spoon.

Mustard Ring Mold

> 1 envelope (¼ ounce) unflavored gelatin
> 1½ cups cole slaw salad dressing
> ⅓ cup dry mustard
> 2 cups whipping cream, whipped

Place gelatin in the top of a double boiler over slowly boiling water. Slowly stir in salad dressing; blend well. Stir in dry mustard. Cook until mixture is hot and gelatin is dissolved. Remove from heat; cool slightly Use a rubber spatula to gently fold the mustard mixture into the whipped cream. Rinse a 6-cup ring mold with cold water. Shake out excess water. Immediately pour mustard mixture into ring mold. Refrigerate 3 to 4 hours.

Texas Cole Slaw

Makes 8 servings

> 1 medium head cabbage, cored and shredded
> 1 large green pepper, thinly sliced
> 1 large onion, thinly sliced
> ½ cup sugar
> 1 cup cider vinegar
> 1 tablespoon sugar
> 1½ teaspoons celery seed
> 1 tablespoon dry mustard
> 1 cup vegetable oil

In a large bowl, combine cabbage, green pepper, and onion. Sprinkle ½ cup sugar over top; toss lightly; set aside. In a medium saucepan, combine vinegar, 1 tablespoon sugar, celery seed, and mustard; bring to boiling, stirring constantly. Remove from heat. Stir in oil. Return to heat; bring to boiling. Pour hot mixture over cabbage mixture; toss lightly. Cover and refrigerate 8 hours or overnight. Before transporting or serving, drain slaw well in a colander.

Seven Layer Salad

Makes 6 to 8 servings

> 1 head lettuce, torn into bite-size pieces
> 1 cup chopped celery
> ½ cup chopped green onions
> 1 cup diced green pepper
> 1 package (10 ounces) frozen peas, cooked
>   and drained
> 4 hard-cooked eggs, sliced, optional
> 2 tablespoons sugar
> 2 cups mayonnaise
> ½ pound sliced bacon, cooked, drained, and crumbled
> 4 ounces Cheddar cheese, shredded

In a large salad bowl, place lettuce. Layer celery, onions, green pepper, peas, and eggs over lettuce. Spread mayonnaise over top. Sprinkle sugar over mayonnaise. Sprinkle on bacon and cheese. Refrigerate until ready to serve.

Deluxe Potato Salad

Makes 6 to 8 servings

> 8 medium potatoes *or* 12 new potatoes
> 1 can (10½ ounces) chicken broth
> 1 large red onion, minced
> 12 cherry tomatoes
> 1 can (4 ounces) artichoke hearts, drained
>   and sliced
> 4 hard-cooked eggs, diced
>   Chopped parsley
>   Salt and pepper
> 1 cup mayonnaise *or* salad dressing

Boil the potatoes in their skins until tender, about 25 minutes; drain and set aside until cool. Peel and slice potatoes; place in a bowl. Pour chicken broth over potatoes; let stand for 1 hour. In a salad bowl, combine onion, tomatoes, artichoke hearts, and eggs. Sprinkle on parsley, and salt and pepper to taste. Just before serving, drain potatoes and add to vegetables; toss lightly. Stir in mayonnaise. If transporting, keep potato salad well chilled.

Salads

Calico Bean Salad

Makes 6 servings

- 2 cups cut green beans, drained
- 2 cups cut waxed beans, drained
- 2 cups kidney beans, drained
- 1 can (16 ounces) garbanzo beans, drained
- ½ large green pepper, sliced
- ½ large onion, sliced
- ¾ cup sugar
- ⅔ cup vinegar
- ⅓ cup vegetable oil
- Salt

In a large bowl, combine all the beans, green pepper, and onion; toss lightly to mix. In a small bowl, combine sugar, vinegar, oil, and salt to taste; blend well. Pour dressing over salad; toss lightly. Chill well, stirring occasionally.

Shrimp Macaroni Salad

Makes 4 to 6 servings

- 1 box (7 ounces) ring macaroni, cooked according to package directions and drained
- 1 cup pitted black olives, sliced
- 1 can (6½ ounces) broken shrimp, drained
- 6 hard-cooked eggs, chopped
- 2 ribs celery, diced
- 2 green onions, diced
- 2 ounces mild Cheddar cheese, cubed
- ½ teaspoon onion salt
- 1 cup mayonnaise or salad dressing

In a large bowl, combine macaroni, olives, shrimp, eggs, celery, onions, and cheese; toss lightly. Stir onion salt into mayonnaise; blend into macaroni mixture. Cover and refrigerate until chilled.

Crunchy Chicken Salad

Makes 4 servings

- 1 cup diced cooked chicken
- 1 cup diced celery
- 1 cup shredded raw carrots
- ¼ cup minced onion
- 1 tablespoon half-and-half or milk
- ½ cup mayonnaise or salad dressing
- 1 tablespoon pickle relish
- 1 can (2 ounces) shoestring potatoes

In a medium bowl, combine chicken, celery, carrots, and onion; toss lightly. In a separate small bowl, stir half-and-half into mayonnaise. Stir in relish. Add dressing to vegetables; blend well. Top with shoestring potatoes and serve.

German Potato Salad

Makes 6 to 8 servings

- 10 medium potatoes
- 1 pound sliced bacon, crisp-cooked, drained, and crumbled; reserve 2 tablespoons drippings
- 1 tablespoon flour
- ¾ cup water
- ¼ cup vinegar
- ¼ cup sugar
- 1 teaspoon salt
- 1 small onion, minced
- 1½ cups diced celery

Boil the potatoes in their skins until tender, about 25 minutes; drain, peel, and cube or slice. In the same pan the bacon was fried in, blend flour into reserved drippings. Cook over low heat 2 minutes, stirring constantly. Gradually stir in water, vinegar, sugar, and salt. Add onion and celery. Simmer over low heat 5 to 10 minutes or until celery is tender. Place sliced potatoes in a large bowl. Pour bacon mixture over potatoes; stir to coat potatoes. Serve hot.

Chef's Salad

Makes 8 servings

- 1½ quarts mixed salad greens, coarsely torn
- 1 cup sliced celery
- 1 cup sliced cucumber
- ½ cup green pepper strips
- 1 cup sliced carrots
- 1 cup cauliflower, broken into flowerets
- 2 large tomatoes, cut in wedges
- 2 hard-cooked eggs, sliced
- 1 cup Cheddar cheese strips
- 1½ cups cooked ham strips
- Spicy French Dressing (recipe on page 47)

In a large salad bowl, combine salad greens, celery, cucumbers, green peppers, carrots, and cauliflower; toss lightly to mix. Arrange tomatoes, eggs, cheese, and ham attractively on top of salad greens. Serve with Spicy French Dressing.

Mustard and Pepper Relish

Makes about 6 pints

- 5 sweet green peppers
- 3 sweet red peppers
- 3 large onions
- 1 cup flour
- 6 cups sugar
- 3 cups vinegar
- 1 cup water
- 1 jar (7 ounces) prepared mustard
- 2 tablespoons salt
- 2 teaspoons turmeric
- 2 teaspoons celery seed

Grind peppers and onions in a food grinder or chop in a food processor. In a large saucepan or Dutch oven, combine peppers, onions, and remaining ingredients; blend well. Cook over medium heat until thickened, stirring often. Pack boiling hot into clean hot jars to within ½ inch of the top. Seal with two-piece vacuum seal lids according to manufacturer's directions. Process in boiling water-bath canner for 10 minutes. Use on hot dogs, hamburgers, sandwiches, in ham salad, or as a dressing for potato salad.

Piccalilli

Makes about 7 pints

- 20 green tomatoes
- 1 medium head cabbage, cored
- 6 large sweet green peppers
- 6 large sweet red peppers
- 6 medium onions
- 1 cup salt
- 3 quarts vinegar
- 8 cups sugar
- 2 tablespoons celery seed
- 2 tablespoons dry mustard
- 2 tablespoons whole cloves

Grind tomatoes, cabbage, peppers, and onions in food grinder or chop in a food processor. In a large bowl, combine vegetables and salt. Cover and let stand overnight. Drain; transfer vegetables to a large saucepan or Dutch oven. Add vinegar, sugar, and spices. Bring to boiling; boil 20 minutes, stirring often. Pack boiling hot into clean hot jars to within ½ inch of the top. Seal with two-piece vacuum seal lids according to manufacturer's directions. Process in boiling water-bath canner for 10 minutes.

Banana Pepper Relish

Makes about 6 pints

- 8 cups banana peppers
- 1 small head cabbage, cored
- 1 tablespoon mustard seed
- 3 tablespoons salt
- 3 cups sugar
- 3 cups vinegar

Grind peppers and cabbage in a food grinder or chop in a food processor. In a large bowl, combine peppers, cabbage, mustard seed, and salt. Let stand overnight. Drain; transfer vegetables to a large saucepan or Dutch oven. Add sugar and vinegar. Bring to boiling; boil for 20 minutes, stirring often. Pack boiling hot into clean hot jars to within ½ inch of the top. Seal with two-piece vacuum seal lids according to manufacturer's directions. Process in boiling water-bath canner for 10 minutes.

Green Tomato and Pepper Relish

Makes about 4 pints

- 1 quart green tomatoes
- 2 medium sweet red peppers
- 2 medium sweet green peppers
- 2 large onions
- 1 small head cabbage, cored
- 3 cups vinegar
- 2 cups firmly packed brown sugar
- 2 tablespoons mixed pickling spices

Grind tomatoes, peppers, onions, and cabbage in a food grinder or chop in a food processor. In a large bowl, combine all vegetables; let stand overnight. Drain well; squeeze out excess liquid. In a large saucepan or Dutch oven, combine vinegar and sugar. Place pickling spices in a spice bag or cheesecloth; tie securely. Add to vinegar mixture. Bring to boiling. Add vegetables; simmer about 30 minutes, stirring occasionally. Remove spice bag. Pack boiling hot into clean hot jars to within ½ inch of the top. Seal with two-piece vacuum seal lids according to manufacturer's directions. Process in boiling water-bath canner for 10 minutes.

Boiled Cole Slaw Dressing

Makes about 1½ cups

- **2 eggs**
- **2 teaspoons flour**
- **2 teaspoons dry mustard**
- **1 cup sugar**
- **1 cup cider vinegar**

In a medium saucepan, combine eggs, flour, and mustard; blend well with a fork. Add sugar and vinegar. Bring to boiling over medium heat, stirring constantly. Remove from heat; let stand until room temperature. Store in a covered container in the refrigerator.

Tomato Soup Salad Dressing

Makes about 2 cups

- **1 can (10¾ ounces) condensed tomato soup, undiluted**
- **¾ cup sugar**
- **⅓ cup vinegar**
- **1 cup vegetable oil**
- **1 teaspoon celery salt**
- **1 teaspoon garlic powder**
- **1 teaspoon instant minced onion**
- **1 teaspoon paprika**
- **½ teaspoon black pepper**
- **1 tablespoon Worcestershire sauce**

In a medium bowl, combine soup, sugar, vinegar, and oil; blend well. Add all seasonings and Worcestershire sauce; blend well. Store in a covered container in the refrigerator.

Sour Cream Blue Cheese Dressing

Makes about 1½ cups

- **½ cup crumbled blue cheese**
- **½ teaspoon salt**
- **⅛ teaspoon black pepper**
- **1 tablespoon minced onion**
  Dash Worcestershire sauce
- **1 teaspoon lemon juice**
- **1 cup dairy sour cream**

In a small bowl, combine blue cheese, salt, pepper, onion, Worcestershire sauce, and lemon juice; blend well. Stir in sour cream; blend well. Chill before serving.

Spicy French Dressing

Makes about 4 cups

- **1 can (10¾ ounces) tomato soup, undiluted**
- **¾ cup vegetable oil**
- **¾ cup sugar**
- **½ cup vinegar**
- **1 small onion, minced**
- **1 teaspoon Worcestershire sauce**
- **1 clove garlic, minced**
- **1 teaspoon salt**
- **¾ teaspoon black pepper**
- **¾ teaspoon paprika**
- **½ teaspoon dry mustard**

In an electric blender or food processor, combine soup, oil, sugar, and vinegar; blend well. Add onion and seasonings; blend well. Store in a covered container in the refrigerator.

Cranberry Orange Fruit Dressing

Makes about 1⅔ cups

- **1 carton (8 ounces) vanilla-flavored yogurt**
- **⅔ cup cranberry-orange sauce**
- **½ teaspoon grated lemon peel**
- **¼ teaspoon lemon juice**

In a small bowl, combine yogurt, cranberry-orange sauce, lemon peel, and juice; blend well. Chill before using. Serve over fruit, such as apple wedges, melon balls, pineapple chunks, orange sections, banana slices, or grapes.

Sweet Sour Cream Dressing

Makes 1 cup

- **1 carton (8 ounces) dairy sour cream**
- **3 tablespoons brown sugar *or* honey**

In a small bowl, combine sour cream and brown sugar or honey; blend well. Serve with assorted fresh fruit.

Quick Russian Dressing

Makes about 1 cup

- **1 cup mayonnaise *or* salad dressing**
- **4 tablespoons catsup**
  Dash Worcestershire sauce

In a small bowl, combine mayonnaise, catsup, and Worcestershire sauce; blend well. Chill before using.

Sauces and Marinades

Super Sauce

Makes about 1½ cups

- ¼ cup vinegar
- ½ cup water
- 2 tablespoons sugar
- 1 tablespoon mustard
- ½ teaspoon black pepper
- 1½ teaspoons salt
- ¼ teaspoon cayenne pepper
- 1 slice lemon
- 1 onion, sliced
- ¼ cup butter *or* margarine
- ½ cup catsup
- 2 tablespoons Worcestershire sauce
- 1½ teaspoons liquid smoke, optional

In a medium saucepan, combine vinegar, water, sugar, mustard, pepper, salt, cayenne, lemon, onion, and butter. Simmer, uncovered, 20 minutes, stirring occasionally. Add catsup, Worcestershire sauce, and liquid smoke, if desired; blend well. Bring to boiling. Remove from heat. Brush on ribs or chicken.

Cranberry Barbecue Sauce

Makes about 1¼ cups

- 1 can (8 ounces) jellied cranberry sauce
- ⅓ cup chili sauce
- 1 tablespoon Worcestershire sauce
- 1½ teaspoons lemon juice

In a small saucepan, place cranberry sauce; break up with a fork. Add remaining ingredients; blend well. Cook over medium-low heat until smooth. Brush on chicken or hamburgers. Pass remaining sauce at the table.

Jiffy Sauce

Makes about 1¼ cups

- 1 can (8 ounces) tomato sauce
- 2 tablespoons vegetable oil
- 1 tablespoon vinegar
- 1 tablespoon Worcestershire sauce
- 1 tablespoon instant minced onion
- 1 teaspoon salt
- ¼ teaspoon hot pepper sauce

In a small bowl, combine all ingredients; blend well. Brush on chicken, ribs, hot dogs, or hamburgers.

Beer-B-Q Sauce

Makes about 2½ cups

- ⅓ cup packed brown sugar
- 1 cup beer
- 1 cup catsup
- ⅓ cup vinegar
- 1 teaspoon dry mustard
- 1 teaspoon paprika
- ½ teaspoon chili powder
- ½ teaspoon salt
- 3 tablespoons Worcestershire sauce
- 1 medium onion, thinly sliced
- ½ lemon, thinly sliced
- 2 tablespoons cornstarch

In a medium saucepan, combine brown sugar, beer, catsup, vinegar, dry mustard, paprika, chili powder, salt, and Worcestershire sauce. Bring to boiling over medium heat, stirring frequently. Reduce heat and cook 5 minutes. Add onion and lemon. Simmer 5 minutes, stirring often. Remove about ¼ cup of sauce from pan. Stir cornstarch into reserved sauce until dissolved. Return to pan; blend well. Cook and stir 2 to 3 minutes or until thickened. Brush on chicken or ribs.

New Orleans Sauce

Makes about 1 cup

- 1 cup water
- 2 ounces bourbon
- 2 teaspoons soy sauce
- Dash Worcestershire sauce

In a small bowl, combine all ingredients. Brush on any kind of beef or game.

Orange and Raisin Sauce

Makes about 2 cups

- 1 can (6 ounces) frozen orange juice concentrate, undiluted
- 1½ cups water
- ½ cup sugar
- 1½ tablespoons cornstarch
- Salt
- ⅓ cup dark raisins

In a small saucepan, combine orange juice concentrate, water, and sugar. Add cornstarch; stir to dissolve. Cook over low heat until thickened, stirring frequently. Season with salt to taste. Stir in raisins. Brush on ham. Pass remaining sauce.

Lemon Barbecue Sauce for Chicken

Makes about 2 cups

    1 cup butter *or* margarine
    1 clove garlic, minced
    4 teaspoons flour
    2/3 cup hot water
    1 tablespoon sugar
    1 teaspoon black pepper
    6 tablespoons lemon juice
    1/4 teaspoon hot pepper sauce
    1/2 teaspoon crushed leaf thyme
    1 tablespoon salt

In a medium saucepan, melt butter. Add garlic; sauté until garlic is fragrant, 3 to 4 minutes. Stir in flour; cook 2 minutes, stirring constantly. Gradually stir in water until smooth. Add remaining ingredients. Cook until slightly thickened, stirring frequently. Let stand until cool. Dip chicken or shrimp in sauce before grilling.

Apricot Ginger Sauce

Makes about 1 1/2 cups

    1 jar (10 ounces) apricot preserves
    3 tablespoons cider vinegar
    2 tablespoons butter, melted
    1/2 teaspoon ground ginger
    1/2 teaspoon salt

In a small saucepan, combine all ingredients. Cook over low heat until preserves are melted and mixture is smooth, stirring constantly. Brush on chicken or pork the last 15 minutes of cooking time.

Country Terrace Barbecue Sauce

Makes about 2 3/4 cups

    1/4 cup butter *or* margarine
    3/4 cup sliced green onions
    1/2 cup chopped celery
    4 cups chopped peeled tomatoes *or* 2 cans
        (15 ounces each) tomato sauce with tomato bits
    1/4 cup chopped parsley
    1/4 cup packed brown sugar
    1/4 cup vinegar
    1 1/2 teaspoons salt
    2 tablespoons Worcestershire sauce

In a medium saucepan, melt butter. Add green onions and celery; sauté until vegetables are tender-crisp. Add tomatoes; simmer until vegetables are tender. Stir in remaining ingredients. Brush on chicken.

Deep South Hot Barbecue Sauce

Makes about 2 1/4 cups

    2 tablespoons olive *or* vegetable oil
    2 tablespoons instant minced onion, rehydrated
    1/4 teaspoon instant minced garlic, rehydrated
    2 tablespoons water
    1 cup chicken broth
    1 can (8 ounces) tomato sauce
    1 can (6 ounces) tomato paste
    3 tablespoons vinegar
    2 tablespoons brown sugar
    2 tablespoons parsley flakes
    1/2 teaspoon ground allspice
    1/4 teaspoon salt
    1/4 teaspoon cayenne pepper

In a medium saucepan, heat oil. Add onion and garlic; sauté 4 minutes or until onion is golden. Remove from heat. Add remaining ingredients; blend well. Simmer, uncovered, 15 minutes, stirring occasionally. Brush on chicken, pork, or fish.

Smoky Barbecue Sauce

Makes about 2 cups

    1 cup packed brown sugar
    1 can (10 3/4 ounces) tomato soup, undiluted
    1/4 cup butter *or* margarine
    1/4 cup catsup
    2 tablespoons prepared mustard
    2 tablespoons liquid smoke
    2 tablespoons lemon juice
    1 tablespoon Worcestershire sauce
    1 teaspoon onion powder
    1/4 teaspoon garlic powder

In a medium saucepan, combine all ingredients; blend well. Bring to boiling over low heat, stirring frequently. Boil 1 minute; remove from heat. Brush on chicken, ribs, hot dogs, or hamburgers.

Western Sauce

Makes about 2 1/4 cups

    1/2 cup packed brown sugar
    3/4 cup catsup
    1/2 cup cider vinegar
    1/3 cup chili sauce
    2 tablespoons prepared mustard
    2 tablespoons steak sauce
    1 tablespoon vegetable oil
        Dash hot pepper sauce
    1 clove garlic, minced

In a small bowl, combine all ingredients; blend well. Brush on chicken, ribs, or hamburgers.

Marinades

Quick Steak Marinade

Makes about ½ cup

- ¼ cup steak sauce
- ¼ cup lemon juice
- 2 tablespoons vegetable oil
- 1 small onion, minced
- 1 clove garlic, crushed

In a small bowl, combine all ingredients; blend well. Place steak in shallow dish or in a double plastic bag. Pour marinade over steak. Cover or seal. Refrigerate 3 to 4 hours, turning steak once. Grill steak to desired doneness.

Lemon Marinade

Makes about 1½ cups

- ¾ cup vegetable oil
- 6 tablespoons soy sauce
- ¼ cup wine vinegar
- 3 tablespoons lemon juice
- 2 tablespoons Worcestershire sauce
- 1 tablespoon dry mustard
- 1 tablespoon salt
- 1½ teaspoons black pepper

In a small bowl, combine all ingredients; blend well. Place steak or roast in a shallow dish or in a double plastic bag. Pour marinade over meat. Cover or seal. Refrigerate 24 hours, turning meat occasionally. Grill meat to desired doneness.

Red Wine Marinade

Makes about 1½ cups

- ½ cup red wine
- ½ cup soy sauce
- ½ cup vegetable oil
- 2 tablespoons lemon juice
- 2 cloves garlic, minced
- 1 teaspoon salt
- ½ teaspoon ground ginger
- ½ teaspoon black pepper

In a small bowl, combine all ingredients; blend well. Place steak in a shallow dish or in a double plastic bag. Pour marinade over steak. Cover or seal. Refrigerate several hours or overnight, turning steak occasionally. Grill steak to desired doneness.

Pineapple Marinade

Makes about 2 cups

- ½ cup packed brown sugar
- 1 cup soy sauce
- ½ cup pineapple juice
- ½ cup vinegar
- 2 teaspoons salt
- ½ teaspoon garlic powder

In a medium saucepan, combine all ingredients; blend well. Bring to boiling; reduce heat and simmer 5 minutes. Refrigerate until chilled. Use to marinate shish kebabs or chicken.

Apple Tarragon Marinade

Makes about 2 cups

- 1 cup apple cider
- ⅓ cup vinegar
- ¼ cup vegetable oil
- 3 tablespoons honey
- 2 tablespoons steak sauce
- ⅓ cup sliced green onion with tops
- 1½ teaspoons crushed leaf tarragon
- 1 teaspoon salt
- ¼ teaspoon black pepper

In a medium saucepan, combine all ingredients. Bring to boiling; reduce heat and simmer, uncovered 20 minutes. Refrigerate until chilled. Use to marinate chicken or lamb.

White Wine Marinade

Makes about 1½ cups

- 1 cup white wine
- ½ cup vegetable oil
- ¼ cup minced celery
- ¼ cup minced onion
- 1 clove garlic, minced
- 1 teaspoon crushed leaf marjoram
- 1 teaspoon crushed leaf thyme
- ¼ teaspoon black pepper

In a small bowl, combine all ingredients; blend well. Place chicken or fish in a shallow dish or in a double plastic bag. Pour marinade over chicken or fish. Cover or seal. Refrigerate 3 to 4 hours. Grill as desired.

Soy-Glazed Cornish Hens, 24

Marinades

Wild Game Marinade

Makes about 1 quart

    2 cups dry red wine
    1 cup wine vinegar
    1 cup water
    1 carrot, chopped
    1 rib celery, chopped
    1 large onion, chopped
    2 cloves garlic, crushed
    1 tablespoon mixed pickling spices
    ½ teaspoon black pepper

In a medium bowl, combine all ingredients; blend well. Place game, such as venison, in a large container. Pour marinade over meat. Cover and refrigerate 3 to 5 days for small cuts; 5 to 10 days for larger quantities. Makes enough marinade for up to 4 pounds of meat.

French Dressing Marinade

Makes about 1 cup

    1 bottle (8 ounces) French dressing
    1 cup dry red wine
    1 clove garlic, minced
    1 teaspoon chopped parsley
    ⅛ teaspoon crushed leaf tarragon
    ⅛ teaspoon crushed leaf thyme

In a small bowl, combine all ingredients; blend well. Place meat, fish, or vegetables in a shallow dish or in a double plastic bag. Cover or seal. Refrigerate 3 to 4 hours, turning once. Grill as desired. Use on chicken, lamb, fish, or vegetables.

Beef Marinade

Makes about 2 cups

    1 cup tomato juice
    ½ cup vinegar
    3 tablespoons chili powder
    1 tablespoon brown sugar
    1 tablespoon onion powder
    1½ teaspoons salt
    ½ teaspoon crushed leaf oregano
    ½ teaspoon garlic powder

In a small bowl, combine all ingredients; blend well. Baste steaks, ribs, or hamburgers during grilling time.

Teriyaki Marinade

Makes about ¾ cup

    ¼ cup soy sauce
    ¼ cup red wine *or* **2 ounces bourbon** *or* **water**
    2 tablespoons sugar
    1 teaspoon ground ginger
    1 clove garlic, minced

In a small bowl, combine all ingredients; stir to dissolve sugar. Place steak in a shallow dish or in a double plastic bag. Pour marinade over steak. Cover or seal. Refrigerate 3 to 4 hours. Grill to desired doneness.

Dilled Wine Marinade

Makes about 3 cups

    2 cups dry red *or* **white wine**
    ½ cup olive *or* **vegetable oil**
    1 onion, thinly sliced
    2 carrots, thinly sliced
    ¼ cup parsley sprigs *or* **4 teaspoons parsley flakes**
    ¼ cup dill sprigs *or* **4 teaspoons dried dillweed**
    ¼ cup minced chives
    Dash pepper

In a medium bowl, combine all ingredients, blend well. Use to marinate fish or vegetables.

Hot Pepper and Herb Marinade

Makes about ¾ cup

    ¼ cup lime juice
    ½ cup vegetable oil
    ½ teaspoon sugar
    1 teaspoon dry mustard
    1 teaspoon salt
    ¼ teaspoon crushed leaf thyme
    ¼ teaspoon crushed leaf rosemary
    ¼ teaspoon crushed leaf basil
    1 bay leaf
    ¼ teaspoon hot pepper sauce

In a small bowl, combine lime juice and oil; blend well. Add remaining ingredients; blend well. Place (beef or lamb) in a shallow pan or in a double plastic bag. Pour marinade over meat. Cover or seal. Refrigerate at least 5 hours, turning occasionally. Grill to desired doneness.

Condiments

Plantation Hot Sauce

Makes about 1½ cups

½ cup honey
½ cup prepared mustard
½ cup cider vinegar
¼ cup Worcestershire sauce
1 tablespoon chopped parsley
2 teaspoons hot pepper sauce
1 teaspoon salt

In a medium saucepan, combine honey and mustard; blend well. Stir in remaining ingredients. Bring to boiling over low heat, stirring often. Remove from heat. Serve warm with smoked fish or shrimp.

Cool Blender Sauce

Makes about 2¼ cups

¾ cup mayonnaise *or* salad dressing
1 egg
3 tablespoons lemon juice
1 teaspoon salt
1 teaspoon sugar
1 teaspoon instant minced onion
1 teaspoon prepared mustard
2 drops hot pepper sauce
⅛ teaspoon black pepper
¾ cup vegetable oil
⅓ cup chopped parsley
1 tablespoon prepared horseradish
1 clove garlic, minced

In an electric blender or food processor, combine first 9 ingredients; blend 3 to 4 seconds. With blender on, gradually add oil; blend until thick and smooth. Add parsley, horseradish, and garlic; blend until smooth. Serve with grilled or smoked fish.

Homemade Tomato Catsup

Makes about 10 pints

1 peck (12½ pounds) ripe tomatoes
8 medium onions, sliced
¼ teaspoon cayenne pepper
2 cups cider vinegar
1½ tablespoons broken stick cinnamon
1 tablespoon whole cloves
3 cloves garlic, minced
1 tablespoon paprika
1 cup sugar
2½ teaspoons salt

Wash and slice tomatoes. Boil tomatoes in a large kettle of water about 15 minutes or until soft. In a separate kettle, place onions. Add water just to cover; cook until tender; drain. Press tomatoes and onions through a sieve or process in an electric blender or food processor. Combine tomatoes and onion in a large saucepan or Dutch oven. Add cayenne; bring to boiling and boil rapidly until mixture is reduced to about half the original volume. While tomatoes are cooking, pour vinegar into a medium saucepan. Combine cinnamon, cloves, and garlic in a spice bag or piece of cheesecloth; tie securely. Add to vinegar. Bring to boiling; reduce heat and simmer 30 minutes. Bring to boiling; remove from heat; discard spice bag. Cover and set aside until ready to use. Add vinegar to tomato mixture. (There should be about 1¼ cups vinegar.) Add paprika, sugar, and salt; bring to boiling. Boil about 10 minutes until desired thickness, stirring often. Pour immediately into clean hot jars to within ½ inch of the top. Seal with two-piece vacuum seal lids according to manufacturer's directions. Process in a boiling water-bath canner for 10 minutes.

Lemon Catsup Sauce

Makes about 1 cup

¾ cup catsup
2 tablespoons steak sauce
1 tablespoon grated lemon peel
1 teaspoon lemon juice

In a small bowl, combine all ingredients. Serve over corned beef hash patties or hamburgers.

Tartar Sauce

Makes about ¾ cup

½ cup mayonnaise *or* salad dressing
1 tablespoon chopped ripe olives, optional
1 tablespoon chopped onion
1 tablespoon minced parsley
1 tablespoon sweet pickle relish

In a small bowl, combine all ingredients; blend well. Chill before serving with fish.

Appetizers

Oregano Dip

Makes about 1 cup

   1 cup dairy sour cream
   1 teaspoon crushed leaf oregano
   ½ teaspoon grated onion
   ¼ teaspoon salt
   Dash hot pepper sauce
   Assorted raw vegetables

In a small bowl, combine all ingredients, except vegetables; blend well. Chill at least 1 hour before serving.

Onion Smoked Fish Spread

Makes about 2 cups

   2 cups flaked smoked fish
   ¾ cup mayonnaise *or* salad dressing
   ½ teaspoon onion powder
   2 tablespoons chopped parsley
   Assorted chips, crackers, or raw vegetables

In a small bowl, combine all ingredients, except chips; blend well. Chill at least 1 hour before serving. Serve with chips, crackers, or raw vegetables.

Beach Balls

Makes 6 servings

   1 can (7½ ounces) minced clams; drained; reserve liquid
   ½ cup butter *or* margarine
   ½ teaspoon poultry seasoning
   ¼ teaspoon salt
   1 cup flour
   4 eggs

Grease a large baking sheet; set aside. Preheat oven to 450° F. Add water to reserved clam liquid to equal 1 cup. In a saucepan, combine clam liquid, butter, poultry seasoning, and salt. Bring to boiling; reduce heat. Add flour; cook until mixture forms a ball, stirring constantly. Remove from heat. Add eggs, one at a time, beating well after each addition. Beat until shiny and smooth. Stir in clams. Drop dough by teaspoonfuls onto the prepared baking sheet. Bake 10 minutes; reduce heat to 350° F. and bake 10 minutes. Serve warm or cold.

Smoked Fish Spread

Makes about 3½ cups

   1½ pounds smoked fish, skinned, boned, and flaked
   1¼ cups mayonnaise *or* salad dressing
   2 tablespoons minced sweet pickle
   2 tablespoons chopped parsley
   1 tablespoon mustard
   2 teaspoons minced onion
   2 teaspoons minced celery
   1 clove garlic, minced
   ⅛ teaspoon Worcestershire sauce
   Assorted chips, crackers, or raw vegetables

In a medium bowl, combine all ingredients, except chips. blend well. Chill at least 1 hour before serving. Serve with chips, crackers or raw vegetables.

Fresh Fruit Dip

Makes about 4 cups

   12 macaroon cookies, coarsely crushed
   ¼ cup firmly packed brown sugar
   2 cups dairy sour cream
   1 large pineapple
   Assorted berries
   Purple *or* red grapes, seeded, if necessary
   Seedless green grapes
   Sliced bananas
   Watermelon wedges
   Peaches, sliced
   Kirsch *or* brandy, optional

In a small bowl, combine macaroons, brown sugar, and sour cream; blend well. Chill several hours to soften macaroons. (Do not stir.) Cut a slice from pineapple about 1 inch below bottom leaves. Use a sharp knife to hollow out center, leaving shell intact. Cut pineapple pulp into bite-size pieces, discarding hard center core. Spoon sour cream dip into shell. Place pineapple in the center of a large serving platter. Arrange pineapple, berries, grapes, bananas, watermelon wedges, and peaches around pineapple. Sprinkle fruit with kirsch or brandy, if desired.

Appetizers

Pickled Shrimp

Makes 8 to 12 servings

2½ pounds fresh *or* thawed frozen shrimp
   Boiling water
½ cup celery tops
¼ cup mixed pickling spices
5 teaspoons salt, divided
2 cups sliced onions
7 bay leaves
1¼ cups vegetable oil
¾ cup vinegar
2½ tablespoons capers, undrained
2½ teaspoons celery seed
1½ teaspoons salt
   Dash hot pepper sauce

In a large saucepan, cover shrimp with boiling water. Add celery tops, pickling spices, and 3½ teaspoons of the salt. Simmer, covered, 5 minutes. Drain, cool, peel, shell, and devein shrimp. In a shallow dish, arrange shrimp and sliced onion. Add bay leaves. In a small bowl, combine oil, vinegar, capers and liquid, celery seed, remaining 1½ teaspoons salt, and hot pepper sauce; blend well. Pour marinade over shrimp and onions. Cover and refrigerate 24 hours. Drain marinade and serve.

Ham and Broccoli Cups

Makes 36

2 packages (10 ounces each) refrigerated butterflake rolls
1 tablespoon butter, softened
1 teaspoon lemon juice
2 tablespoons chopped onion
2 tablespoons chopped parsley
2 tablespoons prepared mustard
¾ cup shredded Cheddar cheese
¾ cup shredded mozzarella cheese
1 cup minced ham
1 cup minced broccoli, fresh *or* thawed frozen

Separate rolls; cut in halves. Press each half firmly into greased muffin cups. Bake in a 350° F. oven 5 minutes. If biscuits become too puffy, gently reshape. In a small bowl, combine butter, lemon juice, onion, parsley, and mustard; blend well. Add cheeses, ham, and broccoli; blend well. Spoon mixture by tablespoonfuls into partially baked cups. Bake 15 to 20 minutes or until hot and bubbly. These can be made ahead, frozen, thawed, and reheated on the grill.

Chili Dip

Makes about 1¼ cups

1 cup small curd cottage cheese
1 hard-cooked egg, finely chopped
1½ teaspoons grated onion
1 teaspoon chili powder
½ teaspoon salt
3 tablespoons pickle relish
1 tablespoon chopped stuffed olives
   Assorted chips, crackers, or raw vegetables

In a small bowl, combine cottage cheese, egg, onion, chili powder, and salt; beat with an electric mixer until smooth. Stir in pickle relish and olives. Cover and chill at least 1 hour before serving. Serve with chips, crackers, or raw vegetables.

Sausage Stuffed Mushrooms

Makes about 24 appetizers

1 pound fresh mushrooms
1 pound bulk pork sausage
1 clove garlic, minced
2 tablespoons chopped parsley
1½ cups shredded sharp Cheddar cheese
   Chopped, drained pimiento, optional
   Chopped parsley, optional

Rinse mushrooms; remove stems and pat dry. Chop stems. In a large skillet, combine chopped stems, sausage, garlic, and 2 tablespoons parsley. Cook until sausage is browned, stirring often; drain fat. Add cheese; stir until softened. Fill mushroom caps with sausage mixture. Place filled caps in a 13 x 9-inch baking dish. Bake at 350° F. 20 minutes or until cheese melts. Garnish with pimiento and parsley, if desired.

Taco Dip

Makes 8 servings

1 package (8 ounces) cream cheese, softened
1 can (10½ ounces) bean dip
1 package (1¼ ounces) taco seasoning mix, divided
2 cups shredded lettuce
2 large tomatoes, chopped
3 cups shredded Cheddar cheese
   Tortilla chips

In a bowl, combine cream cheese, bean dip, and half of the taco seasoning mix; blend well. Spoon into a shallow 8-inch serving dish. Top with lettuce, tomatoes, and Cheddar cheese. Sprinkle with remaining taco seasoning mix. Serve with tortilla chips.

Beverages

Golden Glow Punch

Makes 25 servings

    1 can (6 ounces) frozen lemonade concentrate,
      thawed
    1 can (6 ounces) frozen orange juice concentrate,
      thawed
    1 can (6 ounces) frozen tangerine juice concentrate,
      thawed
    2 cups water
    2 bottles (28 ounces each) ginger ale, chilled
      Ice cubes

In a punch bowl or large pitcher, combine all juice concentrates and water; blend well. Just before serving, add ginger ale and ice cubes.

Spiced Iced Tea

Makes 12 to 16 servings

    2 quarts water
    12 tea bags
    1 cup water
    ½ cup sugar
    ½ cup strained orange juice
    1 cup strained lemon juice
    12 whole cloves
    2 cinnamon sticks

In a large saucepan, boil 2 quarts water. Add tea bags; let stand 5 minutes. Remove tea bags. In a small saucepan, combine 1 cup water and sugar; bring to boiling, stirring to dissolve sugar. Remove from heat. Add orange and lemon juices and spices to sugar water. Add spiced mixture to tea. Chill well before serving over ice in tall glasses.

Sea Foam Punch

Makes 12 to 16 servings

    1 envelope (1½ ounces) unsweetened lemon-lime
      soft drink powder
    ½ cup sugar
    1 quart cold milk
    1 pint vanilla ice cream
    2 bottles (7 ounces each) lemon-lime carbonated
      beverage, chilled

In a large bowl, combine soft drink powder, sugar, and milk; stir to dissolve soft drink powder and sugar. Add ice cream by spoonfuls. Carefully pour in lemon-lime carbonated beverage. Serve immediately.

Strawberry Rhubarb Punch

Makes 8 servings

    3 cups sliced rhubarb
    3 cups water
    1 cup sliced strawberries
    1 can (6 ounces) frozen pink lemonade concentrate,
      thawed
    ¾ cup sugar
    1 cup ice cubes
    2 bottles (7 ounces each) lemon-lime carbonated
      beverage
      Lemon slices, optional
      Strawberries, optional

In a large saucepan, combine rhubarb, water, strawberries, lemonade concentrate, and sugar; bring to boiling over high heat. Reduce heat and simmer, covered, 10 to 15 minutes or until rhubarb is very soft. Press through colander with back of spoon; discard pulp. Cover and refrigerate until cold. Pour strawberry-rhubarb syrup over ice cubes in a punch bowl. Add lemon-lime carbonated beverage. Garnish with lemon slices and strawberries, if desired.

Orange Blossom Punch

Makes 25 servings

    1 cup cold water
    1 jar (4 ounces) maraschino cherries, drained
    1 can (8 ounces) pineapple chunks, drained
    2 quarts orange juice
    1 bottle (24 ounces) champagne

Fill a 6-cup ring mold with cold water. Drop in cherries and pineapple chunks. Place in freezer until frozen solid. At serving time, pour orange juice and champagne into a punch bowl. Unmold ice ring and slide into punch.

Cranberry Punch

Makes 12 to 16 servings

    1 can (16 ounces) jellied cranberry sauce
    ¾ cup orange juice
    ¼ cup lemon juice
    1 bottle (12 ounces) ginger ale, chilled
      Ice cubes

In a large pitcher, combine cranberry sauce and both juices. Chill. Just before serving, add ginger ale and ice cubes.

Desserts

Zucchini Banana Cake

Makes 12 to 16 servings

> 3 cups flour
> 2 teaspoons baking powder
> 1 teaspoon baking soda
> 1½ teaspoons cinnamon
> ½ teaspoon salt
> 1 cup vegetable oil
> 2 cups sugar
> 4 eggs
> 1½ cups grated zucchini
> 1½ cups mashed bananas (about 3 medium)
> 1 cup chopped nuts, optional

Grease and flour a 10-inch fluted tube pan. Preheat oven to 350° F. In a large bowl, combine flour, baking powder, baking soda, cinnamon, and salt; set aside. In a separate large bowl, combine oil and sugar; blend well. Add eggs; blend well. Blend in zucchini and bananas. Gradually blend in flour mixture. Stir in nuts, if desired. Pour into prepared pan. Bake for 1 hour 15 minutes or until a toothpick inserted in the center comes out clean. Cool in pan on a wire rack. Frost with a white or cream cheese frosting or glaze, if desired.

Summer Fruit Pie

Makes 4 to 6 servings

> ¾ cup graham cracker crumbs
> 2 tablespoons butter or margarine, melted
> 1 teaspoon sugar
>   Dash cinnamon
> 1 cup green or red grapes
> 1 cup blueberries
> 1 cup strawberry halves
> 1 peach, peeled and sliced

In a small bowl, combine graham cracker crumbs, butter, sugar, and cinnamon; blend well. Press into a 9-inch quiche pan or pie plate. Bake at 350° F. 10 minutes or until lightly browned. Arrange fruit over crust. Brush on Currant Glaze. Store in the refrigerator.

Currant Glaze

> ¼ cup red currant jelly
> 1 tablespoon water

In a small saucepan, combine jelly and water; cook over low heat 3 minutes or until jelly melts, stirring constantly.

Fresh Fruit Tart

Makes 12 servings

> 1 package (9 ounces) lemon cake mix
> ⅔ cup graham cracker crumbs
> ½ cup chopped nuts
> ½ cup butter or margarine, softened
> 1 egg
> 1 package (3 ounces) cream cheese, softened
> ⅓ cup sugar
> ¼ teaspoon orange or vanilla extract
> 1 cup whipping cream, whipped
> 4 cups assorted sliced fresh fruit
> ⅓ cup apple jelly, melted

Preheat oven to 350° F. In a large mixing bowl, combine cake mix, graham cracker crumbs, nuts, and butter; blend at low speed until crumbly. Add egg; blend well. Press into a 14-inch pizza pan or 10 x 15-inch jelly-roll pan. Bake 10 to 15 minutes or until golden. Cool in pan on a wire rack. In a small bowl, combine cream cheese, sugar, and orange extract; beat until fluffy. Fold in whipped cream until well blended. Spread over crust. Arrange fruit decoratively on top. Brush with melted jelly. Store in the refrigerator.

Chocolate Cheese Dessert

Makes 12 servings

> ¾ cup shortbread cookie crumbs
> ⅓ cup ground nuts
> 1 tablespoon sugar
> ¼ cup butter or margarine, melted
> 1 carton (8 ounces) vanilla-flavored yogurt
> 1 cup ricotta cheese
> 1 can (16½ ounces) ready-to-spread milk-chocolate frosting
>   Chopped nuts, optional

Preheat oven to 350° F. Grease a 9-inch springform pan; set aside. In a small bowl, combine cookie crumbs, nuts, sugar, and butter; blend until crumbly. Press mixture into bottom of prepared pan. Bake 8 minutes; let stand until cool. In a large bowl, combine yogurt, ricotta cheese, and frosting; beat on high speed 2 minutes or until smooth. Pour over cooled crust. Place in freezer 3 hours or until firm. Sprinkle nuts on top, if desired.

Desserts

Blueberry Parfait

Makes 8 servings

1 package (3 ounces) lemon-flavored gelatin
1 cup boiling water
1 tablespoon grated lemon peel
1 container (8 ounces) frozen whipped nondairy
　　dessert topping, thawed
1½ cups fresh blueberries

In a small bowl, dissolve gelatin in boiling water. Stir in lemon peel. Refrigerate until slightly thickened. Beat with an electric mixer until thick and fluffy. Fold in whipped topping until well blended. Spoon one-third of the gelatin into 8 tall dessert glasses. Top with about 1½ tablespoons blueberries. Repeat layers, ending with blueberries. Chill before serving.

Cherry Freeze

Makes about 10 servings

1 package (3 ounces) cherry-flavored gelatin
1 cup boiling water
½ cup sugar
2 cups milk
1 container (4 ounces) frozen whipped nondairy
　　dessert topping, thawed

In a small bowl, dissolve gelatin in boiling water. Add sugar; stir until completely dissolved. Stir in milk. (Mixture will appear curdled, but will become smooth when frozen.) Pour into a 9 x 13-inch pan. Freeze about 1 hour or until ice crystals begin to form 1 inch from edge. Transfer to chilled bowl; beat with an electric mixer until smooth. Fold in whipped topping until well blended. Return to pan. Place in freezer about 4 hours or until firm. Scoop into individual serving dishes.

Bananas Foster

Makes 4 servings

4 bananas
¼ cup butter or margarine
¼ cup packed brown sugar
2 teaspoons rum extract
¼ teaspoon cinnamon
　　Vanilla ice cream

Tear off 4 sheets of heavy-duty aluminum foil. Slice bananas lengthwise in half, then crosswise. Place bananas in center of foil. Dot each with butter. Sprinkle brown sugar, rum extract, and cinnamon over each. Wrap securely as shown on page 32. Grill over medium-hot coals 15 to 20 minutes or until bananas are tender. Remove bananas from foil; place in serving dishes. Top with scoops of vanilla ice cream.

Quick Orange Mousse

Makes 9 servings

1¼ cups graham cracker crumbs
⅓ cup butter or margarine, melted
¼ cup sugar
1 can (6 ounces) frozen orange juice concentrate,
　　thawed
1 jar (7 ounces) marshmallow creme topping
1 cup whipping cream, whipped

In an 8-inch square baking pan, combine graham cracker crumbs, butter, and sugar; blend well. Press firmly onto bottom of pan. In a small bowl, combine orange juice concentrate and marshmallow creme; blend well. Fold whipped cream into marshmallow mixture. Pour into prepared pan. Place in freezer until frozen. Cut into squares.

Peaches 'n Cream Cheesecake

Makes 6 to 8 servings

¾ cup flour
1 teaspoon baking powder
½ teaspoon salt
1 package (3¼ ounces) vanilla-flavored pudding mix
3 tablespoons butter or margarine, softened
1 egg
½ cup milk
1 can (16 ounces) sliced peaches, drained;
　　reserve 3 tablespoons syrup
1 package (8 ounces) cream cheese, softened
½ cup sugar
1 tablespoon sugar
½ teaspoon cinnamon

Grease a 10-inch pie plate; set aside. In a large mixing bowl, combine flour, baking powder, salt, pudding mix, butter, egg, and milk; beat on low speed just until all ingredients are moistened. Beat on medium speed 2 minutes. Pour into prepared pie plate. Arrange peach slices on top of batter. In a small bowl, combine cream cheese, sugar, and reserved peach syrup; blend well. Spread cream cheese mixture over peaches. Preheat oven to 350° F. Combine sugar and cinnamon; sprinkle over cheesecake. Bake 30 to 35 minutes or until golden. Cool to room temperature. Serve warm or chilled. Store in the refrigerator.

Apple Upside-Down Cake

Makes 9 servings

 2 tablespoons butter *or* margarine
 ½ cup packed brown sugar
 1¼ cups sliced apples
 Pecan halves
 1 teaspoon cinnamon
 1 package (9 ounces) yellow cake mix

In a 9-inch baking pan, melt butter over low heat. Sprinkle brown sugar over bottom of pan. Arrange apple slices and pecans over brown sugar. Sprinkle cinnamon on top. Preheat oven to 350° F. Prepare cake mix according to package directions. Pour carefully over fruit. Bake 45 to 55 minutes or until top springs back when lightly touched. Cool in pan 5 minutes. Turn out of pan onto serving plate.

Peanut Butter Picnic Cake

Makes 12 to 16 servings

 2¼ cups flour
 2 cups packed brown sugar
 1 cup peanut butter
 ½ cup butter *or* margarine, softened
 1 teaspoon baking powder
 ½ teaspoon baking soda
 1 cup milk
 1 teaspoon vanilla
 3 eggs
 1 package (6 ounces) semisweet chocolate chips

Grease bottom only of a 9 x 13-inch baking pan; set aside. Preheat oven to 350° F. In a large mixing bowl, combine flour, brown sugar, peanut butter, and butter; beat until crumbly. Reserve 1 cup. Add baking powder, baking soda, milk, vanilla, and eggs; blend until smooth. Pour batter into prepared pan. Sprinkle reserved crumbs on top. Sprinkle chocolate chips over crumbs. Bake 35 to 40 minutes or until a toothpick inserted in the center comes out clean. Let stand in pan until cool. Cut into squares.

Lemon Fluff Pie

Makes 6 to 7 servings

 3 eggs, separated
 1 cup sugar, divided
 Grated peel and juice of 1 lemon
 3 tablespoons hot water
 1 baked 9-inch piecrust

In a mixing bowl, beat egg yolks until thick and light-colored. Gradually beat in ½ cup of the sugar, lemon peel and juice, and hot water. Pour into top of a double boiler. Cook until slightly thickened, stirring often. In a small mixing bowl, beat egg whites until foamy. Gradually beat in remaining ½ cup sugar; beat until stiff peaks form. Fold egg whites into custard. Spoon into piecrust. Chill until set.

Rhubarb Surprise Cake

Makes 12 to 16 servings

 3 cups cut-up fresh *or* thawed frozen rhubarb
 1½ cups water
 1 cup sugar
 1 package (3 ounces) strawberry-flavored gelatin
 2 cups miniature marshmallows
 1 package (18½ ounces) white cake mix
 Sweetened whipped cream, optional

In a large saucepan, combine rhubarb, water, and sugar. Bring to boiling; remove from heat. Add gelatin; stir to dissolve; set aside. Grease bottom only of a 9 x 13-inch baking pan. Sprinkle marshmallows over bottom of pan; set aside. Preheat oven to 350° F. Prepare cake mix according to package directions, using whole eggs. Pour batter over marshmallows. Pour rhubarb mixture evenly over batter. Bake 45 to 50 minutes or until lightly browned. Serve warm or cold topped with whipped cream, if desired.

Chocolate Chip Nut Squares

Makes 9 servings

 2 eggs, lightly beaten
 ¾ cup packed brown sugar
 ½ cup flour
 ½ teaspoon baking powder
 ¼ teaspoon salt
 ½ cup butter *or* margarine, melted
 1 cup semisweet chocolate chips
 ½ cup chopped walnuts, optional

Preheat oven to 325° F. In a mixing bowl, combine eggs and sugar; blend well. Add remaining ingredients; blend well. Spread batter in an 8 x 8-inch square baking pan. Bake 25 minutes or until sides begin to pull away from edge of pan. Cut into squares; let cool in pan.

Raspberry Dipped Fruits

Makes 10 to 12 servings

- ¼ cup shredded coconut
- 2 tablespoons finely chopped pecans
- 1 cup dairy sour cream
- ¼ cup raspberry preserves
- 2 tablespoons milk
  Assorted fresh fruit, such as apple and pear wedges, banana pieces, strawberries, grapes, and melon balls
  Lemon juice

In a small bowl, combine coconut, pecans, sour cream, preserves, and milk; blend well. If using apples, pears, or bananas, dip in lemon juice to prevent browning. Arrange fruit around edge of a large serving platter. Place dip on a bed of ice in center.

Strawberry Cheese Pie

Makes 8 to 10 servings

- ½ cup butter *or* margarine
- 1 cup flour
- 1 tablespoon sugar
- 1 egg yolk
  Pinch salt
- 1 package (8 ounces) cream cheese, softened
- ½ cup sugar
- 2 eggs
- 1 teaspoon vanilla
- 1 quart strawberries, hulled

In a small bowl, cut butter into flour and sugar with a pastry blender or two knives. Add egg yolk and salt; blend with a fork. Pat dough into a 9-inch pie plate. Bake at 375° F. 15 to 20 minutes or until golden. Let stand until cool. In a small bowl, combine cream cheese, sugar, eggs, and vanilla. Beat with an electric mixer until smooth. Pour into cooled piecrust. Bake at 375° F. 15 to 20 minutes or until set. Let stand until cool. Stand strawberries in pie shell. Spoon Glaze over berries. Refrigerate until well chilled.

Glaze

- 1 cup sugar
- 3 tablespoons cornstarch
- ¼ teaspoon salt
- ¾ cup fruit juice *or* water
- 1 teaspoon lemon juice

In the top of a double boiler, combine all ingredients; blend well. Simmer over slowly boiling water 20 minutes or until thickened, stirring frequently.

Banana Split Dessert

Makes 12 to 16 servings

- 2 cups graham cracker crumbs
- 5 to 6 bananas, sliced lengthwise
- ½ gallon French vanilla ice cream, slightly softened
- 1 cup chopped walnuts
- 1 package (6 ounces) semisweet chocolate chips
- ½ cup butter *or* margarine
- 2 cups powdered sugar
- 1½ cups evaporated milk
- 1 teaspoon vanilla
- 1 cup whipping cream, whipped

Butter a 9 x 13-inch pan. Reserve ½ cup of the graham cracker crumbs. Spread remaining crumbs in bottom of prepared pan. Arrange bananas on top of crumbs. Gently spread the ice cream on top of the bananas. Sprinkle nuts on top. Place in freezer until frozen. In a small saucepan, melt chocolate chips and butter over low heat, stirring constantly. Add powdered sugar and evaporated milk; blend well. Cook until thick and smooth, stirring often. Stir in vanilla. Pour sauce over ice cream. Return to freezer. Remove ice cream dessert from freezer 10 minutes before serving. Spread whipped cream over the top. Sprinkle on reserved graham cracker crumbs.

Fudge Brownies

Makes 18

- 1 package (12 ounces) semisweet chocolate chips
- 1 cup butter *or* margarine
- 4 eggs
  Pinch salt
- 1 cup sugar
- 1 cup sifted flour
- 1 teaspoon baking powder
- 2 teaspoons vanilla
- 1 cup chopped nuts, optional

Grease a 9 x 13-inch baking pan; set aside. Preheat oven to 375° F. Combine chocolate chips and butter in a large saucepan. Melt over low heat, stirring constantly. Remove from heat. In a small bowl, combine eggs, salt, and sugar; blend well. Add to chocolate mixture; blend well. Stir in flour, baking powder, and vanilla until well blended. Stir in nuts, if desired. Pour into prepared pan. Bake for 25 minutes or until brownie begins to pull away from edge of pan. Let stand until cool. Cut into bars.

Book I Index

Book II

Old-Fashioned
Family Cookbook

By Clarice L. Moon

Ideals Publishing Corp.
Nashville, Tennessee

Contents

Appetizers and Beverages

ANCHOVY PECANS

Toast pecan halves in a 350° oven for 5 minutes. Spread bottoms with thin layer of anchovy paste. Press each 2 halves together. Serve immediately.

CAVIAR ROUNDS

Rye bread, toasted rounds
Caviar
Finely minced onion
Hard-boiled egg

Butter rounds of rye toast. Press on these rounds, slices of the egg white. Fill the inside of the egg white with caviar. Sprinkle finely minced onion over caviar. Surround egg white with grated yolk.

ASPARAGUS CANAPÉ

2 T. mayonnaise
2 hard-boiled eggs
  Pimiento strips
5 asparagus tips
  Toast triangles

Spread toast with mayonnaise. Chop egg yolks and whites separately. Arrange the chopped egg white and the chopped egg yolk in alternate rows across toast. Lay asparagus tips on top. Garnish with pimiento strips.

HOT TUNA CANAPÉS

Mix flaked tuna with mayonnaise or salad dressing. Add chopped stuffed olives. Add a few drops of Worcestershire sauce. Spread on toast strips and sprinkle with American cheese. Place under broiler until cheese melts. Serve hot.

CORNUCOPIAS

2 3-oz. pkgs. cream cheese
1 T. pickle relish
1 T. minced onion
12 thin slices boiled ham

Mash cheese with onion and drained pickle relish. Spread on a slice of boiled ham. Roll cornucopia fashion. Chill.

CHEESE SAVORY CANAPÉS

4 T. Roquefort cheese
2 T. butter
½ t. salt
⅛ t. pepper
  Mayonnaise
  Gherkins, thinly sliced
  Celery, minced
  Pimiento strips

Cream cheese and butter together. Add salt and pepper. Spread on toasted bread. Cover with celery mixed with a little mayonnaise. Garnish with sliced gherkins and a cross made of pimiento strips.

CHEESE BEEF STICKS

Cut American cheese in strips 2 inches long and ⅜ inch wide. Wrap each stick in a dried beef square. Place rolls on a cookie sheet, 3 inches below broiler. Broil until cheese is slightly melted.

EGGNOG

12 eggs, separated
1½ pt. cream or half and half
4 c. sugar
1½ c. whisky
1 t. nutmeg
1 t. salt
6 qts. milk

Beat egg yolks until lemon colored. Beat in sugar and salt. Slowly add whisky, cream, nutmeg and milk. Fold in well-beaten egg whites. Makes 2 gallons.

DIET SHAKE

1 12-oz. can diet soda, any flavor
⅓ c. instant nonfat dry milk
½ c. fresh fruit
⅛ t. artificial sweetener
½ t. vanilla
½ t. extract, strawberry, almond, rum or brandy
1 c. coarsely crushed ice

Combine all ingredients in blender. Whirl at high speed until frothy and blended.

SKINNY FRUIT WHIRL

1 12-oz. can diet creme soda
½ c. nonfat milk
1 t. lemon juice
⅛ t. artificial sweetener
⅛ t. salt
2 c. sliced nectarines, peaches or other fruit

Whirl all ingredients together in blender until smooth. Makes about 1 quart. Mixture may be frozen to make sherbet.

HOT TODDY

Juice of 1 lemon
2 T. honey or sugar
3 oz. bourbon or rye whisky
Boiling water

Put juice of 1 lemon in tall glass or mug. Sweeten with honey or sugar. Add whisky or rye. Fill glass with boiling water. Stir and drink.

RUSSIAN TEA

1 c. Tang
1 t. cinnamon
¼ c. instant tea
½ t. cloves
½ pkg. lemonade mix with sugar

Mix all ingredients together and keep in a tightly sealed jar. Use 1½ teaspoonsful in a teacup of hot water or 2 heaping teaspoonsful in a mug.

SKINNY MARY

¾ c. tomato juice
1 T. Worcestershire sauce
¼ c. sauerkraut juice
Ice cubes

Pour tomato and sauerkraut juice over ice cubes in glass. Add Worcestershire sauce and stir. Serve at once. Makes 1 serving.

LEMONADE

½ c. lemon juice (2 lemons)
3 c. cold water
½ c. sugar
Ice cubes

Add sugar to juice. Stir in cold water. Pour over ice in glasses. For hot lemonade, use hot water instead of cold.

Note: Roll lemons on table to make more juice.

Salads and Dressings

STUFFED PRUNE SALAD

12 large cooked prunes
2 3-oz. pkgs. cream cheese
2 c. grapefruit sections
¼ c. mayonnaise
¼ c. chopped nuts
   Lettuce

Drain prunes and remove the pits. Blend cream cheese and mayonnaise; fill centers of prunes. Sprinkle with nuts. Arrange on lettuce leaves with grapefruit sections and serve with a salad dressing of your choice. Serves 4.

GERMAN POTATO SALAD

¼ c. sugar
1 T. flour
2 t. salt
¼ t. pepper
¼ c. vinegar
⅔ c. water
4 slices bacon, diced and browned
¼ c. bacon drippings
4 c. cold, cooked, cubed potatoes
1 hard-boiled egg
2 T. chopped onion
   Sprig parsley

Combine sugar, flour, salt and pepper in the top of a double boiler. Stir in vinegar, water, bacon and bacon drippings. Cook, stirring constantly, about 5 minutes, or until thick. Place potatoes, onions, egg and parsley in a greased casserole or baking pan. Pour dressing over and mix to coat all. Heat in a 350° oven for 30 minutes. Serves 6 to 8.

PERFECTION SALAD

2 T. unflavored gelatin
2½ c. cold water
1 c. boiling water
⅓ c. sugar
1 t. salt
¼ c. tarragon vinegar
2½ T. lemon juice
½ t. prepared horseradish
3 carrots, grated
1 c. thinly sliced celery
1 2-oz. jar diced pimiento
2 c. finely shredded cabbage
½ green pepper, chopped
2 green onions and tops, thinly sliced

Soften gelatin in ½ cup cold water. Stir in boiling water, sugar and salt. Stir until dissolved. If necessary, place over low heat to dissolve. Add remaining 2 cups cold water, vinegar, lemon juice, and horseradish. Chill to a soft set. Fold in remaining ingredients. Turn into a 6-cup mold. Chill overnight. Unmold to serve. Serves 6.

CELEBRATION SALAD

2 c. diced cooked chicken
2 c. diced cooked ham
2 c. diced celery
1 c. salted almonds
½ c. mayonnaise
1 hard-boiled egg
2 T. pimiento slices
   Lettuce

Combine chicken, ham, celery, almonds and mayonnaise. Serve on lettuce leaves. Cut egg lengthwise into eighths. Garnish salad with egg wedges and pimiento. Serve with hot biscuits. Serves 6.

Pictured opposite
Celebration Salad
(page 6)

FROSTED FRUIT SALAD

1 3-oz. pkg. lemon gelatin
1 3-oz. pkg. orange gelatin
　Juice of 1 lemon
2 c. boiling water
2 c. cold water
2 bananas, diced
1 No. 2 can crushed pineapple, drained
1 c. minature marshmallows

Dissolve gelatin in boiling water. Add cold water and lemon juice. Chill until partly set. Fold in pineapple, marshmallows and bananas. Pour into a 9 x 12 x 3-inch loaf pan. Chill until set. When gelatin is firm frost with Frosting. Serves 8.

FROSTING

2 T. flour
½ c. sugar
1 egg, beaten
½ c. milk
1 c. pineapple juice
1 c. heavy cream, whipped

Combine flour and sugar. Slowly stir in egg and milk. Stir in pineapple juice. Cook, stirring constantly, until thickened. Cool. Fold in whipped cream.

HAM SALAD

1 3-oz. pkg. lemon gelatin
1⅔ c. boiling water
1 T. lemon juice
¼ t. salt
1 c. chopped, cooked ham
¼ c. chopped celery
2 T. chopped green pepper
½ t. chopped onion
2 T. chopped pimiento

Dissolve gelatin in boiling water; add lemon juice and salt. Cool until slightly thickened. Pour half the gelatin into individual molds or one large mold, filling molds only half full. Chill just until set. Stir ham and vegetables into remaining gelatin and gently pour on top of set gelatin. Refrigerate until completely set. Unmold on rings of pineapple or garnish with pineapple. Serves 8.

JELLIED BEET SALAD

1 3-oz. pkg. lemon or lime gelatin
1 c. boiling water
1 c. cold beet juice
3 T. vinegar
2 T. minced onion
1 T. horseradish
¾ c. celery
1 16-oz. can diced beets, drained

Dissolve gelatin in boiling water. Stir in beet juice and vinegar. Add onion, horseradish, celery and diced beets. Refrigerate overnight. Serve on a bed of lettuce. Serves 4.

POTATO SALAD

4 c. potatoes, cooked and diced
6 hard-boiled eggs, chopped
½ c. chopped green pepper
2 T. chopped ripe olives
1½ to 2 c. mayonnaise
1 t. salt
1 c. diced celery
½ c. diced pimiento
1 large onion, chopped
　Paprika

Mix together all ingredients, stirring thoroughly to coat all with mayonnaise. Place in serving dish. Sprinkle with paprika. Refrigerate until serving time. Serves 6.

THREE BEAN SALAD

1 16-oz. can green beans
1 16-oz. can wax beans
1 16-oz. can kidney beans
½ c. sugar
½ c. vinegar
½ t. celery seed
1 T. vegetable oil
1 medium onion, chopped

Combine beans. Slowly stir vinegar into sugar, blending until smooth. Add celery seed, oil and onion. Refrigerate.

SEA SALAD SURPRISE

2 c. tuna fish
1 c. lobster meat
2 c. shrimp, cooked and deveined
1 lemon, cut in wedges
2 c. diced celery
¾ c. mayonnaise
1 bunch watercress

Clean and slice fish. Reserve 12 whole shrimp for garnish. Combine all with mayonnaise and serve on watercress. Garnish with whole shrimp and lemon wedges. Serve with hot hard rolls. Serves 6.

MOLDED CRANBERRY SALAD

1 16-oz. can whole cranberry sauce
1 c. boiling water
1 3-oz. pkg. strawberry gelatin
1 T. lemon juice
¼ t. salt
½ c. mayonnaise
1 apple, diced
½ c. finely chopped celery
¼ c. chopped nuts

Heat cranberry sauce. Strain. Mix cranberry liquid, boiling water and gelatin, stirring until gelatin is dissolved. Add lemon juice and salt. Chill mixture until slightly thickened. Stir in mayonnaise; beat until fluffy. Fold in reserved cranberries, apple, celery and nuts. Pour into a mold or a flat pan; cut in squares to serve. Refrigerate until firm. Makes 6 servings.

FRENCH DRESSING

¼ c. vegetable oil
1 T. sugar
½ t. pepper
2 T. cider vinegar
1 t. salt
½ t. paprika

Place all ingredients in a pint jar; shake vigorously until thick. Serves 4.

LO-CAL TOMATO JUICE DRESSING

½ c. canned tomato juice
2 T. lemon juice or vinegar
1 t. salt
1½ T. Worcestershire sauce
2 to 4 T. vegetable oil
½ t. dry mustard
1 t. minced onion
3 T. sugar substitute

Combine all ingredients and beat until well blended. Makes 1 cup. Contains 25 calories per tablespoon.

BOILED SALAD DRESSING

2 T. flour
1 t. salt
¾ t. dry mustard
1 T. sugar
⅛ t. pepper
½ t. paprika
1 egg, slightly beaten
1 c. milk
¼ c. cider vinegar
2 T. butter or margarine

In the top of a double boiler, mix together flour, salt, mustard, sugar, pepper and paprika. Gradually stir in egg and milk. Cook over boiling water, stirring constantly, until thick. Add vinegar and butter. Cool. Makes 1⅔ cups.

NEW ORLEANS DRESSING

½ t. salt
½ t. dry mustard
¼ c. vinegar
¼ t. sugar
¾ c. vegetable oil
¼ t. pepper

Combine all ingredients in a screw-top jar. Shake vigorously. Rub bowl with clove of garlic before tossing green salad with dressing.

CELERY SEED DRESSING

2½ c. sugar
4 t. dry mustard
4 t. salt
1¼ c. vinegar
1 small onion, grated
4 c. vegetable oil
¼ c. celery seed

Combine sugar, mustard and salt. Add half the vinegar and onion to dry mixture. Beat on medium speed of mixer for 15 minutes. Stir in oil, then remainder of vinegar. Mix until well blended. Fold in celery seed. Refrigerate. Makes 3 pints.

MAYONNAISE

2 egg yolks
1 t. salt
1 t. dry mustard
2 c. vegetable oil
2 T. lemon juice or vinegar

Beat egg yolks, salt and mustard until light and lemon colored. Add oil, a small amount at a time. Beat until mixture is emulsified. Stir in lemon juice or vinegar. Refrigerate until needed. Makes 1 pint.

FRENCH DRESSING

1 10¾-oz. can tomato soup
1 c. sugar
1 c. cider vinegar
1 c. vegetable oil
2 T. Worcestershire sauce
1 t. salt
1 t. dry mustard
1 t. paprika
1 t. dry onion flakes *or* 1 T. minced onion

Place all ingredients in a screw-top jar. Shake well. Store in refrigerator. Makes 1 quart.

Pictured opposite
from left
Mrs. Smith's Salad Dressing
Russian Dressing
Roquefort Cheese Dressing (on salad)
(page 11)

ROQUEFORT CHEESE DRESSING

1 t. salt
1 t. celery seed
1 t. paprika
1 t. dry mustard
1 t. minced onion
4 T. sugar
¼ c. grated Roquefort cheese
⅔ c. vegetable oil
4 T. lemon juice

Mix dry ingredients together. Blend with a little of the oil. Stir in remaining oil, alternating with lemon juice. When ready to serve, add cheese.

MRS. SMITH'S SALAD DRESSING

3 whole eggs, slightly beaten
1 T. flour, rounded
¾ t. salt
2 T. butter
⅓ c. sugar
½ t. dry mustard
½ c. cider vinegar

Mix all ingredients in top of a double boiler. Cook over boiling water, stirring constantly, until thick and smooth. Cool.

RUSSIAN DRESSING

¼ c. white corn syrup
½ t. salt
½ t. celery seed
1 T. vinegar
1 T. Worcestershire sauce
1 medium onion, finely chopped
⅓ c. sugar
½ t. paprika
2 T. lemon juice
½ c. catsup
1 c. salad oil

Combine all ingredients in a screw-top jar. Shake well. Refrigerate.

Vegetable Dishes

FRIED GREEN TOMATOES

4 medium-size green tomatoes
1 t. salt
½ c. flour
2 T. vegetable oil

Wash and slice green tomatoes in ½-inch thick slices. Sprinkle with salt. Roll each slice in flour until coated on each side. Place oil in a skillet and heat. Place floured tomato slices in skillet. Fry over low heat until browned on both sides. Serve hot. Serves 4.

STUFFED CUCUMBER

1 large cucumber
2 3-oz. pkgs. cream cheese
1 T. chopped pimiento
3 T. mayonnaise
1 T. chopped stuffed olives
1 T. chopped ripe olives
Lettuce leaves

Cut cucumber in half lengthwise. With a spoon scoop out seeds and membrane. Soften cream cheese with mayonnaise. Mix in olives and pimiento. Fill the cucumber cavity with the cream cheese mixture until level. Press cucumber halves together. Refrigerate for at least 2 hours. To serve, slice thin and place on lettuce leaf. Serve with Roquefort cheese dressing.

GLAZED PARSNIPS

3 c. parsnips, sliced diagonally in ½-inch slices
¾ c. boiling water
½ t. salt
2 T. butter
¼ c. orange juice
1 t. grated orange rind

Place parsnips in water with salt. Bring to a boil. Simmer, covered, about 20 minutes. Drain. Heat remaining ingredients together in a saucepan. Pour over parsnips in serving dish. Serves 6.

SPINACH BALLS

2 c. chopped spinach, cooked and drained
2 T. grated cheese
2 T. melted butter
1½ c. bread crumbs
2 eggs
¼ c. water
⅓ t. pepper
½ t. salt
¼ c. margarine
Bread crumbs

Combine spinach, cheese, butter, bread crumbs and 1 beaten egg. Roll into balls. To other egg, add water and seasoning and beat. Dip spinach balls into additional bread crumbs, then into egg mixture, and again in bread crumbs. Brown balls on both sides in margarine. Serves 4.

POTATO CROQUETTES

2 c. mashed potatoes
1 egg
1 t. salt
¼ t. black pepper
2 T. chopped parsley
1 T. Parmesan cheese
1 clove garlic, minced (optional)
¾ c. bread crumbs
1 egg, beaten
1 T. water

Thoroughly mix potatoes, 1 egg, salt, pepper, parsley, cheese and garlic, if desired. Shape into small balls. Dip balls in bread crumbs, then into egg mixed with water, and again in the bread crumbs. Let stand on waxed paper 20 minutes. Fry in deep fat until browned on all sides. Serves 4.

SAUERKRAUT STUFFING FOR GOOSE

2½ lbs. sauerkraut
1 grated carrot
1 c. salami or other sausage
1 T. goose or bacon fat
1 potato, grated
1 onion, minced
½ c. dried bread crumbs

Mix all ingredients together. Stuff into goose that has been prepared for roasting. Sew up. Place in roasting pan. Roast, uncovered, in a 350° oven for 2 hours or until goose is done. Pour off fat occasionally.

POLENTA

3 c. water
1½ t. salt
1 c. yellow cornmeal
1 c. cold water
2 T. vegetable oil
1 lb. Italian sausage, casings removed
1 lb. mushrooms, cleaned and sliced lengthwise
2½ c. tomatoes
1 t. salt
¼ t. pepper
½ c. grated Parmesan or Romano cheese

Bring water and salt to a boil. Mix cornmeal with cold water; gradually stir into boiling water. Continue boiling, stirring constantly, until mixture thickens. Cover; lower heat. Simmer 10 minutes. Meanwhile, to make sauce, place oil in heavy skillet. Crumble sausages in skillet; add mushrooms. Cook until mushrooms and sausages are lightly browned. Stir in tomatoes, salt and pepper; simmer 20 to 30 minutes. To serve, transfer cooked cornmeal to a warm platter. Top with tomato sauce and sprinkle with grated Parmesan or Romano cheese. Serves 6 to 8.

MAPLE-GLAZED SQUASH AND PARSNIPS

8 parsnips (1½ lbs.)
2 small acorn squash
1¼ c. maple syrup
Water
1 t. salt
3 T. butter or margarine
1 T. chopped parsley
¼ t. nutmeg

Pare parsnips; cut in quarters, lengthwise then crosswise into thirds. Halve squash crosswise; scoop out seeds and stringy membrane. Cut squash into ½-inch slices. Do not peel. Cook parsnips and squash in a large skillet in boiling salted water for 10 minutes or until almost tender. Drain. Heat maple syrup in same skillet. Add butter or margarine. Stir until melted. Return parsnips and squash to skillet. Simmer over medium heat, basting frequently, until vegetables are tender and glazed. Remove squash with slotted spoon. Arrange slices around edges of heated platter. Spoon parsnips into the center. Drizzle remaining syrup over vegetables. Sprinkle with parsley and nutmeg. Serves 8.

STUFFED CABBAGE LEAVES

12 large cabbage leaves
1 lb. ground beef
1 c. cooked rice
⅔ c. milk
1 egg
¼ c. onion, finely chopped
1 t. chopped parsley
1 t. salt
½ t. sage
2 T. brown sugar
⅔ c. water
4 whole cloves
1 10½-oz. can condensed tomato soup

Drop cabbage leaves into boiling water. Boil for 5 minutes; drain. Cut thick vein from each leaf. Brown ground beef. Mix beef, rice, milk, egg, 2 tablespoons of the onion, parsley, salt and sage. Place a spoonful on each leaf. Roll up the leaf and secure with a toothpick. Place rolls in a buttered 13 x 9 x 2-inch pan. Sprinkle with brown sugar. Mix the remaining onion with soup, water and cloves. Pour over cabbage rolls. Bake uncovered in a 325° oven for 1½ hours. Serves 6.

RED CABBAGE

3 strips bacon
1½ lbs. red cabbage
1 medium onion, finely chopped
7 bay leaves
2 T. mixed pickling spice
3 T. honey *or* sugar
Juice of 2 lemons *or* ¼ c. vinegar
½ t. salt
⅛ t. pepper

Fry bacon until crisp. Remove from pan and break into small pieces. Shred cabbage leaves in ¼-inch wide strips. Add to bacon grease along with crumbled bacon. Cover tightly and simmer for 20 minutes. Add onion, bay leaves and pickling spice, tied in cheesecloth. Stir in honey, lemon juice or vinegar. Cover and simmer slowly for about 1½ hours. Add salt and pepper and steam ½ hour. Serves 4.

Pictured opposite
Red Cabbage (page 15)
with a pork roast and potatoes

CORN AND TOMATOES

6 large, fresh tomatoes
2 c. fresh corn
½ t. salt
1 t. chopped chives
½ t. pepper
¼ t. sweet basil

Pour boiling water over tomatoes. Cool slightly; slip off tomato skins. Chop tomatoes. Combine corn and tomatoes in a saucepan. Add salt, pepper, chives and basil. Simmer over low heat for 20 minutes or until vegetables are tender. Serves 6.

STUFFED GREEN PEPPERS

4 large green peppers
1 lb. ground beef
¼ c. vegetable oil
½ t. salt
¼ t. pepper
1 T. minced parsley
⅔ c. cooked rice
1½ c. tomatoes, sieved
¼ c. minced onion
½ t. salt
¼ c. water
¼ t. pepper
2 slices mozzarella cheese

Grease a 2-quart baking dish. Rinse peppers. Cut a thin slice from the stem end of each green pepper and remove inner white fiber and seeds. Rinse cavity. Drop peppers in boiling salted water to cover. Simmer for 5 minutes. Remove and set aside to drain. Brown ground beef in oil. Stir in parsley, salt, pepper and cooked rice. Lightly fill pepper shells with the mixture, heaping slightly. Place in a baking dish. Combine tomatoes, onion, salt, water and pepper, mixing well. Pour over peppers. Place a strip of cheese on top of each pepper. Bake in a 350° oven for 30 minutes. Serves 4.

EGGPLANT WITH SHRIMP OR HAM FILLING

1 1½ to 2-lb. eggplant
2 T. butter or margarine
¼ c. chopped onion
2 T. chopped green pepper
1 clove garlic, minced
2 c. shrimp or ham
1 c. soft bread crumbs
2 T. pimiento, chopped
½ t. salt
¼ t. pepper
1 c. Buttered Bread Crumbs

Split eggplant in half lengthwise. Cook, covered, in a small amount of boiling water for 10 minutes or until slightly tender. Remove from water and drain. Scoop out pulp from center of eggplant, leaving ¼-inch shell. Set shells aside. Finely chop the pulp. Melt butter; add pulp, onion, green pepper and garlic. Sauté until onion is transparent. Chop shrimp or ham. Add shrimp, bread crumbs, pimiento, salt and pepper to onion mixture. Blend thoroughly. Spoon mixture into eggplant shells, heaping slightly. Cover tops with buttered bread crumbs. Bake in a 375° oven for 20 to 30 minutes or until crumbs are browned. Serves 6 to 8.

BUTTERED BREAD CRUMBS

2 T. melted butter
1 c. soft bread crumbs

Melt butter. Add bread crumbs and sauté until slightly browned.

PAPRIKA BROWNED POTATOES

2 c. boiled potatoes, thinly sliced
3 T. margarine
¼ t. pepper
½ t. salt
1 t. paprika

Melt margarine in a heavy skillet. Add potatoes, salt, pepper and paprika. Mix well and brown lightly over low heat until potatoes are warmed through and reddish brown in color. Serves 4.

BAKED STUFFED TOMATOES

2 T. vegetable oil
1 t. chopped onion
¼ c. ground beef
½ c. grated cheese
1 t. salt
1 c. cooked rice
6 large ripe tomatoes

Grease an 8 x 8 x 2-inch baking dish. Heat oil in skillet; brown onion and ground beef. Stir in cheese, seasonings and rice. Set aside. With a sharp knife, cut a ¼-inch slice from top of each tomato. Cut around inside of tomatoes, being careful not to cut through the bottom. Scoop out center pulp. Sieve the tomato pulp and set aside the liquid. Sprinkle each tomato with salt. Lightly fill the tomatoes with filling. Place tomatoes in baking dish. Pour the tomato juice over tomatoes. Bake in a 375° oven for 20 to 25 minutes. Garnish with parsley. Serves 6.

STUFFED GRAPE LEAVES

12 large grape leaves
½ lb. ground beef
1 medium onion, minced
2 T. vegetable oil
1 T. grated lemon rind
1 t. salt
⅛ t. pepper
½ c. white raisins
2 c. cooked rice

Grease a 1½-quart casserole. Wash grape leaves. Blanch the grape leaves in boiling water for 30 seconds. Drain. Plunge in cold water; drain and set aside. Brown ground beef and onion in oil. Stir in lemon rind, salt, pepper, raisins and rice. Place one-third cup filling on each grape leaf. Fold leaves around the filling. Place in the casserole with folded side down. Continue until all grape leaves and filling are gone. Add 1 cup water. Cover and bake in a 350° oven 20 to 30 minutes until liquid is almost gone. Serves 4.

GREEN BEAN CASSEROLE

3 6-oz. pkgs. frozen green
  beans, French cut
1 8-oz. can water chestnuts
½ c. butter
4 green onions *or* 1 medium onion,
  chopped
2 4-oz. cans mushrooms
½ c. flour
2 c. milk
¾ c. shredded Cheddar cheese
2 t. soy sauce
½ t. Tabasco sauce
1 t. salt
¾ c. slivered almonds

Cook frozen beans according to package directions. Drain. Chop water chestnuts and add to beans. Sauté onion and mushrooms in butter. Stir in flour, milk and cheese. Cook over low heat until thickened, stirring occasionally. Stir in soy sauce, Tabasco sauce and salt. Pour sauce over beans and mix gently. Turn into a 2-quart buttered casserole. Sprinkle almonds over top. Bake for 20 minutes in a 375° oven. Serves 8 to 10.

SCALLOPED POTATOES

3 or 4 large white potatoes, thinly sliced
1 small onion, sliced
½ t. pepper
1 t. salt
⅓ c. flour
½ c. bread crumbs
2 c. milk or more
4 to 5 T. butter or margarine

Grease a 2-quart casserole. Alternate layers of sliced potatoes and onion. Sprinkle each layer with salt, pepper and flour. Dot with butter. Repeat until casserole is full. Pour milk over, barely covering potatoes. Sprinkle top with bread crumbs and dot with additional butter. Bake in a 375° oven 45 to 60 minutes or until potatoes are tender. Serves 4.

LEFSE

1 T. melted butter
1 T. sugar
¼ t. salt
1 c. cream
10 c. mashed potatoes
  Flour

Add butter, sugar, salt and cream to mashed potatoes. Blend well. Add enough flour to handle without being sticky. Dough will be similar to pie dough. Cool completely and roll very thin in 8 to 9-inch circles. (To prevent sticking, dough must be rolled with a covered rolling pin.) Bake dough on *lefse* grill or pancake grill. Turn only once when underside is brown spotted. Makes about 35 circles. To serve, cut circles into wedges. Butter and roll up. The *lefse* pieces were traditionally used to wrap around a piece of fish or meat before eating. Serves 8 to 10.

BAKED FILLED SWEET POTATOES

6 medium-size yams
1 T. shortening
12 pork sausage links
½ c. hot orange juice
3 T. butter or margarine
2 T. brown sugar
1 t. grated orange peel
1 t. salt
½ t. nutmeg

Rub potato skins with shortening. Bake in a 450° oven for 45 to 60 minutes. While potatoes are baking, pan broil pork sausage links. Drain on paper towels and keep warm. When sweet potatoes are tender, cut each potato in half lengthwise. Scoop out inside of the potato without breaking skin. Mash or rice potato; whip in hot orange juice, butter, brown sugar, orange peel, salt and nutmeg. Pile mixture lightly into potato shells. Top each with 2 sausage links. Bake in a 350° oven 8 to 10 minutes longer, or until potatoes are reheated and browned lightly. Serves 6.

BLUSHING CAULIFLOWER

1 head cauliflower
½ t. salt
2 T. butter
1 clove garlic, crushed
1 10-oz. can condensed tomato soup
½ c. grated American cheese
1 T. chopped parsley

Place cauliflower in a large kettle. Add salted water to cover bottom of the pan. Simmer over low heat for about 20 to 30 minutes, or until tender. Melt butter in a saucepan. Sauté garlic until lightly browned. Add soup and cheese; heat, stirring occasionally, over low heat until cheese is melted. Pour sauce over cauliflower; sprinkle with parsley. Serves 6.

POTATO CAKES

6 large potatoes
¼ c. milk
3 eggs, beaten
½ t. salt
3 T. butter
1 t. baking powder
2 c. flour
　Cream Sauce

Peel and boil potatoes in salted water until tender. Drain and mash. Beat in milk, eggs, salt, flour and baking powder. Form into patties. Brown potato patties lightly in hot butter. Serve with Cream Sauce. Serves 6.

CREAM SAUCE

4 c. milk, heated
3 T. flour
⅓ c. sugar
¼ c. cold milk
2 T. butter
1 t. caraway seed

Heat milk in saucepan. Mix flour and sugar with the cold milk. Stir into hot milk, stirring until mixture boils and thickens. Add butter and caraway seed, stirring to melt butter.

BAKED STUFFED MUSHROOMS

1 lb. mushrooms with 1 to 2-inch caps
2 T. vegetable oil
¼ c. chopped onion
⅓ c. bread crumbs
3 T. grated Parmesan cheese
1 T. chopped parsley
½ t. salt
⅛ t. oregano
2 T. vegetable oil

Clean mushrooms; remove stems. Place caps, open side up, in a greased 1½-quart casserole. Set aside. Finely chop mushroom stems. In a skillet heat oil; add mushroom stems and onion. Sauté over low heat until onion is lightly browned. Combine bread crumbs, cheese, parsley, salt and oregano. Add to mushroom stems and onions. Pile mixture lightly into mushroom caps. Drizzle remaining oil over caps. Bake in a 400° oven for 15 to 20 minutes or until mushrooms are tender and tops are browned. Serves 6 to 8.

EGGPLANT PARMIGIANA

2 medium-size eggplants
1 c. vegetable oil
2 6-oz. cans tomato paste
2 c. water
½ c. grated Parmesan cheese
1 3-oz. can mushrooms
1 lb. mozzarella cheese

Peel eggplant and slice into ½-inch slices. Fry in oil until lightly browned. Drain on paper towels. Cover bottom of a 13 x 9 x 2-inch buttered pan with a layer of eggplant slices. Combine tomato paste and water, mixing well. Pour over eggplant. Sprinkle with Parmesan cheese, mushrooms and mozzarella cheese. Repeat layers, ending with mozzarella cheese. Bake in a 400° oven for 20 minutes or until cheese is bubbly. Makes 10 servings.

Pictured opposite
Baked Stuffed Onions
(page 19)

BAKED STUFFED ONIONS

- 6 large onions
- ½ t. salt
- 2 T. vegetable oil
- ¼ lb. ground beef
- 1 c. cooked rice
- 1 egg yolk
- ½ c. soft bread crumbs
- ½ t. salt
- ½ t. pepper
- 2 T. melted butter
- 2 T. grated Parmesan cheese
- ½ c. soft bread crumbs
- 1 T. chopped parsley

Cut off root; peel and rinse onions. Cut a ½-inch slice from the top of each onion. Cook onion, uncovered, in salted water to cover for 10 to 15 minutes or until slightly tender. Drain well; cool. Heat oil in skillet; add ground beef and sauté until browned. Scoop centers out of onions; chop and add to ground beef. Sauté until golden. Combine rice, egg yolk, salt, pepper and bread crumbs with meat mixture. Fill onions. Mix together melted butter, cheese, parsley and bread crumbs. Spread over top of onions. Bake in a greased casserole in a 350° oven for 1 hour. Serves 6.

FRIED ZUCCHINI WITH ONIONS

2 T. margarine
2 medium-size onions, sliced
1 fresh zucchini squash
1 t. salt
¼ t. pepper
¼ c. water

In a heavy skillet, melt margarine; lightly sauté onion slices. Wash zucchini; slice in thin rounds, leaving skin on. Add to onion with salt and pepper. Fry over low heat, turning as slices brown. Add water and lower heat. Cover tightly and steam for 20 to 25 minutes, stirring occasionally, until tender. Serves 4.

FRIED PARSNIPS

6 to 8 parsnips (1½ lbs.)
½ t. salt
3 T. butter

Pare parsnips. Cut in half lengthwise and then in half crosswise. Put in kettle with water to cover; add salt. Cook until tender; drain. Melt butter in skillet. Arrange parsnips in one layer in skillet. Brown on all sides, turning to keep from burning. Serves 8. Can use carrots this way, too.

CARROTS AND CELERY

2 c. diced celery
4 to 6 carrots, diced
½ t. salt
  Water
2 T. melted butter
1 t. chopped parsley

Place celery and carrots in a saucepan with enough salted water to cover. Simmer over low heat 30 minutes or until carrots and celery are tender. Drain. Pour into a serving dish. Pour melted butter over carrots and sprinkle with parsley. Serves 4.

POTATO DUMPLINGS

6 large potatoes, boiled and mashed
1 c. flour
1 t. salt
½ t. nutmeg
3 eggs, beaten slightly
½ lb. ground beef

To cooled potatoes, add flour, salt, nutmeg and eggs. Roll ground beef into balls, ½ inch in diameter. Mold potato mixture around meatballs. Drop in boiling water. Cover tightly and continue boiling for 15 minutes. Do not lift lid. Serve with vegetable soup. Serves 6.

HONEYED SWEET POTATOES

1½ lbs. sweet potatoes
⅓ c. butter
⅔ c. honey
  Salted water

Scrub sweet potatoes and cut into quarters. Place in a stewing kettle. Cover with salted water and boil until almost done, about 30 minutes. Drain; cool slightly. Remove skins and slice crosswise in ½-inch slices. Place in a 1½-quart buttered casserole. Mix honey and butter together. Bake in a 350° oven for 20 to 25 minutes or until lightly browned. Serve at once. Serves 4 to 6.

SOUTHERN CORN PUDDING

2 eggs
2 c. fresh corn
2 c. milk
½ t. salt
½ t. pepper
1 T. vegetable oil

Beat eggs until light. Add milk, corn, seasonings and oil in a large mixing bowl. Mix well. Turn into a 1-quart buttered casserole. Bake in a 350° oven for 30 minutes. Serves 6.

CUCUMBERS IN SOUR CREAM

3 medium-size cucumbers
½ c. sour cream
2 T. cider vinegar
1 t. sugar
½ t. salt
½ t. black pepper

Peel cucumbers and slice thin. Layer cucumbers in a medium-size bowl. Cover with 3 cups water, or enough to cover, and 1½ teaspoon salt. Chill. Pour off salted water and rinse in clear water. Drain. Blend sour cream, vinegar, and sugar. Fold into cucumbers. Serve with a sprinkling of salt and pepper.

STEWED SAUERKRAUT

1 30-oz. can sauerkraut
3 T. caraway seed
1 c. water
1 medium onion, sliced
¼ c. sugar
1 medium potato, grated

Mix all ingredients except potato in a saucepan. Let simmer, stirring occasionally, until onion is soft and transparent. Stir in potato. Just bring mixture to a boil; cover. Let stand for 10 minutes before serving. Serves 4 to 6.

SKILLET SALAD

4 slices bacon
¼ c. vinegar
1 T. brown sugar
1 t. salt
1 T. finely chopped onion
4 c. shredded cabbage
¼ c. chopped parsley

Cook bacon until crisp; drain and crumble. To fat in skillet, add vinegar, sugar, salt and onion. Bring to a boil. Remove from heat; toss cabbage and parsley in hot mixture. Makes 6 servings.

BROCCOLI PARMESAN

1 bunch fresh broccoli
2 T. butter
2 T. minced onion
¼ t. pepper
½ t. dry mustard
½ c. grated Parmesan cheese
½ t. salt
¼ t. marjoram
3 T. flour
1 chicken bouillon cube
2½ c. milk
2 T. grated Parmesan cheese
1 t. paprika

Cook broccoli in boiling salted water until tender. Drain. Arrange broccoli in a shallow greased baking dish. Melt butter in a saucepan. Add onion and sauté over low heat until tender. Blend in seasonings and flour. Add bouillon cube and milk. Cook over medium heat, stirring constantly, until mixture thickens and comes to a boil. Add cheese and stir well, until melted. Pour sauce over broccoli. Sprinkle with paprika and additional Parmesan cheese. Bake in a 375° oven for 20 to 25 minutes or until browned. Serves 4 to 6.

RAW FRIED POTATOES

6 to 8 medium-size potatoes, peeled and thinly sliced
3 T. shortening
1 t. salt
½ t. pepper
1 c. chopped onion, optional
¼ c. water

Heat shortening in large skillet. Add sliced potatoes, salt and pepper and onion, if desired. Fry on medium-low heat, stirring potatoes up from the bottom as they brown. Fry about 15 minutes. Add water and cover tightly. Cook over low heat until potatoes are tender, stirring occasionally. Serves 4 to 6.

HOT COLE SLAW

½ c. cider vinegar
¼ c. water
½ t. salt
¼ c. sugar
¼ t. paprika
¼ t. dry mustard
¼ c. vegetable oil
¼ c. heavy cream
2 eggs, slightly beaten
1 head cabbage, shredded fine
½ c. pickle relish
1 2-oz. jar pimiento, diced

Place vinegar, water, salt, sugar, paprika, mustard and oil in a pan and bring to a boil. Remove from heat. Combine eggs and cream. Stir a little of the hot mixture into egg-cream mixture. Continue stirring and slowly pour remaining hot mixture into the egg mixture. Return to pan and cook on low heat for 5 minutes, stirring constantly. Mix together cabbage, pimiento and pickle relish. Pour hot dressing over and toss lightly. Serve immediately. Serves 8.

BROCCOLI CUSTARD

1 bunch broccoli
½ lb. fresh mushrooms
3 T. butter
1 c. grated Cheddar cheese
3 eggs, well beaten
1 10¾-oz. can condensed cream of celery soup
⅓ c. milk
1 t. grated onion
½ t. salt
1 t. Worcestershire sauce
¼ t. pepper
⅓ c. French bread crumbs

Trim and wash broccoli. Cook until barely tender. Drain and set aside. Sauté whole mushrooms in butter. Arrange broccoli and mushrooms in a shallow, greased 1½-quart baking dish. Combine ½ cup of the cheese, eggs, soup, milk and seasonings. Pour over the vegetables. Sprinkle with remaining cheese and bread crumbs. Set dish in shallow pan of water. Bake in a 350° oven for 45 minutes, or until custard is set. Serves 6.

CORN PUDDING

3 eggs, beaten
1 c. milk
2 c. corn
3 T. chopped green pepper
1 t. grated onion
1 T. minced parsley
½ t. salt
¼ t. pepper

In a large mixing bowl, combine eggs and milk; mix well. Add corn, green pepper, onion, parsley and seasonings. Turn into a buttered 1½-quart casserole. Bake in a 350° oven for 1 hour or until firm. Serves 6.

STUFFED ZUCCHINI

4 zucchini squash
1 green pepper, diced
1 small onion, chopped
1 T. butter
½ lb. ground beef
2 c. fresh corn
1 tomato, chopped
1 pimiento, diced
1 egg, slightly beaten
1 c. bread crumbs
1 T. Worcestershire sauce
¼ t. pepper
1 t. salt

Split zucchini in halves lengthwise and scoop out seeds and membrane. Set aside. Sauté green pepper and onion in butter until onion is transparent. Remove and set aside. Brown ground beef, separating with a fork. Add green pepper, onion and remaining ingredients. Place zucchini halves in a well-greased baking pan. Fill each half with corn stuffing. Pour one-half cup water in the bottom of the pan; cover with foil. Bake in a 350° oven until zucchini is tender. Remove foil and bake an additional ½ hour. Serves 6 to 8.

Pictured opposite
Stuffed Zucchini
(page 22)

SQUAW CORN

2 c. whole kernel corn
2 T. margarine
1 green pepper, diced
2 medium onions, chopped
1 small jar pimiento, diced
¼ t. pepper

Melt margarine in skillet. Add green pepper and onion. Sauté slowly over low heat until tender and onion is transparent. Add drained corn, pimiento and seasonings. Cook over low heat for 20 minutes. Serve in a warm bowl. Serves 4.

CARROTS SUPREME

4 c. carrots, chopped
½ t. salt
  Water
½ lb. bacon, diced
1 medium onion, diced
¼ t. pepper

Cook carrots in boiling, salted water until tender. Drain and set aside. Brown bacon in skillet. Drain and set aside. Sauté onion in bacon fat. Remove to dish. Mash carrots with potato masher; stir in bacon, onions, drippings and seasoning. Mix well. Serve hot. Serves 4.

BUTTERED PARSNIPS

8 parsnips (1½ lbs.)
½ t. salt
2 T. melted butter
2 T. parsley, chopped

Pare the parsnips and quarter. Split in half lengthwise. Place in a kettle with salted water to cover. Simmer until tender; drain. Pour melted butter over parsnips in serving dish. Mix to coat all sides. Sprinkle with parsley and serve. Serves 6.

VEGETABLE DISH

2 16-oz. cans green beans
2 16-oz. cans small, whole onions
2 16-oz. cans potatoes
1 16-oz. can small carrot pieces
2 2½-oz. jars mushrooms
1 head cauliflower, broken into flowerets
½ t. salt
½ t. pepper
  Paprika
  Cheese Sauce

Drain all vegetables and combine in a buttered 9 x 13 x 2-inch baking dish. Stir in Cheese Sauce and sprinkle top with paprika. Bake in a 350° oven for 1 hour. Serves 6.

CHEESE SAUCE

4 T. butter
4 T. flour
2 c. milk
1 t. salt
¼ t. pepper
½ lb. Cheddar cheese

Melt butter in saucepan. Add flour, salt and pepper. Gradually stir in milk. Simmer 2 to 3 minutes, or until thickened. Add cheese, stirring to melt. Blend thoroughly.

PEAS AND CARROTS

1 10-oz. pkg. frozen peas *or* 2 c. fresh peas
4 carrots, diced
2 c. water
½ t. salt
2 T. melted butter *or* 2 c. White Sauce

Cook peas and carrots in salted water until carrots are tender, about 15 minutes. Drain. Add melted butter or White Sauce. Serve hot. Serves 8.

WHITE SAUCE

2 T. butter
2 T. flour
2 c. milk

Melt butter in saucepan; add flour. Stir in milk and cook, stirring, until thick.

SNOW PEAS

4 c. fresh snow peas *or* 2 6-oz. pkgs. frozen snow peas
2 c. water
½ t. salt
2 T. melted butter

Prepare fresh snow peas by breaking off tips and tails. Wash and place in saucepan in salted water. Drain. Drop frozen snow peas in boiling salted water and cook until tender. Drain. Add melted butter and serve. Serves 4.

SNOW PEAS AND MUSHROOMS

1 6-oz. pkg. frozen snow peas *or* 2 c. fresh snow peas
Water to cover
1 t. salt
1 4-oz. can mushroom bits and pieces
2 T. melted butter

Cook frozen snow peas or fresh snow peas in salted water to cover for 20 minutes or until tender. Add drained mushrooms. Mix well. Heat through. Drain. Pour into warm serving dish. Pour melted butter over peas. Serve hot. Serves 4.

CAULIFLOWER WITH BUTTERED CRUMBS

1 head cauliflower
1 t. salt
Water to cover
3 T. margarine
¾ c. bread crumbs

Soak cauliflower in salted cold water, head down for 30 minutes. Rinse in clear water. Place in kettle. Add salt and enough water to cover. Simmer slowly for 20 to 30 minutes, until tender but still firm. Drain. Carefully remove cauliflower to a warm serving dish. Melt margarine in saucepan or small skillet and mix with bread crumbs. Heat through, but do not burn. Pour over cauliflower and serve hot. Serves 6.

STEWED TOMATOES WITH BREAD CUBES

1 30-oz. can tomatoes *or* 2 c. fresh tomatoes
1 c. stale bread, cut in cubes
1 t. salt
1 T. butter
½ t. pepper

Heat tomatoes in a saucepan or cook fresh tomatoes 20 minutes. Add bread cubes, butter, and seasonings. Bring to a boil. Serve hot. Serves 4.

STEWED TOMATOES

1 30-oz. can tomatoes *or* 2 c. fresh tomatoes
1 t. salt
1 T. butter
½ t. pepper

Combine tomatoes, seasonings and butter in a saucepan. Bring to a boil. Serve hot. Serves 4.

PARSNIP PATTIES

8 to 10 parsnips
½ t. salt
Boiling water
½ t. onion salt
⅛ t. pepper
½ t. salt
1 egg, beaten
⅓ c. fine bread crumbs
2 T. butter or margarine
¼ c. bread crumbs

Peel parsnips and cook in boiling salted water until tender. Drain and mash. Beat in seasonings and egg. Add bread crumbs. Chill well. Make into 6 patties. Coat with additional bread crumbs and fry in melted butter until golden brown on both sides. Serves 6.

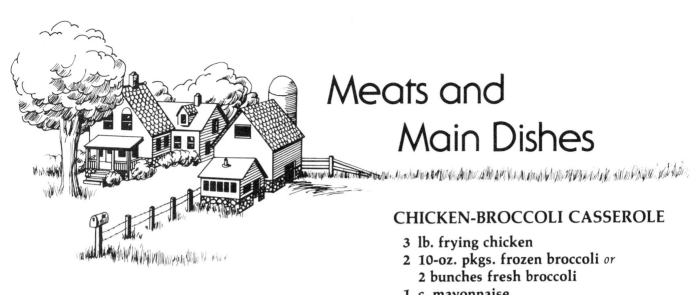

Meats and Main Dishes

CHICKEN-BROCCOLI CASSEROLE

- 3 lb. frying chicken
- 2 10-oz. pkgs. frozen broccoli *or* 2 bunches fresh broccoli
- 1 c. mayonnaise
- 2 10¾-oz. cans condensed cream of chicken soup
- ¼ t. curry powder
- 1 T. lemon juice
- ½ c. grated Cheddar cheese
- ½ c. bread crumbs
- 1 T. melted butter

Stew chicken; cool and bone. Steam broccoli until tender; drain. Grease an 11 x 7-inch casserole. Place chicken on the bottom, broccoli on top. Combine mayonnaise, soup, curry powder and lemon juice. Pour over broccoli. Sprinkle with a mixture of cheese and bread crumbs combined with butter. Bake in a 350° oven for 30 minutes. Serves 6.

SAUERBRATEN

- 5 lbs. boneless round, chuck or rump roast
- 2 onions, sliced
- 2 carrots, pared and sliced
- 1 stalk celery, chopped
- 1 T. meat tenderizer
- 1 T. salt
- 2 T. sugar
- 6 peppercorns
- 3 bay leaves
- 6 whole cloves
- 1½ c. red wine vinegar
- 1½ c. water
- 2 T. flour
- 4 T. butter
- ½ c. gingersnap crumbs

Place meat in earthenware, glass or enamel bowl. Add vegetables, meat tenderizer, seasonings, vinegar and water. Cover and refrigerate for 2 to 4 days, turning meat each day. When ready to cook, remove meat from marinade and pat dry. Strain marinade and save both marinade and vegetables. Flour meat. In a deep pot, melt butter and brown meat on all sides. Add 2 cups marinade and the vegetables. Cover tightly and simmer over low heat for 3½ to 4 hours, or until meat is tender. Add a bit more marinade if needed to replenish liquid. Remove meat to a heated platter and keep warm. To make gravy, strain vegetables from marinade. Add enough of the marinade to make 2 cups. Bring to a boil; add gingersnap crumbs. Cook, stirring constantly until thickened. Serve with vegetables, gravy and potato dumplings. Serves 12.

BIG BOY PIE

- ½ c. chopped onion
- ¼ c. shortening
- 1 lb. ground beef
- 2 T. catsup or chili sauce
- 1 t. salt
- 2 c. biscuit mix
- ⅔ c. milk
- 1 c. cooked tomatoes, drained
- 1 c. grated cheese

Sauté onion in shortening until golden. Add meat and brown. Stir in catsup and salt. Set aside. Stir milk into the biscuit mix, stirring until well blended. Turn onto a lightly floured board. Knead six times. Roll into a circular shape and place in a 9-inch pie pan. Fill with meat and onion. Cover with tomatoes and top with grated cheese. Bake in a 450° oven for 30 minutes. Serves 6.

Pictured opposite
Chicken-Broccoli Casserole
(page 27)

LASAGNA

    1 lb. ground beef
    ¼ c. butter
    1 c. chopped onion
    1 garlic bud, minced
    3 6-oz. cans tomato paste
    2 c. water
2½ T. salt
    1 No. 2 can tomatoes
    1 lb. broad noodles, boiled
    1 lb. mozzarella cheese, shredded
    2 lbs. dry cottage cheese
    1 c. Parmesan cheese

Brown meat in butter. Add onion and garlic. Stir in tomato paste, water, salt, and tomatoes. Cook over low heat for 45 minutes. Cook noodles, rinse and drain. Butter a 13 x 9 x 2-inch baking dish. Line dish with layer of noodles, sauce and cheese, ending with sauce and cheese. Bake in a 375° oven for 30 minutes. Let stand for 10 minutes before cutting. Serves 8 to 10.

VEAL PARMIGIANA

1½ lbs. veal, thinly sliced
    3 T. vegetable oil
    ½ c. chopped onion
    2 8-oz. cans tomato sauce
    ¼ t. crushed basil leaves
    ½ t. oregano
    ¼ t. thyme
    ½ lb. sliced mozzarella cheese
    ¼ c. grated Parmesan cheese

Over medium heat, brown veal lightly on both sides in the hot oil. Remove meat to a shallow 2-quart buttered dish. Add more oil as needed. Add onion and sauté until tender. Stir in tomato sauce, basil, oregano and thyme. Remove from heat. Pour sauce over veal and top with mozzarella and Parmesan cheese. Bake in a 350° oven for 40 minutes or until browned and tender. Serves 6.

CHOW MEIN CASSEROLE

    1 lb. ground beef
    1 onion, chopped
    1 large can chow mein noodles
    2 c. diced celery
    2 T. vegetable oil
    1 10¾-oz. can condensed cream of
      mushroom soup
    1 10¾-oz. can condensed tomato soup
    1 10¾-oz. can condensed cream of
      chicken soup

Brown beef and onion in oil. Pour into a greased 2-quart casserole. Add celery, noodles and soup. Bake in a 350° oven for 1 hour. Serves 6.

HAM LOAF

2½ c. soft bread crumbs
    1 c. milk
    1 lb. ground ham
    1 lb. ground beef
    2 eggs
    ½ green pepper, chopped
    2 T. chopped onion
    1 t. salt
    ½ t. pepper

Soak bread crumbs in milk. Add to meat and mix well. Add remaining ingredients and mix thoroughly. Pack in a greased loaf pan. Bake in a 350° oven for 1½ hours. Serves 6.

BAKED SPARERIBS AND DRESSING

    1 c. chopped apple
    1 c. hot water
    4 c. dry bread crumbs
    1 t. sage
    ½ c. chopped onion
    1 t. salt
    4 lbs. meaty pork spareribs

In a large bowl, combine all ingredients except spareribs. Add more water if a moist stuffing is desired. Place dressing in the bottom of a greased baking dish. Place ribs on top. Cover tightly with foil. Bake in a 350° oven for 2 hours or until meat is tender. Serves 4 to 6.

CORNED BEEF HASH

4 c. cooked corned beef, diced
2 T. butter
4 c. cooked potatoes, diced
1 medium onion, diced
1 t. salt
½ t. pepper
½ to 1 c. milk
6 poached eggs

Melt butter in a heavy frying pan; add chopped meat, potatoes, onion, seasonings and enough milk to moisten. Stir until well blended. Cook slowly for 1 hour. When brown on bottom, fold over like an omelet and serve on a warm platter. Garnish with poached eggs. Serves 6.

TAMALE PIE

1 onion, chopped
1 green pepper, diced
1 T. shortening
2 8-oz. cans tomato sauce
1 12-oz. can whole kernel corn
½ c. ripe olives, chopped
1 clove garlic, minced
1 T. sugar
1 t. salt
½ t. pepper
1 t. chili powder
1½ c. shredded American cheese
¾ lb. ground beef
¾ c. cornmeal
½ t. salt
2 c. cold water
1 T. butter

Cook onion and green pepper in shortening until tender. Add meat and brown. Add tomato sauce, corn, olives, garlic, sugar, salt, pepper and chili powder. Simmer for 20 to 25 minutes. Add cheese, stirring until melted. Pour into a 10 x 6-inch greased baking dish and set aside. Stir cornmeal and salt into water. Cook and stir until thick. Add butter. Spoon over meat mixture in strips. Bake in a 375° oven for about 40 minutes. Serves 6 to 8.

JAMBALAYA

½ lb. bacon
½ c. finely chopped onion
2 large green peppers, chopped
1 c. uncooked rice
1 clove garlic, minced
1 large can tomatoes
1 t. salt
1 bay leaf
¼ t. thyme
½ lb. baked or cooked ham, cubed
2 T. chopped parsley
½ t. pepper
½ t. Tabasco sauce
2 c. chicken broth, strained
1 lb. shrimp, cooked, shelled, and deveined

Preheat oven to 350°. Cut bacon into ½-inch pieces and cook in a heavy, oven-proof pan or Dutch oven with cover. When browned, remove with slotted spoon to paper towel to drain. Sauté onion until transparent, stirring as needed. Add green pepper; cook for 1 minute. Add rice; stir and cook rice for 3 minutes. Add remaining ingredients and bring to a boil. Cover pot and place in oven. Bake, covered, for 15 to 20 minutes or until liquid is absorbed and rice is tender. Sprinkle with parsley. Serves 4 to 6.

BEEF AND SAUERKRAUT

1 qt. sauerkraut
2 T. flour
3 lbs. beef brisket
1 small onion, minced
1 tart apple, grated
1 T. brown sugar
½ t. salt
¼ t. pepper

In a large Dutch oven, layer half of the sauerkraut; sprinkle with flour. Add meat, onion, apple and sugar. Sprinkle with salt and pepper. Lay remaining sauerkraut on top of meat. Add boiling water to just cover. Cover tightly and simmer for 1½ to 2 hours over low heat. Serves 6.

LAMB STEW WITH MUSHROOM DUMPLINGS

3 lbs. lamb stew meat, cubed
3 T. shortening
½ c. sliced onion
3 carrots, sliced diagonally
5 c. boiling water
1 c. flour
2 t. baking powder
½ c. condensed mushroom soup
3 T. water
3 T. parsley, chopped

Roll lamb in flour. Melt shortening and brown lamb cubes and onion. Add carrots and boiling water. Simmer slowly for 2 hours. To make dumplings, sift together flour and baking powder. Add mushroom soup and water. Mix well. After stew has simmered for 2 hours, drop dumplings by spoonfuls into boiling stew. Cover tightly and cook for 20 minutes. Remove stew to hot platter and surround with dumplings. Garnish with parsley. Serves 6.

BEEF STROGANOFF

3 beef bouillon cubes
1 c. boiling water
2 lbs. round or sirloin steak, cubed
3 T. flour
½ t. salt
⅛ t. pepper
½ c. shortening
1 c. chopped onion
1 14-oz. can mushrooms
1 c. sour cream
1 T. Worcestershire sauce

Dissolve bouillon cubes in water. Set aside. Dredge meat in flour and seasonings. In a large skillet, brown in ¼ cup of the shortening. Sauté onion in remaining shortening; add onion and bouillon to meat. Mix thoroughly. Cover pan and cook slowly for 1½ hours or until meat is tender. Add mushrooms and Worcestershire sauce; fold in sour cream. Heat thoroughly but do not boil. Serve hot on buttered noodles. Serves 6.

LAMB STEW

2 lbs. lamb shoulder, cubed
1 t. salt
4 carrots, cut up
3 potatoes, quartered
1 t. sugar
2 T. flour
1 T. shortening
1 6-oz. can peas

Salt meat thoroughly and place in a stewing pan; add water to cover. Bring to a boil. Reduce heat and simmer until meat is almost tender. Add carrots, potatoes and sugar. Simmer until vegetables and meat are tender. Melt shortening; stir in flour. Add about a cup of hot stew liquid to flour mixture, stirring well. Add to stew, stirring until thickened. Add drained peas. Heat through. Serves 4 to 6.

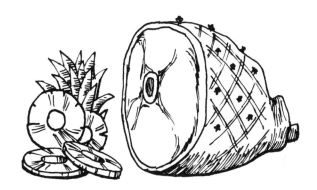

BAKED HAM

5 to 6-lb. ham
½ c. whole cloves
⅓ c. prepared mustard
½ c. brown sugar
6 to 8 pineapple slices
½ c. pineapple juice

Bake ham in roasting pan, uncovered, in a 350° oven for 1½ hours. Remove from oven and cut off skin. With a sharp knife, score fat into diamond shapes. Place a whole clove in the center of each diamond. Spread mustard over ham. Then press on brown sugar. Secure pineapple slices on ham with toothpicks. Bake an additional 30 minutes, basting frequently with pineapple juice. Serves 10 to 12.

Pictured opposite
Beef Stroganoff
(page 31)

NOODLE, KRAUT AND WIENER CASSEROLE

6 wieners
1 c. sauerkraut, rinsed and drained
½ t. caraway seed
⅛ t. celery salt
1 c. cooked noodles
½ t. pepper
½ t. salt
½ t. nutmeg
4 oz. Cheddar cheese, shredded
1 T. margarine

Place wieners in a buttered 1½-quart casserole. Combine sauerkraut, caraway seed and celery salt. Combine noodles, pepper, salt, and nutmeg. Mix well. Place half of the sauerkraut on top of wieners. Cover with noodles. Arrange cheese and margarine over noodles. Top with rest of the sauerkraut. Bake in a 375° oven for 25 minutes. Makes 2 servings.

CHOP SUEY

1 c. pork or veal, cubed
½ c. chopped onion
3 T. shortening
1½ c. water
½ t. salt
1½ c. celery, cut diagonally
1 1-lb. can bean sprouts
1 1-lb. can chop suey vegetables, drained
1 4-oz. can mushrooms
3 T. cornstarch
⅓ c. cold water
1 T. brown sugar
2 T. soy sauce
2 c. cooked rice

Brown cubed meat and onion in shortening. Place in stewing kettle. Add water, salt and celery; simmer until meat is tender. Add bean sprouts, chop suey vegetables, and mushrooms. Heat to boiling. Mix cornstarch and cold water until smooth. Add to boiling mixture, stirring constantly, until thickened and transparent. Add brown sugar and soy sauce. Serve over cooked rice or Chinese noodles. Serves 4.

SAN FRANCISCO STEW

1½ lbs. hamburger
2 T. shortening
1 1-lb. can tomatoes
4 c. Great Northern beans, cooked
1 large onion, sliced
1 c. brown sugar, firmly packed
4 bacon slices

Brown meat in shortening. Drain beans; add to meat with tomatoes. Mash. Pour half the mixture in a 4-quart greased baking dish. Slice a layer of onion to cover; sprinkle brown sugar over onions. Add remaining bean mixture. Bake in a 350° oven for 1 hour. Place bacon slices over top. Bake until bacon is done and juice is absorbed. Serves 6.

PARSNIP CASSEROLE

3 c. mashed, cooked parsnips
½ t. pepper
½ t. salt
1 c. cubed ham
1 c. sliced mushrooms
1 c. shredded cheese
½ c. crushed cornflakes

Season hot parsnips. Mix ham, mushrooms and cheese. Alternate layers of parsnips and ham mixture in a greased 2-quart casserole. Sprinkle top with cornflakes. Bake in a 350° oven for 25 minutes. Serves 6.

MACARONI CASSEROLE

1 lb. ground beef
2 t. dry onion flakes
2 c. elbow macaroni
1 T. diced pimiento
1 3-oz. can tomato sauce
⅔ c. water
2 T. vegetable oil

Brown ground beef in oil. Add onion flakes. Cook macaroni in salted water until done. Drain and rinse with hot water. Combine macaroni and meat. Add tomato sauce, water and pimiento. Pour into a greased baking dish. Cover with foil. Bake for 1 hour in a 350° oven. Serves 6.

ORIENTAL HAMBURGER

1½ lbs. ground beef
2 T. shortening
1 medium onion, chopped
2 t. garlic salt
2 c. water
4 T. soy sauce
1½ T. molasses
1 8-oz. pkg. frozen green beans
4 T. cornstarch
½ c. water
6 to 7 c. cooked rice

Brown ground beef and onion in shortening. Stir in garlic salt, 2 cups water, soy sauce and molasses. Heat to boiling; add green beans. Simmer 20 to 30 minutes until beans are tender. Blend cornstarch with ½ cup water. Stir into meat mixture; cook until thickens. Serve over rice. Serves 4 to 6.

HUNTER'S STEW

2 lbs. lean meat, beef or venison, cubed
Shank bone of beef
½ lb. suet
1½ gal. cold water or 24 c.
1 bunch celery
3 onions, chopped
1½ c. peas
1½ c. corn
1½ c. tomatoes
1½ c. lima beans
5 potatoes, diced
1½ c. diced carrot
¼ c. rice
½ c. chili sauce

Combine meat, bone, suet, celery, onion and water. Simmer 2½ hours. Remove celery and bone. Add vegetables with rice and simmer over low heat until vegetables are done. Before serving, season with ½ cup chili sauce and more salt and pepper if needed. Should be a thick soup. Serves 8 to 10.

SAVORY STEW

2 lbs. beef chuck, cut in 1-inch cubes
1 t. lemon juice
1 clove garlic, minced
1 small bay leaf
¼ t. allspice
8 small whole onions
3 c. water
1 t. Worcestershire sauce
1 medium onion, sliced
2 t. salt
¼ t. pepper
6 carrots, quartered
3 medium potatoes, cut up
½ c. flour
1 c. water

In Dutch oven, combine all ingredients except 1 cup of the water and the flour. Cover and bake in a 325° oven for 4 hours or until meat is tender. Remove stew from oven. In a covered jar, shake 1 cup water and flour until blended. Stir into stew. Heat to boiling, stirring constantly for 1 minute. Serve hot. Serves 4 to 6.

PRIME RIBS AU JUS

5 lbs. prime ribs
1 c. water
¼ c. vinegar
2 stalks celery, diced
1 c. water
⅛ c. vegetable oil
2 carrots, diced
1 onion, chopped
2 bay leaves
½ t. sage
½ t. salt
4 raw potatoes, cut up
1 green pepper, diced
1 clove garlic
½ t. thyme
2 c. tomatoes
¼ t. pepper
1 t. paprika

Place beef in roasting pan with water. Add ingredients in order as above. Bake in a 300° oven for 2½ hours. Baste meat every 30 minutes. Serves 6.

SOY-MARINATED CHUCK STEAK

- 3½ to 4 lbs. beef blade chuck roast, 2 inches thick
  Unseasoned meat tenderizer
- 3 T. brown sugar
- 4 t. white vinegar
- ¾ c. soy sauce
- 3 T. Worcestershire sauce

Early in the day, trim excess fat from steak. Prepare steak with meat tenderizer as label directs. Combine brown sugar, vinegar, soy sauce and Worcestershire sauce in a deep bowl or pan. Add meat, turning to coat. Cover and refrigerate at least 4 hours, turning occasionally. Barbecue, basting with marinade, until tender and browned. Serves 4 to 6.

SWEET-SOUR RIBS

- 3 lbs. beef short ribs
- 1 c. sliced onion
- 1 clove garlic
- 1 small bay leaf
- 3 T. brown sugar
- ¼ c. raisins
- ⅛ t. pepper
- 1½ c. hot water
- ¼ c. vinegar
- ⅓ c. catsup
- 1 t. salt

Wipe short ribs with damp cloth. Cut into individual serving pieces. Remove excess fat. Dredge in seasoned flour and brown well on all sides in hot fat in skillet. Remove ribs. Sauté onion and garlic. Combine remaining ingredients; pour over ribs. Cover and simmer 2 to 2½ hours or over low heat until tender. Serves 6.

BAKED HAM HASH

- ½ lb. boiled ham, ground
- 1 6-oz. can peas
- 5 hard-boiled eggs, chopped
- 1½ c. soft bread crumbs
- 1 T. melted butter
- 1 c. milk
- 2 T. flour
- ⅛ t. pepper
- ½ t. salt

In a buttered casserole, layer ham, peas, eggs and bread crumbs. Melt butter in a saucepan. Stir in flour. Gradually add milk, stirring constantly. Cook over medium heat, stirring constantly, until thickened. Add salt and pepper. Pour over casserole. Bake in a 350° oven for 30 minutes or until top is brown. Serves 4 to 6.

PIGSPAGOOT

- 2 T. shortening
- 2 lbs. pork, cubed
- 1 stalk celery, chopped
- 1 27-oz. can tomatoes
- 1 9-oz. pkg. spaghetti, cooked
- 1 6-oz. can mushrooms, drained
- 1 8-oz. can lima beans
- 1 3-oz. jar stuffed olives and liquid

Slightly brown pork in shortening. Salt very lightly. Sauté celery in 1 tablespoon shortening. Add to browned pork. Mix in tomatoes. Simmer until meat is tender. Add cooked spaghetti, mushrooms, lima beans, olives and liquid. Heat through; serve hot. Serves 4 to 6.

HORSERADISH MOLD FOR COLD MEAT

- 1 3-oz. pkg. lime gelatin
- 1 c. boiling water
- 1 c. cold water
- ¾ c. grated horseradish
- 1 c. shredded cabbage

Dissolve gelatin in boiling water; add cold water. Stir in horseradish and cabbage. Pour into tiny individual molds and chill until firm. Serve in lettuce nests as a garnish for a platter of cold meat.

*Pictured opposite
Sweet-Sour Ribs
(page 34)*

NEW ENGLAND BOILED DINNER

2 lbs. ham hocks
6 small beets
3 small turnips
3 carrots
1 t. salt
6 small onions
2 c. shredded cabbage
3 small parsnips
3 small potatoes
½ t. pepper

Wash ham hocks and put in a stewing kettle with enough water to cover. Simmer for 1 hour. Add vegetables in serving sized portions and seasonings. Cover and cook 30 minutes more or until vegetables and meat are tender. Place ham hocks in middle of platter and arrange vegetables around edge. Serves 4 to 6.

STUFFED FLANK STEAK

2 lbs. flank steak
1½ t. salt
1 onion, chopped
2 apples, sliced
6 or 8 prunes
Strips of fat salt pork
2 T. shortening
3 T. flour
½ t. pepper
1 c. cream
Toothpicks

Pound meat; salt. Sprinkle evenly with onions, apples, and prunes and roll tightly. Tie or fasten with toothpicks. Insert strips of pork. Sear on all sides in hot shortening. Cover and simmer, basting with the stock. Cook for 2 hours. Remove meat; add flour to liquid in pan. Add cream and pepper. Simmer until thick. Pour over meat. Serves 4 to 6.

LIVER LOAF

1 lb. ground liver
¼ lb. ground pork
¼ lb. ground beef
2 t. salt
¼ t. nutmeg
4 T. chopped onion
2 T. shortening
2 eggs
2 c. thin cream
¼ t. cinnamon
1 t. pepper
2 c. flour, sifted

Combine all meats, salt and nutmeg; mix well. Sauté onion in shortening until tender. Add to ground meat with eggs. Blend in remaining ingredients. Put mixture in a well-greased loaf pan. Set in a pan with hot water 1-inch deep. Cover loaf pan with foil. Bake in a 350° oven for 1 hour. Uncover and bake 1 additional hour. Serve hot or cold. Serves 8 to 10.

CREAMED CHIPPED BEEF

¼ lb. dried beef
2 T. minced onion
1 4-oz. can mushrooms
¼ c. butter
3 T. flour
1 c. milk
1 c. shredded Cheddar cheese
1 t. salt
⅛ t. pepper
1 c. sour cream

Cut dried beef in strips. Sauté beef, onion and drained mushrooms in butter. Cook over low heat until onions are transparent. Blend in flour. Add milk, stirring constantly. Cook until sauce is thick and smooth. Add cheese, sour cream, salt and pepper. Heat to serving temperature. Serve in popovers, on buttered toast triangles, toasted English muffins, rice or buttered noodles. Garnish with additional cheese, if desired. Serves 5 to 6.

SPANISH RICE

1 lb. ground beef
2 T. vegetable oil
1 green pepper, chopped
1 onion, chopped
1 1-lb. can tomatoes
3 T. parsley
1 c. diced celery
1 c. raw rice
1 c. water
½ t. salt
¼ t. pepper
½ t. chili pepper

Brown ground beef in oil. Add pepper and onion and cook until onion is transparent. Add remaining ingredients, mixing well. Pour mixture into a greased 1½-quart casserole. Bake in a 350° oven for 45 minutes. Serves 4.

SATURDAY NOODLE BAKE

1 lb. ground beef
½ lb. ground pork
2 T. butter or margarine
⅔ c. chopped onion
2 10¾-oz. cans condensed tomato soup
1 3-oz. pkg. cream cheese
2 T. sugar
¼ t. pepper
1 t. salt
1½ T. Worcestershire sauce
2 c. wide noodles
1 c. crushed cornflakes
½ c. melted butter or margarine

Combine meats and brown lightly in butter. Add onion and cook until tender, but not brown. Add soup, cheese, sugar, Worcestershire sauce and seasonings. Simmer for 15 minutes. Cook noodles in boiling water until tender; drain. Place noodles in a 11 x 7 x 1-inch buttered baking dish; pour sauce over noodles. Mix cornflakes with melted butter; sprinkle over the top. Bake in a 350° oven for 20 minutes or until heated through. Serves 8.

PORK ROAST

4 to 5-lb. fresh pork shoulder
½ t. pepper
1 t. salt
¼ c. flour
6 potatoes, quartered
6 medium onions, quartered
6 carrots, halved

Place pork shoulder, fat side up, in a roasting pan. Sprinkle with salt and pepper. Sprinkle flour on fat part of roast. Roast in a 350° oven for 1½ hours. Prepare vegetables and place around meat. Bake an additional 45 minutes or until vegetables are tender and pork is well done. Serves 6 to 8.

PORK, SAUERKRAUT AND DUMPLINGS

3 or 4 pork shanks *or* 3 lbs. meaty spareribs
1 large onion, chopped
1 T. caraway seed
1 t. salt
½ t. pepper
1½ lbs. sauerkraut

Wash pork. Place in a large pot; cover with water. Bring to a boil and simmer for about 15 minutes. Add onion, caraway seed, salt and pepper. Simmer for 60 minutes. Rinse sauerkraut; add to the meat. Bring to a boil and add dumplings. Cover tightly and boil an additional 30 minutes.

Potato Dumplings

1 egg, slightly beaten
½ c. flour
4 large potatoes, peeled and grated
½ t. salt

Drain excess water from grated potatoes by placing on cloth and squeezing out excess water. Place potatoes in a bowl and add egg, salt and flour; mix thoroughly. Drop by spoonfuls on top of pork and sauerkraut mixture. Simmer about 30 minutes. Serves 4 to 6.

STEAK AND KIDNEY PIE

1 lb. round steak
1 beef kidney
¼ c. flour
⅛ t. pepper
1 t. salt
3 T. shortening
1 onion, chopped
¼ c. pimiento, chopped
2 T. Worcestershire sauce
¼ t. thyme
1½ c. water
    Pastry for 1 pie

Cut round steak in ¾ to 1-inch cubes. Remove tubes and fat from kidney. Cut in ¾ to 1-inch cubes. Combine flour, salt and pepper. Dredge steak and kidney cubes in flour, reserving any extra flour. Brown meat in shortening. Remove meat from skillet. Add onion to drippings in skillet and sauté over low heat until transparent. Drain grease. Add pimiento, Worcestershire sauce, thyme and water. Bring to a boil. Stir in browned meat cubes and any remaining seasoned flour. Make crust for pie. Roll out and line pie pan. Roll out top crust, cutting design for steam to escape. Turn meat mixture into crust in pie pan. Moisten edges. Cover with top crust. Seal top crust to edge and flute edges. Paint top with milk. Bake in a 325° oven for 1½ hrs. Makes 6 servings.

SAUERKRAUT CASSEROLE

2 lbs. sauerkraut
½ c. diced smoked sausage
1 large carrot, diced
1 onion, chopped
12 peppercorns
1 c. dry white wine
2 c. diced smoked ham
½ c. diced bacon
1 large apple, diced
1 large potato, pared and grated
1 c. stock or water

Drain sauerkraut. Combine all ingredients and pour in a buttered 2-quart casserole. Cover tightly and bake in a 350° oven for 1½ to 2 hours. It should be fairly dry. Serves 6.

TUNA-POTATO CHIP CASSEROLE

2 c. tuna, flaked
2 T. butter
1 c. sliced fresh mushrooms
½ green pepper, diced
1 t. minced onion
½ c. sliced stuffed olives
1 3-oz. bag potato chips
2 c. White Sauce

Melt butter in skillet. Sauté mushrooms, pepper and onion over low heat for 5 minutes. In a greased casserole, lightly combine all ingredients. Top with crushed potato chips. Bake in a 375° oven for 30 minutes. Serves 4.

WHITE SAUCE

2 T. butter
2 T. flour
2 c. milk

Melt butter; stir in flour. Slowly add milk, blending until smooth. Cook slowly until thickened, stirring constantly.

HUNGARIAN VEAL CUTLET

1 veal steak, 1½-inch thick
1 c. soft bread crumbs
1 egg, slightly beaten
1 T. water
1 clove garlic
¼ c. shortening
1 t. paprika
2 c. sour cream

Cut veal into six serving-size pieces. Dip into crumbs, in egg that has been beaten with water, and again into crumbs. Rub frying pan with garlic; melt shortening. Brown breaded veal quickly on both sides. Add paprika to sour cream. Pour over veal. Cover; and bake in a 325° oven for 1½ hours or until tender. Uncover for the last 15 minutes to brown. Serves 6.

Pictured opposite
Ingredients for
Sauerkraut Casserole
(page 38)

PORK CHOPS
SPANISH STYLE

6 pork chops *or* pork steaks
   Pepper
   Salt
2 T. shortening
2 16-oz. cans stewed tomatoes
1 c. uncooked rice
2 T. butter
1 t. salt

Sprinkle meat with salt and pepper. Brown meat in hot shortening. Drain. Preheat oven to 350°. In a 1½-quart greased baking dish, combine tomatoes with liquid, rice, butter and 1 teaspoon salt. Arrange meat over rice. Bake for 1 hour or until meat is tender. Serves 4.

MEATBALLS WITH SAUERKRAUT

1 lb. ground beef
1 egg
¼ c. coarse bread crumbs
½ t. salt
¼ t. pepper
1 c. catsup
1 c. water
½ c. gingersnap crumbs
¼ c. brown sugar, firmly packed
½ t. salt
1 8-oz. can sauerkraut

Mix together meat, egg, bread crumbs, salt and pepper. Shape into 1-inch balls. Simmer catsup, water and cookie crumbs for 5 minutes. Add brown sugar, salt and sauerkraut. Heat to boiling; add meatballs. Lower heat and simmer for 45 minutes. Serves 4 to 6.

ENGLISH BEEF STEW

1½ lbs. round steak, cubed
⅛ t. pepper
½ t. salt
3 T. shortening
2 medium onions, sliced
2 c. boiling water
2 c. tomatoes
3 c. sliced potatoes
1 T. Worcestershire sauce
1 c. sliced carrots
3 T. flour
¼ c. water
   Pastry or biscuits for topping

Season meat with salt and pepper and roll in flour. Brown in shortening. Add onions and boiling water. Simmer for ½ hour. Add tomatoes, potatoes, Worcestershire sauce and carrots. Simmer over low heat until meat and vegetables are tender. Remove meat and vegetables to a casserole and thicken stock with flour mixed with water. Pour thickened stock over meat and vegetables. Cover with biscuits. Bake in a 425° oven for 20 to 25 minutes. Serve hot. Serves 6.

FRANKY NOODLE

1 lb. frankfurters
1 onion, chopped
½ green pepper, chopped
3 T. margarine
1½ c. tomato juice
¾ c. water
1 T. sugar
2 T. flour
3 c. cooked noodles

Cut frankfurters into 1-inch pieces. Sauté franks, onion and green pepper in margarine. Add tomato juice, water, flour and sugar. Stir until thickened. Simmer slowly for 20 minutes; serve hot over noodles. Serve with salad and rolls. Serves 4.

PORK BIRDS

1 onion, chopped
½ c. chopped celery
1 T. shortening
1 t. sage
2 c. dry bread cubes
2 bouillon cubes
½ to ¾ c. hot water or enough to moisten bread
6 boneless pork steaks
2 T. shortening

Brown onion and celery in shortening. Add sage, onion and celery to bread cubes. Dissolve bouillon cubes in hot water and pour over bread mixture. Stir with a fork until moistened. Place a heaping tablespoon of stuffing in middle of pork steak. Roll up and fasten with toothpicks. Brown each steak in additional shortening until all sides are browned. Place in a casserole or baking dish; add ¾ cup water to bottom of pan. Cover and bake in a 350° oven 1½ hours. Serves 6.

FRANKFURTER SPAGHETTI

⅓ c. chopped onion
¼ c. shortening
3 T. flour
¼ t. oregano
½ t. salt
¼ t. pepper
¾ c. water
1 c. evaporated milk
1 t. Worcestershire sauce
1 c. grated American cheese
1 lb. wieners, cut up
1½ c. cooked spaghetti

Sauté onion in shortening until tender. Remove from heat and stir in flour, oregano, salt and pepper. Heat until thick; gradually add water, milk, Worcestershire sauce and cheese. Stir over low heat until cheese melts. Add wieners and spaghetti. Place in 1½-quart greased baking dish. Bake in a 350° oven for 30 minutes. Serves 4 to 6.

QUICK CHILI MAC

1 c. macaroni
1 green pepper, chopped
1 large onion, chopped
2 T. margarine
1 lb. ground beef
1 10¾-oz. can condensed tomato soup
1 1-lb. can kidney beans
½ t. salt
½ t. chili powder

Boil macaroni as directed on package. Drain and set aside. Sauté green pepper and onion in margarine until transparent. Add ground beef and brown. Add tomato soup, kidney beans, salt and chili powder. Simmer over low heat for 20 minutes. Add macaroni and heat through. Serves 4.

THRIFTY TUNA CASSEROLE

1 10¾-oz. can condensed cream of mushroom soup
½ c. milk
1 7-oz. can tuna, drained and flaked
1¾ c. potato chips, crushed
1 c. canned peas, drained

Empty soup into small bowl. Add milk and mix. Add tuna, crushed potato chips and peas. Stir well. Turn into a greased 1½-quart casserole. Sprinkle top with crushed potato chips. Bake in a 375° oven for 25 minutes. Serves 4.

VEAL SCALLOPINI

1 c. mushrooms
¼ c. olive oil or vegetable oil
¾ c. flour
2 lbs. veal steak, cut thin
½ t. pepper
1 t. salt
1½ c. white wine

Sauté mushrooms in hot oil. Remove and set aside. Flour meat lightly; brown in hot oil. Add mushrooms, salt, pepper and wine. Cover and simmer 20 minutes. Serves 6.

Quick Breads and Yeast Breads

CRANBERRY NUT LOAF

2 c. flour
1½ t. baking powder
1 t. salt
½ t. baking soda
1 egg
1 c. sugar
¾ c. orange juice
3 T. vegetable oil
1½ c. cranberries, chopped
1 c. chopped nuts

Sift together flour, baking powder, salt and soda. Put egg, sugar, orange juice and oil in blender. Blend only until mixed. Add cranberries and nuts; blend. Add dry ingredients and stir until barely moistened. Turn into a greased 9 x 5 x 3-inch loaf pan. Bake in a 350° oven for 45 minutes or until a tester inserted into the middle comes out clean. Turn out of pan onto a wire rack and cool before slicing.

BANANA BREAD

1 c. sugar
½ c. butter or margarine
1 t. baking soda
1 T. sour milk or orange juice
2 eggs, well beaten
3 mashed, ripe bananas
2 c. flour
¼ c. chopped nuts

Cream together butter and sugar. Stir soda into sour milk or orange juice. Add eggs, bananas, soda mixture and flour, beating thoroughly. Stir in nuts. Pour into a buttered loaf pan. Bake in a 350° oven for 1 hour. Cool before slicing. Freezes well. Makes 1 loaf.

CLUSTER COFFEE CAKE

2 pkgs. dry yeast
¼ c. warm water
1¼ c. milk, scalded and cooled to lukewarm
3½ to 4 c. flour
2 eggs, well beaten
½ c. sugar
½ c. melted butter and margarine
1 t. salt
2 T. grated orange rind
¾ c. sugar
¾ c. pecans, finely chopped

Soften yeast in water for 5 minutes. Add milk and 1 cup of the flour, beating well. Let mixture stand for 20 minutes or until light and bubbly. Blend beaten eggs, ½ cup sugar, melted butter and salt. Add to yeast mixture; mix well. Work in remaining flour and 1 tablespoon orange rind. Knead on floured board until dough is smooth and elastic. Place in a greased bowl and let rise in a warm place, until doubled in bulk. Divide dough in half; form each half into a long roll. Cut each roll into 24 pieces. Roll each piece into a ball. Mix remaining sugar and orange rind. Dip balls into melted butter, then into sugar mixed with rind, then into chopped nuts. Place in a greased tube pan, close together and in layers. Let stand in a warm place for 40 minutes. Bake in a 350° oven for 45 minutes. Turn out of pan onto a cake rack to cool. Break off pieces and butter. The coffee cake may be made in layer cake pans, if desired.

Pictured opposite
Cranberry Nut Loaf (upper shelf)
Banana Bread (lower shelf)
(page 43)

REFRIGERATOR ROLLS

1 c. milk, scalded
¼ c. sugar
1 t. salt
⅓ c. shortening *or* vegetable oil
2 pkgs. dry yeast
½ c. lukewarm water
2 eggs, beaten
5 c. sifted flour (about)

Scald milk. Add sugar, salt, shortening or oil. Stir until dissolved. Cool to lukewarm. Dissolve yeast in lukewarm water; add to milk mixture. Add eggs. Gradually add flour; mix to a smooth, soft dough. Knead on a lightly floured board until smooth and satiny. Shape into a ball and place in a greased bowl; cover with a cloth. Let rise in a warm place until doubled in bulk. (If it is not to be used immediately, dough can be set in refrigerator until needed; then let it rise until doubled in bulk.) Shape into rounds or crescents. Cover. Let rise until doubled in bulk. Bake in a 425° oven for 15 to 20 minutes. Makes 2½ dozen.

POPOVERS

1 c. flour
¼ t. salt
⅞ c. milk
1 t. melted butter or margarine
2 eggs

Sift together flour and salt. Gradually add milk to flour in a bowl. Add butter. Beat eggs well and add to batter. Beat batter for 2 minutes with mixer. Fill hot muffin pans two thirds full. Bake in a 450° oven for 14 minutes. Reduce heat to 350° and bake 20 more minutes. Serve hot. Can be filled with creamed vegetables or creamed meat.

PUMPKIN BREAD

1 c. brown sugar
½ c. sugar
1 c. cooked or canned pumpkin
½ c. vegetable oil
2 eggs, beaten
2 c. sifted flour
1 t. baking soda
½ t. salt
½ t. nutmeg
½ t. cinnamon
¼ t. ginger
1 c. raisins
½ c. chopped nuts
¼ c. water

Combine sugars, pumpkin, oil and eggs. Beat until blended. Sift together flour, soda, salt and spices. Add to pumpkin mixture and mix well. Stir in raisins, nuts and water. Spoon into a well-oiled 9 x 5 x 3-inch loaf pan. Bake in a 350° oven for 65 to 75 minutes or until a toothpick inserted into the bread comes out clean. Turn out on a wire rack to cool thoroughly before slicing.

BAKING POWDER BISCUITS

2 c. flour
1 t. salt
2 T. sugar
4 t. baking powder
2 T. shortening
½ c. milk, or enough to make a stiff dough

Sift flour, salt, sugar and baking powder into a bowl. Cut in shortening. Add milk, a little at a time, to make a stiff dough. Turn out on a floured board. Sprinkle flour over the top if sticky and pat into a circle about 1 inch thick. Cut into rounds with a biscuit cutter dipped in flour. Place in a greased pan; bake in a 400° oven for 15 to 20 minutes. Serve hot with butter and honey. *Note:* For shortcake, bake recipe in a 9-inch pie tin and split into wedges. Top with crushed berries and whipped cream.

BOSTON BROWN BREAD

1 egg
1 t. salt
2 T. sugar
1 T. shortening
1 c. sour milk
1 t. baking soda
2 T. dark molasses
2 T. white flour
1 c. raisins
1½ to 2 c. graham flour

Mix ingredients in order given. Care must be given that not too much graham flour is used as it makes the bread crumble when sliced. The dough should be a little thicker than cake batter. Bake in a greased loaf pan in a 350° oven for 50 to 60 minutes. Turn on wire rack to cool before slicing. Makes 1 loaf.

BRAN MUFFINS

1 c. whole bran
1 c. sour milk
1 c. flour
1 t. baking powder
½ t. salt
½ t. baking soda
½ t. cinnamon
¼ c. sugar
2 T. shortening
1 egg, well beaten

Pour milk over bran and set aside. Sift together flour, baking powder, salt, soda, cinnamon and sugar. Set aside. In a large bowl, beat shortening and egg; add bran mixture, mixing thoroughly. Add dry ingredients, stirring only until moistened. Fill muffin cups two-thirds full. Bake in a 400° oven for 20 to 25 minutes.

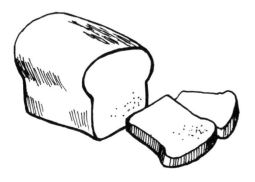

CHEESE BLINTZES

2 eggs
½ t. salt
1 c. water
1 c. sifted flour
¾ lb. cottage cheese
2 T. melted butter
2 T. light cream
⅛ t. salt
Butter for frying

Put 1 egg, salt, water and flour in blender container. Cover and process at mix until smooth. Pour 2 tablespoons of the batter onto a hot griddle. Fry on one side only until lightly browned, using low heat. Remove each pancake onto a clean cloth, cooked side up. Cool. Stir ¾ of the cottage cheese and remaining egg and butter together. Spread a little on each pancake. Fold over from both sides, then roll loosely. Sauté in hot butter. Put the cream, remaining cottage cheese and salt into blender container. Process at blend until smooth. Spoon onto hot blintzes and serve at once. Makes 4 servings.

CREAM PUFFS

¾ c. water
⅓ c. butter or margarine
¾ c. flour
⅛ t. salt
3 eggs

In a small saucepan combine water and butter and bring to a boil over medium heat. Remove from heat and beat in flour and salt, all at once. Over low heat, stir until mixture forms a ball and leaves the sides of the pan. Remove from heat. Add eggs all at once. Beat until smooth and satiny looking. Place dough by large spoonfuls on an ungreased cookie sheet. Bake in a 400° oven for 40 minutes without opening door. Remove from oven and cool in a draft-free place. To serve, cut tops from puffs and take out doughy substance in the middle of each puff and discard. Fill puff with cold vanilla pudding or ice cream. Place tops back on. Can be frosted with chocolate frosting.

DOUGHNUT DROPS

2 c. sifted flour
⅓ c. sugar
3 t. baking powder
½ t. salt
1 t. nutmeg
1 egg, slightly beaten
¾ c. milk
3 T. vegetable oil
Oil for frying
Confectioners' sugar or cinnamon and sugar mixture

Sift together dry ingredients. Add egg, milk and oil; stir until smooth. Heat 1 inch oil to 365°. Drop dough by teaspoons into hot oil. Turn after a few seconds and fry until browned on both sides, turning once more. Remove with slotted spoon. Drain on paper towels over a pan. Roll in sugar and serve warm. Makes about 3 dozen.

RAISED DOUGHNUTS

½ c. warm water
2 pkgs. dry yeast
½ c. shortening
1½ c. warm milk
½ c. sugar
2 eggs
6 to 6½ c. flour

Dissolve yeast in warm water. Heat shortening, milk and sugar until shortening melts. Remove from heat. Cool slightly; then stir in eggs. Stir in yeast mixture. Add 4 cups flour, mixing well. Add more flour as needed to make a soft dough. Knead until smooth and satiny. Place in a greased bowl and let rise in a warm place for 1 hour and 15 minutes. Punch down. Let rise 55 more minutes. Roll out on floured board to about a ¼-inch thickness. Cut with a doughnut cutter. Let rise for 30 minutes. Deep fry in hot grease at 400° until light brown. Turn to brown other side. Drain on paper towels. Sprinkle with confectioners' sugar, granulated sugar or frost.

POTATO BREAD

3 or 4 large potatoes
2 pkgs. dry yeast
¼ c. warm water
½ c. sugar
2 T. salt
½ c. melted shortening
4 c. scalded milk, cooled
4 to 6 c. flour or more

Dissolve yeast in warm water. Peel and cook potatoes. Drain and save potato water. Mash potatoes until fluffy. Add potato water, sugar, salt, yeast, shortening and milk. Add enough flour to make a thick sponge. Let set overnight in a warm place. In the morning, add enough flour to make a dough that isn't sticky. Make into loaves, biscuits or rolls. Let rise about 1 hour. Bake in a 350° oven 30 minutes for rolls and biscuits, about 1 hour for loaves. Remove from pans and wipe tops with butter, then cover with cloth to soften crust.

POTATO PANCAKES

2 eggs
½ small onion
½ t. salt
⅛ t. pepper
2 T. flour
¼ t. baking powder
3 c. cubed raw potatoes

Put eggs, onion, salt, pepper, flour, baking powder and ½ cup of the potato cubes into blender container. Process at grate until potatoes have gone through the blades. Stop blender and add remaining potatoes. Cover and process at chop just until all potato cubes have passed through the blades. Use a rubber spatula to help guide potatoes into the blades. Do not overblend. Pour onto a hot, well-greased griddle. Cook until golden brown. Drain on absorbent paper. Yield 12 pancakes. Serve hot with applesauce.

Note: Potatoes can be raw grated to make 1 cup. Drain well and use in above recipe.

Cakes and Frostings

BRANDIED FRUIT CAKE

3 c. sifted flour
1 t. salt
1 t. baking soda
1 t. nutmeg
1 t. cinnamon
¾ c. shortening
½ c. honey
½ c. brown sugar, firmly packed
2 eggs
½ c. brandy
1 lb. mixed candied fruit, diced
1 c. whole glacé cherries
1 c. light raisins
1 c. broken walnuts

Sift flour with salt, soda, nutmeg and cinnamon. Cream shortening, honey and sugar until fluffy. Add eggs, one at a time, beating well after each. Stir in brandy, fruits and nuts. Gradually add dry ingredients. Beat well with a spoon until well blended. Spoon into a greased and floured 9-inch tube pan. Bake in a 300° oven for 2½ hours or until a toothpick inserted in center comes out clean. Cool in pan for 15 minutes. Remove to rack to finish cooling. Wrap in foil and store to ripen. Once a week, open foil and sprinkle thoroughly with more brandy. Just before serving, brush with glaze and decorate with candied fruits.

COFFEE CLOUD SPONGE CAKE

1 T. instant coffee
1 c. boiling water
2 c. flour
3 t. baking powder
½ t. salt
6 eggs, separated
½ t. cream of tartar
2 c. sugar
1 t. vanilla
1 c. pecans, chopped

Dissolve instant coffee in boiling water. Set aside to cool. Sift together flour, baking powder and salt. Beat egg whites with cream of tartar. Add ½ cup of the sugar. Set aside. Beat egg yolks until blended. Add sugar and vanilla. Beat 4 to 5 minutes. Add dry ingredients, cooled coffee and egg whites. Fold in pecans. Bake in a greased and floured 10-inch tube pan or a 13 x 9 x 2-inch pan. Bake in a 350° oven for 60 to 70 minutes.

COFFEE ICING

2 T. butter, softened
2 c. confectioners' sugar
1½ t. instant coffee
2 T. milk

Mix the ingredients to a spreading consistency and spread on cake.

FRUIT CAKE GLAZE

2 T. brown sugar
1 T. light corn syrup
2 T. water

Combine ingredients in a saucepan. Bring to a boil and boil for 2 minutes. Cool before using.

SALAD DRESSING CAKE

2½ c. flour
1¼ c. sugar
⅓ c. cocoa
1½ t. baking soda
½ t. salt
¾ c. salad dressing
1 c. cold water
1 t. vanilla

Sift together flour, sugar, cocoa, soda and salt. Stir in salad dressing, cold water and vanilla, mixing well. Pour into two greased and floured 9-inch cake pans. Bake in a 400° oven for 35 to 40 minutes.

CARROT CAKE

2 c. sugar
2 c. flour
2 t. baking soda
1 t. salt
3 t. cinnamon
1½ c. vegetable oil
4 eggs
3 c. grated carrot
1 c. chopped nuts (optional)
1 t. vanilla

Sift together sugar, flour, soda, salt and cinnamon. Stir in oil. Add eggs, one at a time, mixing well after each addition. Add carrots, nuts and vanilla, mixing thoroughly. Pour into a floured and greased 13 x 9 x 2-inch cake pan. Bake in a 350° oven for 30 minutes. Cool in pan. Spread with Cream Cheese Icing.

CREAM CHEESE ICING

½ c. melted butter
1 8-oz. pkg. cream cheese, softened
1 t. vanilla
1 1-lb. box confectioners' sugar

Combine butter, cream cheese and vanilla, mixing well. Gradually add confectioners' sugar, beating until smooth. Spread on cooled cake.

LIGHTNING CAKE

2 eggs
  Sweet milk
½ c. shortening
1 c. sugar
2 c. flour
2 t. baking powder
¼ t. salt
1 t. vanilla

Drop eggs in measuring cup and add enough milk to make one cup. Add to sugar and shortening in a mixing bowl. Mix well. Sift together flour, baking powder and salt. Add to batter with vanilla. Mix well. Pour into 2 greased and floured 8-inch cake pans. Bake in a 350° oven for 35 minutes or until done. Frost with favorite icing.

TAKE-ALONG CAKE

1 No. 303 can fruit cocktail
2 eggs
1½ c. sugar
2 c. flour
2 t. baking soda
2 t. baking powder
1 t. salt

Mix all ingredients together, including juice from fruit cocktail. Pour into a greased and floured 13 x 9 x 2-inch cake pan. Bake in a 350° oven for 1 hour. Frost warm cake with Coconut Icing.

COCONUT ICING

1 c. sugar
1 c. coconut
½ c. margarine
1 14½-oz. can evaporated milk
1 t. vanilla

Combine all ingredients and bring to a boil. Take fork and stab holes all over cake. Pour hot frosting over cake as soon as the cake is taken from the oven. When cool, cut and serve.

FLORENCE'S DEVIL'S FOOD

3 T. cocoa
½ c. boiling water
1 t. baking soda
1 c. sugar
½ c. shortening
2 eggs
2 c. flour
½ t. salt
½ c. sour milk
1 t. vanilla

Place cocoa in medium-size bowl; add boiling water. Stir in soda and set aside to cool. Cream sugar and shortening. Beat in eggs and mix well. Mix flour and salt and add to sugar and shortening with sour milk. Add vanilla and cocoa mixture. Spoon into a greased and floured 12 x 9-inch cake pan. Bake in a 350° oven for 35 to 40 minutes. Frost with white, caramel or chocolate icing.

PUZZLE CAKE

1½ c. flour
½ c. brown sugar, firmly packed
¾ c. softened butter

Mix together the flour, sugar and butter until crumbly. Set aside one-half of the crumb mixture. Spread remaining crumb mixture in an 8 x 12-inch pan and pat down. Bake in a 350° oven for 10 minutes. Remove from oven and spread on Filling. Sprinkle reserved crumbs on top. Bake for an additional 25 minutes.

FILLING

½ c. cut-up dates
1 c. shredded coconut
½ c. chopped nuts
2 egg whites
¾ c. sugar
1 t. vanilla

Combine dates, coconut and nuts. Whip egg whites until stiff and add sugar and vanilla. Fold in the date mixture.

RHUBARB CAKE

2 c. flour
2 t. baking powder
½ t. salt
½ c. sugar
1 T. butter
1 egg
½ c. milk
3 c. rhubarb, finely sliced
2 c. sugar
1 T. butter
3 T. flour
1 egg
½ t. nutmeg

Sift flour with baking powder, salt and ½ cup sugar. Stir in butter, egg and milk until dry ingredients are moistened. Spread in a buttered and floured 13 x 9 x 2-inch cake pan. Mix rhubarb, sugar, butter, flour, egg and nutmeg. Spread on top of the batter. Bake in a 350° oven for 45 minutes. Cool and serve.

EGGLESS, MILKLESS, BUTTERLESS CAKE

1 c. water
1 c. brown sugar, firmly packed
2 c. raisins
¼ t. nutmeg
⅓ c. lard or shortening
¼ t. salt
1 t. cinnamon
½ t. cloves
2 c. flour
1 t. baking soda
½ t. baking powder

Put water, brown sugar, raisins, lard, salt and spices in a saucepan and mix. Bring to a boil. Cook for 3 minutes; cool. Sift together flour, soda and baking powder. Stir into cooled mixture, mixing well. Pour into a greased loaf tin. Bake in a 350° oven for 1 hour. Frost, if desired, or serve plain.

Pictured opposite
Puzzle Cake
(page 50)

CHOCOLATE GLAZE

1 1-oz. square unsweetened chocolate
1 T. butter
¾ c. confectioners' sugar
½ t. salt
2 T. hot milk (about)

Melt chocolate with butter over low heat. Stir in sugar and salt. Add milk, a small amount at a time, until mixture is of glaze consistency. While glaze is still warm, pour on cake, spreading with spatula. Makes ½ cup.

CHOCOLATE POUND CAKE

1 c. butter or margarine, softened
1 t. vanilla
2¾ c. sifted cake flour
1½ t. cream of tartar
¾ t. baking soda
½ t. salt
1¾ c. sugar
¾ c. milk
3 eggs
1 egg yolk
3 squares chocolate, melted
Chocolate glaze

Cream butter and vanilla. Sift together flour, cream of tartar, soda, salt and sugar. Add dry ingredients to butter, alternating with milk. Mix until all flour is moistened. Then beat for 2 minutes at medium speed of electric mixer or 300 vigorous strokes by hand, scraping the sides of bowl. Add eggs, egg yolk and melted chocolate. Beat 1 minute longer with mixer or 150 vigorous strokes by hand. Pour batter into a 10-inch tube pan which has been buttered and lined on the bottom with waxed paper. Grease paper. Bake in a 350° oven for 65 to 70 minutes or until cake springs back when lightly pressed. Cool cake in pan for 10 minutes. Remove from pan. Cool thoroughly on rack. Glaze, if desired.
Note: This cake may also be baked in a 9 x 4 x 2-inch loaf pan for 60 to 65 minutes. Cool in pan 10 minutes before turning out to cool.

TOMATO SOUP CAKE

½ c. butter
1 c. sugar
½ t. nutmeg
½ t. cloves
½ t. salt
½ t. cinnamon
2 c. flour
2 t. baking powder
1 t. baking soda
1 c. tomato soup
1 c. dates, cut up
1 c. chopped nuts

Melt butter. Add sugar and cream well. Add spices and salt. Sift flour and baking powder together. Dissolve soda in soup and add alternately with flour to sugar mixture. Beat well. Add dates and nuts, slightly floured. Bake in two 9-inch buttered layer cake pans in a 350° oven for 45 minutes or until the cakes test done. Cool on cake rack when turned out of pans. Spread with icing.

ICING FOR TOMATO SOUP CAKE

1 3-oz. pkg. cream cheese
1½ c. confectioners' sugar
1 t. vanilla or lemon juice

Mix thoroughly and spread on cake.

BOILED CHOCOLATE FROSTING

1 c. sugar
2 T. cocoa
½ c. cream *or* evaporated milk
1 t. vanilla

Mix all ingredients in a saucepan. Boil to the soft-ball stage (234°-238° on a candy thermometer). Remove from heat and beat until thick enough to spread on the cake.

MAGIC CHOCOLATE FROSTING

1⅓ c. sweetened condensed milk
2 1-oz. squares unsweetened chocolate
⅛ t. salt
1 T. water
½ t. vanilla

Cook milk and chocolate in double boiler stirring constantly until thick. Gradually add water and salt. Cool. Stir in vanilla. Spread on cooled cake.
Note: To make a chocolate sauce, add ½ to 1 cup hot water.

CHOCOLATE FROSTING

⅔ c. softened butter or margarine
½ t. salt
6 c. sifted confectioners' sugar
1 egg yolk
3 1-oz. squares melted chocolate
½ c. milk
1 t. vanilla

Beat butter with salt and 1 cup of the sugar. Stir in egg yolk and chocolate. Gradually beat in remaining 5 cups sugar. Add milk and vanilla, beating until smooth. Frost top and sides of cake.

CONFECTIONERS' SUGAR FROSTING

¼ c. butter or margarine
2 c. confectioners' sugar
3 T. milk (about)
¼ t. salt
¾ t. vanilla

Cream butter or margarine. Sift sugar; add gradually until of creamy consistency. Add enough milk to make mixture of spreading consistency. Add salt and vanilla. Makes enough for 2 layer cakes or 12 medium-size cupcakes.

VARIATIONS

Chocolate frosting: Add 2 tablespoons cocoa or 1 1-oz. square melted chocolate.
Mocha frosting: Add 2 tablespoons cocoa and 3 tablespoons strong coffee.
Orange frosting: Add 3 tablespoons orange juice and 1 teaspoon grated orange rind.
Caramel frosting: Add 3 tablespoons brown sugar, moistened with 3 tablespoons milk. Add ¼ cup melted butter or margarine and ½ teaspoon maple flavoring. Add enough confectioners' sugar until of spreading consistency.

BOILED WHITE FROSTING

⅓ c. water
1 c. sugar
1 t. vinegar
2 egg whites
¾ t. vanilla

Boil water, sugar and vinegar to 238° on a candy thermometer, or until syrup spins a long thread when dropped from tip of spoon. Beat egg whites stiff. Gradually add syrup to egg whites, beating constantly until frosting holds its shape. Add vanilla. Use to frost one 8-inch layer cake.

BROWN SUGAR BOILED FROSTING

1½ c. brown sugar, firmly packed
⅓ c. water
2 egg whites
¼ t. salt
1 t. vanilla

Boil sugar and water to 240° on candy thermometer or until a small quantity dropped in cold water forms a medium firm ball. Beat egg whites stiff. Gradually add syrup to egg whites, beating constantly until frosting holds its shape. Add salt and vanilla. Makes enough to fill and frost one 8-inch layer cake.

Pies and Piecrusts

GRAHAM CRACKER CRUST

1½ c. graham cracker crumbs
2 T. sugar
¼ c. melted butter

Mix all ingredients and press in bottom and sides of a 9-inch pie pan. Can be baked 10 minutes in a 350° oven or placed in refrigerator for ½ hour to set.

PASTRY FOR TWO-CRUST PIE

1½ c. flour
½ c. shortening
½ t. salt
¼ c. water

Combine flour and salt. Cut in shortening until mixture resembles grains of rice. Add water, a little at a time, mixing to a workable dough. Use more water if needed. Divide dough in half; roll out top and bottom half of crust on a floured board.

MOLASSES PECAN PIE

3 eggs, slightly beaten
¾ c. unsulphured molasses
¾ c. light corn syrup
2 T. melted butter or margarine
⅛ t. salt
1 t. vanilla
1 T. flour
1 c. pecans
1 unbaked 8-inch pastry shell

Combine the eggs, molasses, corn syrup, butter, salt and vanilla; mix well. Mix the flour with a small amount of egg mixture. Stir into remaining egg mixture. Add pecans. Turn into pastry shell. Bake in a 325° oven for 60 minutes or until done. Serve cold.

PUMPKIN CHEESECAKE PIE

15 graham crackers
2 T. brown sugar
¼ c. melted butter or margarine
8 oz. cottage cheese
1 c. canned pumpkin
2 egg yolks
¾ c. sugar
½ t. nutmeg
3 T. cornstarch
¾ c. milk
1 T. grated lemon rind
2 T. lemon juice
1 t. lemon extract
2 egg whites

Roll graham crackers into fine crumbs. Combine with brown sugar and melted butter or margarine. Set aside ¼ cup of the crumb mixture. Press remaining crumb mixture into a deep 9-inch pie pan. Bake in a 350° oven for 9 minutes. Cool. Press cottage cheese through a fine sieve. Combine with pumpkin, egg yolks, sugar and nutmeg. Mix well. Combine cornstarch with some of the milk, blending to a thin paste. Add remaining milk. Combine with cheese mixture. Add lemon rind, juice and extract. Beat egg whites stiff and fold into the pumpkin mixture. Spoon into crust; sprinkle top with reserved crumbs. Bake in a 350° oven for 30 minutes, or until a knife inserted comes out clean. Allow pie to cool before serving. Serves 6 to 8.

54

Pictured opposite
Molasses Pecan Pie
(page 54)

GRASSHOPPER PIE

1½ c. chocolate wafer crumbs
¼ c. melted butter
25 large marshmallows
⅔ c. cream
1 c. heavy cream, whipped
4 T. green creme de menthe
4 T. white creme de cacao

Reserve 2 tablespoons crumbs for topping. Mix remaining crumbs and butter. Press evenly on bottom and sides of a 9-inch pie pan. Chill in refrigerator while preparing filling. Combine marshmallows and cream. Heat slowly until marshmallows have melted; cool. Fold in liqueurs and whipped cream. Pour into chilled crust. Sprinkle remaining crumbs over top. Freeze until firm. Makes 1 pie.

KEY LIME PIE

1 baked 9-inch pastry shell
1 T. unflavored gelatin
1 c. sugar
¼ t. salt
4 eggs, separated
½ c. water
1 T. grated lime peel
  Green food color
½ c. lime juice
1 c. heavy cream, whipped

Mix gelatin, ½ cup sugar and salt in a saucepan. Beat together egg yolks and water; stir into gelatin mixture. Cook over medium heat, stirring constantly, until mixture boils. Remove from heat and stir in grated peel and lime juice. Add enough food coloring to make a pale green color. Chill, stirring occasionally, until thick. Beat egg whites until stiff peaks form. Gradually add remaining sugar. Fold gelatin mixture into egg whites and fold in whipped cream. Spoon into pastry shell. Chill until firm. Spread with additional whipped cream and sprinkle additional grated lime peel around edge of pie. Serve cold.

DUTCH APPLE PIE

Pastry for single-crust, 9-inch pie
4 c. peeled, sliced tart apples
¾ c. sugar
½ t. cinnamon
¼ t. nutmeg
¾ c. flour
½ c. brown sugar, firmly packed
½ t. cinnamon
½ c. butter

Combine apples, sugar, ½ teaspoon cinnamon and nutmeg. Pour in a pastry-lined, 9-inch pie pan. Blend flour, brown sugar, cinnamon and butter by mixing with fingers to make coarse crumbs. Place on top of apple mixture in pie pan. Bake in a 425° oven for 45 minutes. Serve with whipped topping. Serves 6 to 8.

LEMON MERINGUE PIE

1 baked 9-inch pastry shell
1 c. sugar
¼ c. flour
⅛ t. salt
¼ c. water
3 egg yolks
¾ c. water
3 T. butter or margarine
¼ c. lemon juice
2 t. grated lemon rind
3 egg whites
½ t. salt
9 T. sugar

Mix sugar, flour, salt and ¼ cup water until smooth. Beat egg yolks, add with ¾ cup water. Cook over hot water, stirring constantly, until thick. Cover and cook for 10 minutes. Add butter or margarine, lemon juice and rind. Pour into pastry shell. Beat egg whites until stiff but not dry. Add salt. Gradually add sugar, beating constantly. Swirl on pie filling. Bake in a 325° oven for 20 minutes, until lightly browned.

MOTHER'S OLD-FASHIONED APPLE PIE

4 to 5 c. peeled and sliced tart apples
1½ c. sugar
⅓ c. flour
1 t. cinnamon
¼ c. water
1 T. butter
Pastry for double-crust, 9-inch pie

Prepare pastry. Roll out half and line pan. Combine sugar, flour and cinnamon in a bowl; stir in water. Add apples, mixing to coat thoroughly. Pour into pan and dot with butter. Roll out top crust; cut a design in the center to allow steam to escape. Place top crust on pie, pressing around the edge to seal. Brush pastry with milk and sprinkle with sugar. Bake in a 350° oven 45 to 60 minutes or until apples are tender and crust is browned.

CHESS PIE

½ c. butter
1½ c. sugar
3 eggs
1 t. vanilla
1 unbaked 9-inch pie shell

Cream together butter and sugar until mixture is light and fluffy. Add eggs, one at a time, beating well after each addition. Add vanilla and blend. Pour into unbaked pie shell. Bake in a 350° oven for 35 to 40 minutes or until filling has set. Remove from oven and cool on wire rack.

RHUBARB PIE

Pastry for 9-inch 2-crust pie
3 c. rhubarb, cut fine
1½ c. sugar
1 egg
¼ c. flour
½ t. cinnamon
1 T. butter

Place rhubarb in large bowl. Add sugar, egg, flour and cinnamon. Mix well. Spoon into pastry lined pie pan. Dot with butter. Place top crust on pie; crimp edges. Brush with milk and sprinkle with sugar. Bake in a 350° oven 45 to 50 minutes or until rhubarb is done and crust is brown. Makes 1 pie.

PUMPKIN PIE

1 c. canned pumpkin
1 c. brown sugar, firmly packed
2 eggs, beaten
¼ t. ginger
½ t. nutmeg
1 t. cinnamon
1 T. butter, melted
1 c. milk
1 unbaked 9-inch pie crust

Mix all ingredients until well blended. Pour into crust. Bake in a 350° oven for 60 minutes or until done in center. Serve with whipped cream or whipped topping mix.

HERSHEY PIE

1 10-inch graham cracker crust
20 marshmallows
6 small Hershey bars
½ c. milk
1 c. whipped cream

Combine marshmallows, Hershey bars, and milk in top of double boiler. Heat until chocolate and marshmallows melt. Cool, then fold in whipped cream. Pour mixture into pie crust; sprinkle a few graham cracker crumbs on top. Refrigerate. Serve cold.

Candies

CARAMEL CORN

1 c. butter
½ c. white corn syrup
2 c. brown sugar, firmly packed
1 t. salt
1 t. butter flavoring
1 t. burnt sugar flavoring
½ t. baking soda
8 qts. popped corn
2 c. peanuts

Melt butter, syrup, brown sugar and salt in a saucepan. Boil for 5 minutes. Add flavorings and soda. Put popped corn and peanuts in a large pan. Pour syrup over popcorn and nuts, stirring well to coat each kernel. Bake for 1 hour in a 250° oven. Stir every 10 or 15 minutes. Remove from oven and cool, stirring often.

DIVINITY

5 egg whites, at room temperature
¼ t. salt
5 c. sugar
1 c. white corn syrup
2 c. water

Add salt to egg whites and beat until stiff and dry. Set aside. Combine sugar, syrup and water. Cook until it forms a hard ball in cold water (265° to 270° on a candy thermometer). Slowly add syrup to egg whites, beating all the time. Do not scrape sides of pan when pouring. Beat until mixture holds its shape. Pour into a buttered 13 x 9 x 2-inch pan. After it cools, cut into squares; or drop by teaspoons onto waxed paper to cool. *Note:* One cup chopped nuts, chopped candied fruit or shredded coconut may be added just before beating.

MILLION-DOLLAR FUDGE

4½ c. sugar
Pinch salt
2 T. butter
1 13-oz. can evaporated milk
1 12-oz. pkg. chocolate chips
1 12-oz. bar German sweet chocolate
2 8-oz. jars marshmallow creme
2 c. nut pieces

Combine sugar, salt, butter and milk. Boil for 6 minutes. Remove from heat and add chocolate chips, German chocolate, marshmallow creme and nuts. Beat until all chocolate is melted. Pour into a buttered 13 x 9 x 2-inch pan. Let stand a few hours before cutting. Store in a tin box with waxed paper between layers.

FAIRY FOOD

1 c. sugar
1 c. white corn syrup
1 T. vinegar
1½ T. baking soda
1 6-oz. pkg. semisweet chocolate chips

Combine sugar, syrup and vinegar in a 3-quart saucepan. Cook to a hard-crack stage (300°). Turn off heat and add soda, mixing quickly. Pour immediately into a greased 11 x 7 x 1½-inch pan. Cool. Then invert on a tray. Spread with melted chocolate. Break into chunks. Yields about 1 pound.

Cookies

BANANA COOKIES

¾ c. shortening
1 c. sugar
1 egg
1 t. vanilla
1½ c. flour
½ t. baking soda
1 t. salt
¼ t. nutmeg
¾ t. cinnamon
1 c. mashed banana
1 c. rolled oats
½ c. chopped nuts

Cream shortening and sugar. Add egg and vanilla. Sift flour, soda, salt and spices. Stir into sugar mixture. Add banana, oats and nuts. Drop by teaspoons onto a greased cookie sheet. Bake in a 400° oven for 12 minutes. Yields 3½ dozen cookies.

WASHBOARD COOKIES

1 c. sugar
1 c. brown sugar, firmly packed
1 c. shortening
2 eggs, well beaten
3¼ c. flour, sifted
2 t. baking soda
2 t. cream of tartar
1 t. vanilla
1 t. lemon extract
1 c. coconut
1 c. raisins
½ c. chopped nuts

Cream together sugars and shortening until smooth. Add eggs and mix well. Sift together flour, soda and cream of tartar. Set aside a small part in which to dredge the raisins, nuts and coconut. Add dry ingredients to batter and mix. Add flavorings, raisins, nuts and coconut. Mix well. Shape dough into small balls. Place on a greased cookie sheet and press flat with a fork. Bake in a 350° oven about 12 minutes.

MARSHMALLOW FUDGE SQUARES

½ c. shortening
¾ c. sugar
2 eggs
¾ c. flour
¼ t. baking powder
¼ t. salt
2 T. cocoa
1 t. vanilla
½ c. chopped nuts, if desired
12 marshmallows, cut in halves

Cream shortening with sugar. Add eggs and mix well. Sift together flour, baking powder, salt and cocoa. Add to creamed mixture. Stir in vanilla and chopped nuts. Spread in a 13 x 9 x 2-inch greased pan. Bake in a 350° oven for 25 to 30 minutes. Remove from oven and arrange the marshmallow halves evenly over the top. Turn off oven; return pan to oven for 3 minutes. Make Topping and spread on top. Cool and cut into squares.

TOPPING

½ c. brown sugar, firmly packed
⅓ c. water
2 1-oz. squares chocolate
3 T. butter
1 t. vanilla
1½ c. confectioners' sugar

Boil brown sugar, water and chocolate for 3 minutes in a saucepan. Remove from heat and stir in butter, vanilla and sugar.

DROP DATE COOKIES

3 c. flour
1 t. salt
1 t. cinnamon
1 t. cloves
2 t. baking powder
¼ t. baking soda
1 c. lard or shortening
1½ c. brown sugar, firmly packed
3 eggs
1 T. cold water
1 c. dates, cut up

Sift together flour, salt, baking powder, cinnamon, cloves and baking soda. Set aside. Cream shortening and sugar. Beat in eggs and water. Gradually add dry ingredients, beating well after each addition. Stir in dates. Drop by teaspoonfuls onto greased baking sheets. Bake in a 350° oven for 20 minutes, or until done. Cool on a wire rack. Makes 6 dozen.

ICEBOX COOKIES

3 c. flour
½ t. salt
1½ t. baking soda
1½ t. cream of tartar
1½ c. brown sugar, firmly packed
½ c. sugar
½ c. lard or shortening
2 eggs
1½ t. vanilla
1 c. chopped nuts

Sift flour with salt, soda and cream of tartar. Set aside. Cream sugars and shortening; add eggs. Gradually add dry ingredients, beating well after each addition. Stir in vanilla and nuts; mixture will be stiff. Form into several rolls and wrap in waxed paper. Refrigerate overnight. Slice ½ inch thick and place on greased cookie sheets. Bake in a 350° oven for 10 minutes or until light brown around the edges.

CHRISTMAS COOKIES

1 c. butter
1 c. sugar
3 eggs
1 t. vanilla
3 c. flour
2 t. cream of tartar
1 t. baking soda
1 t. nutmeg
Colored sugar

Cream butter and sugar; mix well. Add beaten eggs and flavoring. Sift together flour, cream of tartar, soda and nutmeg. Mix with sugar mixture, stirring well. Roll out on floured board. Cut with assorted Christmas cookie cutters. Sprinkle with colored sugar. Bake in a 425° oven for 10 minutes.
Note: If dough is refrigerated overnight it is easier to handle and roll.

OLD-FASHIONED SUGAR COOKIES

½ c. butter or margarine
1 c. sugar
1 egg *or* 2 egg yolks, beaten
1 T. milk
½ t. vanilla
1½ c. sifted flour
1 t. baking powder
¼ t. salt

Cream butter or margarine. Beat in sugar, egg or egg yolks, milk and vanilla. Sift together flour, baking powder and salt; add to butter mixture. Mix well. Cover and refrigerate 3 to 4 hours or until dough is firm. Heat oven to 375°. Roll dough into small balls about ¾-inch in diameter. Place 2 inches apart on lightly greased cookie sheets. Lightly flatten tops with the bottom of a glass that has been dipped in sugar. Bake 8 to 10 minutes or until cookies are lightly browned around the edges. Transfer to wire racks. Cool. If desired, lightly brush warm cookies with melted butter or margarine and dust with confectioners' sugar. Makes 3 dozen.

Desserts

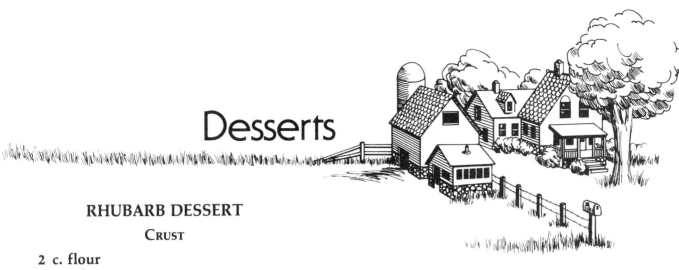

RHUBARB DESSERT

CRUST

2 c. flour
¼ t. salt
2 egg yolks
2 T. sugar
1 c. butter or margarine

Mix ingredients together and spread in a 13 x 9 x 2-inch pan. Bake in a 350° oven for 10 to 15 minutes.

FILLING

4 c. rhubarb, chopped
4 egg yolks, beaten
2 c. sugar
2 T. flour

Mix the above ingredients and spread over the crust. Bake in a 350° oven for 30 minutes.

TOPPING

6 egg whites
1 c. sugar
½ t. cinnamon

Beat egg whites until stiff. Gradually add sugar and cinnamon. Spread on top of rhubarb. Bake in a 350° oven for 30 minutes. Serves 8 to 10.

VANILLA SAUCE

1 c. milk
3 egg yolks, beaten
½ c. sugar
1 t. vanilla
3 egg whites, beaten stiff

Scald milk; remove from heat. Stir some of the milk into the egg yolks; add yolks to milk. Add sugar and cook until thick, stirring to melt. Remove from heat. Fold in beaten egg whites and vanilla. Serve, hot or cold, over pudding.

SUET PUDDING

1 lb. ground suet
4 c. flour
1 t. salt
1 c. water
2 lbs. ground beef
2 medium-size onions, chopped
1 c. finely chopped celery
1 t. salt
½ t. pepper
4 T. catsup
1 c. water

Mix suet, flour and salt in a large bowl. Mix in water to form a dough. Roll out with a rolling pin on a floured board. Place cloth on a large bowl. Put dough on top of the cloth. In a bowl mix the ground beef, onion, celery, seasonings, catsup and water. Put the mixture inside the dough. Tie up cloth and put in a kettle of water. Bring to a boil and boil for 2 hours.

APPLE BROWN BETTY

5 or 6 medium-size apples, peeled
½ c. flour
¼ c. brown sugar, firmly packed
¼ c. soft margarine or butter
½ t. cinnamon
¾ c. granola

Slice apples into 1½-quart greased casserole. In a bowl, mix flour, brown sugar, margarine or butter, cinnamon and granola. Spread the crumbs over the top of the apples. Bake in a 350° oven for 35 to 40 minutes. Serves 4.

Pictured opposite
Apple Brown Betty
(page 63)

Book II Index

Book III
Light Menus

By Louise Mariano

ideals

Ideals Publishing Corp.
Nashville, Tennessee

Contents

Published by Ideals Publishing Corporation
Nelson Place at Elm Hill Pike
Nashville, Tennessee

Menus for Brunch

Mexican Breakfast
Orange Papaya Smoothie

Mexican Breakfast

Makes 4 servings

2 teaspoons safflower oil
1 small red onion, chopped
½ green pepper, seeded and diced
2 12-ounce jars salsa
8 eggs, lightly beaten
¼ cup sliced jalapeño peppers

1 tablespoon butter *or* margarine
4 large corn tortillas
½ cup grated medium Cheddar cheese
Sliced green onion
Sliced jalapeño peppers
Chopped fresh cilantro *or* parsley

Heat oil in medium saucepan. Sauté onion and green pepper in oil. Add salsa and simmer, uncovered, about 10 minutes. Remove sauce from heat. In a bowl, mix eggs and jalapeños. In a large skillet melt butter *or* margarine over medium heat. Scramble egg mixture in butter *or* margarine until eggs are cooked but still moist.

Dip tortillas in salsa mixture until soft. Spoon ¼ of the scrambled eggs down center of each tortilla; roll up and place enchilada, seam side down, in a casserole dish. Repeat with each tortilla. Reheat remaining sauce to boiling. Pour evenly over enchiladas and sprinkle with cheese. Place under broiler, 4 inches from heat source, until cheese melts. Garnish with onion, jalapeños, and cilantro.

Orange Papaya Smoothie

Makes 4 servings

1 ripe papaya, peeled, seeded, and chopped
2 cups orange juice
1 cup plain yogurt

1 cup cracked ice
1 banana, mashed
1 teaspoon lime *or* lemon juice

Purée or process all ingredients until smooth. Serve in tall glasses.

Sunny Fruit Salad with
Ginger Dressing
Oranged Borscht
Breakfast Sandwiches

Sunny Fruit Salad

Makes 4 servings

2 small head Bibb *or* butterhead lettuce
½ avocado, sliced
1 nectarine, peeled and sliced into rounds
½ grapefruit, peeled and sliced into rounds
1 orange, peeled and sliced into rounds
Ginger Dressing (below)

Separate lettuce into leaves. Arrange avocado, nectarine, grapefruit, and orange slices attractively over lettuce. Top with Ginger Dressing.
Note: Slices of peaches and papaya may be substituted for the nectarine, grapefruit, *or* orange.

Ginger Dressing

Makes 1 cup

1 cup plain yogurt
¼ cup orange juice
Sugar to taste
½ teaspoon minced fresh ginger

Stir all ingredients together. Let dressing stand at least 5 minutes before serving to blend flavors.

Variation

Omit minced ginger and add 2 teaspoons grated orange peel and a dash of ground cloves.

Oranged Borscht

Makes 4 servings

1 pound cooked beets, sliced
1 14½-ounce can low-sodium chicken broth
¼ cup coarsely chopped red onion
1 clove garlic

3 to 4 tablespoons orange juice
½ cup plain yogurt *or* Neufchatel cheese, softened
1 cucumber, peeled and diced
Orange slices

Process or blend first 5 ingredients until smooth. Stir in yogurt and cucumber. Chill and garnish with orange slices before serving.

Breakfast Sandwiches

Makes 4 servings

4 croissants, warmed and split in half
4 Open Omelets (page 11)

4 large mushrooms, thinly sliced
12 avocado slices

Layer all ingredients into croissants.

Variations

Ham and Cheese: Substitute omelets and mushrooms with 8 ounces sliced ham, 4 slices Swiss cheese, and 8 ounces sliced pineapple.

BLT: Substitute omelets and mushrooms with 8 cooked bacon strips, 4 lettuce leaves, and 4 tomato slices.

English Muffin Variation

2 English muffins, split
¼ cup butter *or* margarine
4 Open Omelets (page 11)

4 large mushrooms, thinly sliced
12 avocado slices

Toast muffins; spread with butter. Top with remaining ingredients. Serve open-faced.

Oranged Borscht, Breakfast Sandwiches, this page; Sunny Fruit Salad with Ginger Dressing, Page 5

Cantaloupe Fruit Boats with
Honey-Lemon Dressing
Spicy Scrambled Egg Pastries
Cornucopia Roll-Ups

Cantaloupe Fruit Boats with Honey-Lemon Dressing

Makes 4 servings

1 ripe cantaloupe *or* honey-dew melon	2 plums, pitted and sliced
4 peaches, pitted and sliced	½ cup blueberries
1 tablespoon lemon juice	½ cup raspberries
2 teaspoons lime juice	1 kiwi fruit, peeled and sliced
	Honey-Lemon Dressing(below)

Cut melon into 4 wedges; discard seeds. Toss peach slices with lemon and lime juice. Mix together all fruits and fill each melon wedge. Top with Honey-Lemon Dressing.

Honey-Lemon Dressing

Makes 1 cup

1 cup plain yogurt	1 teaspoon lemon juice
1 tablespoon honey	1 teaspoon lime juice
½ teaspoon dry mustard	

In a small bowl blend together all ingredients. Cover and chill until serving time.

Spicy Scrambled Egg Pastries

Makes 4 servings

1 tablespoon vegetable oil
⅓ cup julienne cut green pepper
⅓ cup julienne cut red pepper
2 to 3 tablespoons minced onion
1 clove garlic, minced

⅓ cup salsa
¼ cup finely chopped ham
10 eggs, beaten
8 puff pastry shells, baked according to package directions
Salsa

In a medium skillet heat oil and sauté green and red peppers for 1 minute. Add onion and garlic and continue sautéing until onion becomes transparent and soft. Add salsa and ham; cook 5 minutes. Stir in eggs and scramble until firm but still moist. Serve eggs in puff pastry shells and garnish with extra salsa to taste.

Cornucopia Roll-Ups

Makes 4 servings

1 3-ounce package cream cheese
1 tablespoon curry powder
½ cup finely chopped pecans

2 to 3 tablespoons milk
Freshly ground black pepper to taste
12 turkey luncheon meat slices

Combine cheese, curry powder, and pecans. Stir in milk to moisten and season to taste. Spread over turkey slices and roll up into cornucopias.

Variations

Pineapple-Yogurt Cornucopias: Substitute ½ cup yogurt, ¼ cup drained crushed pineapple, and 12 ham slices for the cream cheese, curry, and turkey.

Ham Rolls: Substitute ham slices and 2 to 3 tablespoons finely chopped ginger preserves for the turkey and curry powder.

Open Omelet Variations
Fresh Herb Scones
Apple Slaw

Open Omelet Variations

Makes 4 servings

4 eggs, separated
1/4 teaspoon salt
1/4 teaspoon cream of tartar

2 tablespoons water
1 to 2 teaspoon butter *or* margarine
1/2 to 1 cup topping of your choice

Preheat oven to 350°. Beat egg whites with salt and cream of tartar at high speed until stiff but not dry. Beat yolks with water at high speed until thick and lemon-colored, about 5 minutes. Fold yolks into whites.

Heat butter *or* margarine in 10-inch omelet pan over medium heat until just hot enough to sizzle a drop of water. Pour in omelet mixture and carefully smooth the surface. Cook until puffy and lightly browned on the bottom, about 5 minutes.

Bake in oven for about 10 minutes or until knife inserted in the center comes out clean. Cover surface with chosen topping. Cut in half or in wedges to serve. Garnish as desired.

Omelet Toppings

Light Lox: Drain and chop 2 slices smoked salmon. Combine with 4 ounces Neufchatel cheese until mixed. Spread on omelet. Sprinkle with lemon juice and chopped chives.

Garden Patch: Sauté or steam 1 cup sliced fresh vegetables of your choice. Garnish with lemon wedges.

Italian Sausage: Cook, drain, and crumble 2 Italian sausages. Combine with 1 large tomato, diced, and 2 tablespoons chopped fresh basil *or* 1 tablespoon dried basil. Ladle over omelet; sprinkle with grated Romano cheese.

Fresh Herb Scones

Makes 4 servings

2 cups all-purpose flour
½ cup whole wheat flour
1 to 2 teaspoons sugar
    substitute
2 teaspoons baking powder
1 teaspoon crushed rosemary
1 teaspoon baking soda

1 teaspoon salt
1 teaspoon thyme
1 teaspoon oregano
¼ cup butter *or* margarine
1 egg(reserve 1 tablespoon white)
½ cup plus 2 tablespoons
    buttermilk

Preheat oven to 400°. Combine or blend first 9 ingredients in bowl or food processor. Cut butter *or* margarine into small pieces and work into flour mixture with food processor or pastry blender until blended. In a separate bowl beat egg with buttermilk and stir into mixture. Turn dough out on a floured board and knead for 2 minutes. Shape into 2 thick circles, 5 inches in diameter. Cut each into quarters and place on lightly greased baking sheet with wedges about 1/2 inch apart. Brush with reserved egg white. Bake for 15 to 20 minutes or until nicely browned. Serve warm.

Apple Slaw

Makes 4 servings

⅓ cup plain yogurt
¼ cup sour cream
2 to 3 tablespoons minced chives
1 tablespoon lemon juice
1 teaspoon lime juice
1 tablespoon minced cilantro
    or parsley

1 teaspoon grated lemon rind
Salt to taste
Freshly ground pepper to taste
1 large red apple
1 cup grated peeled celery root
1 cup grated peeled jicama *or* turnip

In large bowl mix first 7 ingredients. Season to taste with salt and freshly ground pepper. Core apple but do not peel. Grate apple and add to yogurt mixture at once to keep apple from browning. Apple peel that does not pass through grater can be finely chopped. Blend in celery root and jicama. Let stand at room temperature for 30 minutes to blend flavors.

Oven Pancake
Sautéed Apples
Suggested Accompaniment:
Honeydew Melon with Lime Wedges

Oven Pancake

Makes 4 servings

6 eggs
1 cup milk
¼ cup butter *or* margarine, melted

1 cup all-purpose flour
¾ teaspoon salt
Melted butter *or* margarine
Sifted powdered sugar

In a blender combine eggs, milk, and melted butter *or* margarine. Cover and blend on low speed until mixed. Add flour and salt; cover and blend on medium speed until smooth. Pour into a well-greased 13 x 9 x 2-inch baking dish.

Bake at 450° for 20 to 22 minutes or until puffed and golden brown. Drizzle with melted butter and sprinkle with powdered sugar. Serve immediately.

Sautéed Apples

Makes 4 servings

4 medium apples, sliced
2 tablespoons butter *or* margarine

2 tablespoons granulated sugar
Dash Cinnamon

In a skillet cook and stir apples in hot butter *or* margarine over medium-high heat for 6 to 8 minutes or until tender. Stir in sugar and cinnamon. Serve hot.

Cheese-Filled Fig Tulips
Spinach Toss

Cheese-Filled Fig Tulips

Makes 4 servings

12 medium-large fresh figs
1/2 cup ricotta cheese
1/2 cup cream cheese
1/2 teaspoon lemon rind

1/2 teaspoon orange rind
1/2 teaspoon vanilla
 3 to 4 tablespoons powdered sugar
12 unblanched whole almonds

Rinse figs and pat dry. Trim off stem. Cut each fig into 4 petals by cutting through fig from stem end to within 1/2 inch of the other end. (Cover and chill if made ahead.)

Process or blend remaining ingredients except almonds. Stand 2 to 3 figs upright on each plate. Gently open each fig and spoon in about 2 tablespoons of cheese mixture. Top each with an almond.

Spinach Toss

Makes 4 servings

1/2 cup salad oil
1/3 cup sugar
 1 small onion, quartered
 3 tablespoons vinegar
 2 teaspoons prepared mustard

1/2 teaspoon celery seed
 6 slices bacon, optional
 6 cups torn spinach
 1 cup sliced fresh mushrooms
 2 hard-boiled eggs, chopped

To make dressing, in a blender container, combine oil, sugar, onion, vinegar, mustard, and celery seed. Cover and blend until smooth. Keep covered and chill. If desired, in a skillet fry bacon until crisp; drain and crumble. In a large salad bowl combine spinach, mushrooms, eggs, and bacon, if desired. Pour dressing over salad. Toss lightly.

Menus with Chicken

Caviar and Olive Toast Rounds
Chicken in Red Pepper Butter
Mini Medley
Crabmeat Canapés

Mini Medley

Makes 4 servings

¼ **pound golden *or* red baby beets**
¼ **pound baby boiling onions**
¼ **pound baby carrots**
¼ **pound miniature zucchini**

Boiling salted water plus 2 tablespoons lemon juice
Minced parsley
Freshly grated Romano cheese

Trim all vegetables. Peel beets, onions, and carrots; steam over lemon-water for 10 minutes. Add zucchini and steam another 5 to 8 minutes. Toss with parsley and Romano.

Crabmeat Canapés

Makes 4 servings

1 **4-ounce can crabmeat, well drained**
2 **tablespoon mayonnaise**
2 **tablespoons plain yogurt**
1 **tablespoon minced chives**

1 **tablespoon parsley**
1 **teaspoon lime juice**
1 **teaspoon Worcestershire sauce**
   Freshly ground black pepper to taste
   Melba toast rounds

Combine all ingredients except toast rounds; blend well. Spread on toast rounds and serve immediately.

Caviar and Olive Toast Rounds

Makes 4 servings

¼ cup caviar
10 to 12 stuffed green olives, finely chopped
2 to 3 tablespoons lemon juice

1 to 2 tablespoon minced red onion
Melba toast rounds
3 hard-boiled egg yolks, sieved

Mix first 4 ingredients. Spread on toast rounds and sprinkle with sieved yolks.

Chicken in Red Pepper Butter

Makes 4 servings

4 boneless skinless chicken breasts, halved
2 tablespoons butter *or* margarine

2 tablespoons vegetable oil
2 cloves garlic, minced
Red Pepper Butter (below)

Pound breasts to a thickness of ¼ inch. Heat butter *or* margarine, oil, and garlic in sauté pan. Sauté chicken breasts over medium-high heat, 3 to 5 minutes per side. Transfer to platter and keep warm in oven. Serve breasts with Red Pepper Butter.

Red Pepper Butter

Makes approximately 3 cups

2 tablespoons butter
2 medium shallots, minced
2½ medium red bell peppers, sliced
3 tablespoons raspberry vinegar *or* red wine vinegar

¼ cup fresh lemon juice
½ cup dry white wine *or* vermouth
1 cup unsalted butter, melted

Melt 2 tablespoons butter in medium saucepan; sauté shallots and peppers. Stew over low heat, stirring often, until shallots and peppers are softened, about 8 minutes. Add vinegar and cook on high heat until reduced by two-thirds. Add lemon juice and wine. Reduce by half. Transfer to food processor and purée until smooth, 1 to 1½ minutes. Add 1 cup melted butter in a thin stream while machine is running. Process 20 seconds longer. Just before serving, whisk sauce over low heat until hot to the touch. Do not simmer. *Note:* Red Pepper Butter can be prepared 3 hours ahead of time. Cover and store at room temperature until serving time.

Chicken Salad Croissants
Swiss Cheese Soup
Suggested Accompaniments:
Carrot Sticks and Apple Wedges

Chicken Salad Croissants

Makes 4 servings

2 cups diced cooked chicken
1 stalk celery, chopped
1 8½-ounce can crushed
  pineapple, drained
2 tablespoons sliced pimiento-
  stuffed olives

½ cup mayonnaise
  Dash salt
  Leaf lettuce
4 croissants, split
¼ cup chopped cashews

In a medium bowl combine chicken, celery, pineapple, and olives. Add mayonnaise and salt; toss together lightly. Cover and chill. To serve, place a lettuce leaf in each croissant. Spoon chicken salad over lettuce; sprinkle with cashews.

Swiss Cheese Soup

Makes 4 servings

3 tablespoons butter *or*
  margarine
¼ cup flour
1 teaspoon instant chicken
  bouillon granules

¼ teaspoon paprika
3½ cup milk
6 slices processed Swiss cheese
1 teaspoon snipped chives

Melt butter *or* margarine in medium saucepan. Stir in flour, bouillon granules, and paprika. Cook and stir over medium heat until bubbly. Add milk all at once. Cook and stir until thick and bubbly; cook and stir 1 minute more. Stir in cheese and chives. Stir over low heat until cheese melts.

Chicken Salad Croissants, this page

Butter-Broiled Chicken
Romaine and Artichoke Toss
Suggested Accompaniment:
Sautéed Mushrooms

Butter-Broiled Chicken

Makes 4 servings

6 tablespoons butter *or* margarine, melted
¼ teaspoon seasoning salt
¼ teaspoon dried oregano, crushed

Dash Garlic powder
Dash paprika
8 to 10 skinless chicken breasts

Preheat broiler. Combine butter *or* margarine, seasoning salt, oregano, garlic powder, and paprika. Place chicken on an unheated rack of a broiler pan. Brush lightly with butter mixture. Broil 5 to 6 inches from heat for 10 minutes, brushing occasionally with butter mixture. Turn; broil for 10 minutes more or until chicken is tender, brushing occasionally.

Romaine and Artichoke Toss

Makes 4 servings

1 6-ounce jar marinated artichoke hearts
¼ cup mayonnaise
2 tablespoons tarragon vinegar

1 tablespoon anchovy paste
1 teaspoon Dijon-style mustard
3 cups torn romaine

Drain artichoke hearts, reserving 2 tablespoons of the marinade. Cut up artichokes; set aside. To make dressing, combine mayonnaise, vinegar, anchovy paste, mustard, and reserved marinade. In a bowl combine romaine and artichokes; add dressing and toss.

Raspberry Glazed Chicken
Gourmet Onions
Suggested Accompaniment:
Steamed Broccoli

Raspberry Glazed Chicken

Makes 4 servings

1 2-pound whole roasting
   chicken
   Cooking oil
1/3 cup raspberry jelly
2 tablespoons lemon juice
1 tablespoon butter *or*
   margarine

1/4 teaspoon salt
   Dash ground cinnamon
1 tablespoon cold water
2 teaspoons cornstarch

Thoroughly rinse chicken; pat dry with paper towel. Place chicken, breast side up, on a rack in a shallow roasting pan. Rub skin with oil. Insert a meat thermometer in the center of the inside thigh muscle but not touching bone. Roast, uncovered, in a 375° oven for 1 1/4 to 1 1/2 hours or until thermometer registers 185°. In a small saucepan over low heat stir together jelly, lemon juice, butter *or* margarine, salt, and cinnamon until jelly melts. Combine water and cornstarch; stir into jelly mixture. Cook and stir over medium heat until thick and bubbly. Cook and stir 1 to 2 minutes more. Brush on chicken several times during the last 15 minutes of roasting.

Gourmet Onions

Makes 4 servings

6 medium onions, sliced
3 tablespoons butter *or*
   margarine

1/4 cup dry sherry
1/2 teaspoon sugar
2 tablespoons grated Parmesan cheese

In a 10-inch covered skillet cook onions in butter *or* margarine about 10 minutes until tender but not brown, stirring occasionally. Add sherry, sugar, 1/2 teaspoon salt, and dash pepper. Cook, uncovered, 2 to 3 minutes. Turn into a serving dish. Sprinkle with Parmesan cheese.

Smoked Salmon á la Russe
Poached Chicken and Vermicelli in Wine
Sherried Endive Salad
Brussels Sprouts and Creamed Carrots

Smoked Salmon á la Russe

Makes 4 servings

1 **thin loaf French bread, sliced**	**Butter lettuce cups**
Sour cream	**Capers**
2 **4-ounce packages smoked**	**Tomato wedges**
salmon, thinly sliced	**Lemon twists**
4 **ounces caviar**	

Spread bread slices with sour cream. Shape salmon slices into coronets; spoon a little caviar into each coronet. Place coronets on bread slices and arrange on lettuce cups. Garnish with remaining ingredients.

Poached Chicken and Vermicelli in Wine

Makes 4 servings

1 **teaspoon butter** *or* **margarine**	½ **teaspoon tarragon**
1 **teaspoon oil**	⅛ **teaspoon pepper**
½ **pound mushrooms, sliced**	2 **tablespoons minced fresh parsley**
4 **boned chicken breasts,**	¾ **cup dry white wine**
skinned and halved	1 **teaspoon arrowroot, optional**
¼ **teaspoon salt**	8 **ounces vermicelli, cooked and drained**

Melt butter *or* margarine and oil in a large skillet over medium-high heat. Sauté mushrooms and chicken until golden brown. Sprinkle with salt, tarragon, pepper, and parsley. Pour wine over chicken. Cover and simmer for 25 to 30 minutes. Remove chicken to serving platter. Deglaze skillet with a little water; thicken with one teaspoon arrowroot, if desired. Serve sauce with chicken and prepared vermicelli.

Poached Chicken and Vermicelli in Wine,
Smoked Salmon á la Russe, this page;
Sherried Endive Salad, Brussels Sprouts
and Creamed Carrots, page 24

Sherried Endive Salad

Makes 4 servings

12 medium *or* 8 large mush-
    rooms, trimmed
2 heads endive *or* escarole, torn
2 green onions, chopped

½ cup plain yogurt
1½ teaspoons Dijon-style mustard
1 to 2 tablespoons dry sherry

Arrange mushrooms on endive *or* escarole. Mix together remaining ingredients and spoon half of dressing over salad. Serve balance of dressing on the side.

Brussels Sprouts and Creamed Carrots

Makes 4 servings

1 pound Brussels sprouts
  Salt and freshly ground pepper

Creamed Carrots (below)

Trim off sprout ends and cut an "X" in the stem of each. Add sprouts to boiling water. Reduce heat; simmer, uncovered, until tender, 10 to 15 minutes. Drain; transfer to a serving platter and season with salt and ground pepper. Fit a pastry bag with a fluted tip. Pipe a rosette of Creamed Carrots on each Brussels sprout. Pipe remaining Creamed Carrots around edge of platter.

Creamed Carrots
Makes 4 servings

3 carrots, sliced diagonally
4 ounces Neufchatel cheese
2 tablespoons plain yogurt

¼ teaspoon tarragon
  Skim milk

Steam carrots until tender, 5 to 8 minutes. Combine with remaining ingredients and purée until smooth. Thin with milk, if necessary. Serve with Brussels sprouts as directed.

Honey Dip with Fruit
Chicken Jambalaya
Broiled Sourdough Slices
Tomato-Carrot Salad

Honey Dip with Fruit

Makes 1 cup

1 tablespoon honey
½ cup Neufchatel *or* ricotta cheese
½ cup plain yogurt

Grated peel of ½ lime *or* ½ lemon
Grated peel of ½ orange
1 tablespoon jam *or* preserves
Choice of fruits

Combine all ingredients; mix well. Serve as a dip with your favorite fruits prepared in bite-size pieces.

Tomato-Carrot Salad

Makes 4 servings

4 lettuce leaves
4 large tomatoes, cut into wedges
2 large carrots, grated
⅔ cup peanut oil
Juice and grated rind of one orange

1 tablespoon red wine vinegar
1 teaspoon Dijon-style mustard
1 teaspoon sugar
Salt and freshly ground black pepper
Orange wedges

Line 4 bowls with lettuce leaves and top with tomatoes and carrots. Combine remaining ingredients. Pour dressing over each salad just before serving and serve the balance on the side. Garnish with orange wedges.

Chicken Jambalaya

Makes 4 servings

2 to 3 cloves garlic, minced
½ cup chopped red onion
1 stalk celery, sliced
2 hot chorizos, casings removed and broken up
2 tablespoons olive oil *or* vegetable oil
1 cup chicken broth
1 cup white wine

1 cup long-grain white rice
1 16-ounce can stewed tomatoes, chopped
1 teaspoon thyme *or* oregano leaves
½ teaspoon turmeric
¼ teaspoon red pepper
½ 20-ounce package frozen peas
1 pound medium-size raw shrimp, in shells *or* frozen shrimp

Sauté first 4 ingredients 3 to 5 minutes in hot oil. Add next 7 ingredients. Bring to a boil. Reduce heat; cover and simmer 15 minutes. Add peas and shrimp. Cover and cook 5 minutes. Toss with a fork to fluff rice and distribute shrimp.
Note: 8 fresh mussels or clams may be substituted for ½ pound of shrimp.

Broiled Sourdough Slices

Makes 4 servings

½ loaf sourdough French bread
½ cup butter *or* margarine, softened
2 to 3 cloves garlic, minced

¼ cup minced fresh parsley
¼ cup freshly grated Romano *or* Parmesan cheese

Preheat broiler. Slice French bread. Blend remaining ingredients and spread evenly over bread slices. Broil until golden and bubbly.

Vegetable Fromage
Gingered Chicken with Apples
Rosemary Macaroni
Fruited Watercress Salad

Vegetable Fromage

Makes 4 servings

2 8-ounce packages cream cheese
¼ cup plain yogurt
¼ cup shredded carrot
¼ cup finely chopped radish
¼ cup finely chopped red pepper
¼ cup finely chopped green pepper
¼ cup finely sliced green onion *or* cilantro
Whole-grain breadsticks

Process cream cheese, yogurt, carrot, radish, red pepper, green pepper, and green onion or blend well with a wooden spoon. Use immediately or refrigerate, covered, up to 2 days. Bring to room temperature before serving with whole-grain breadsticks.

Rosemary Macaroni

Makes 4 servings

2 quarts water
½ teaspoon salt
8 ounces elbow macaroni (whole wheat, yellow, and/or green)
1 tablespoon oil
1 teaspoon lemon juice
Chopped fresh rosemary *or* chives

Bring water and salt to a boil. Add macaroni, oil, and lemon juice and cook until tender but firm. Add rosemary and toss before serving.

Gingered Chicken with Apples

Makes 4 servings

1 tablespoon safflower oil *or* vegetable oil
2½ pounds chicken, cut into pieces
¼ cup Cognac
½ cup evaporated skim milk
½ cup non-fat milk

1 tablespoon chopped gingerroot *or* ½ teaspoon ground ginger
½ teaspoon nutmeg
1½ cups thinly sliced tart apples
1 teaspoon arrowroot, optional
Toasted slivered almonds
Chopped candied ginger

Heat oil in a large skillet. Add chicken, skin side down; brown well on all sides. Remove and set aside. Deglaze pan with Cognac. Flambé if desired. Return browned chicken to skillet.

To make cream sauce, combine next 5 ingredients. Add to skillet and gently simmer 20 to 30 minutes. Remove chicken to serving platter. Add apples to skillet. Cook until just tender, 1 to 2 minutes. Thicken with arrowroot, if desired. Serve apples and sauce over chicken. Garnish with almonds and candied ginger.

Fruited Watercress Salad

Makes 4 servings

2 oranges, peeled and sliced
2 kiwi fruit, peeled and sliced
1 grapefruit, peeled and sliced
2 bunches watercress, tough stems removed

1 head butter lettuce, cleaned and separated into leaves
Lemon *or* lime juice
Vegetable oil

Arrange fruit on a bed of watercress and butter lettuce. Sprinkle with juice and oil to taste.

Menus with Pork

Carrots Purée in Zucchini Boats
Mustard-Broiled Pork Chops
Pasta with Garlic
Grilled Cheese and Walnut Salad
with Mango Dressing

Carrots Purée in Zucchini Boats

Makes 4 servings

1 tablespoon butter *or* margarine
1 pound carrots, thinly sliced
3 tablespoons water
1/2 cup evaporated milk

1 to 2 tablespoons dry sherry
1/4 teaspoon nutmeg
1/4 teaspoon cinnamon
4 medium zucchini, baked until soft

Melt butter *or* margarine in large skillet; add carrots and water. Steam, covered, until tender, 5 to 8 minutes. In a blender combine carrots with next 4 ingredients; blend until smooth. Split zucchini lengthwise and scoop out seeds. Spoon carrot purée into each zucchini shell, or pipe, using a pastry bag fitted with a rosette tip.

Mustard-Broiled Pork Chops

Makes 4 servings

1/4 cup Dijon-style mustard
4 pork loin chops, 3/4 inch thick, trimmed

Freshly ground pepper to taste

Preheat broiler. Spread half of the mustard evenly over chops. Broil 6 inches away from heat source for 8 to 10 minutes. Turn chops; spread with remaining mustard. Grind pepper over chops. Broil another 10 minutes.

Mustard-Broiled Pork Chops, Carrots Purée in Zucchini Boats, this page; Pasta with Garlic, Grilled Cheese and Walnut Salad with Mango Dressing, page 32

—— 31 ——

Pasta with Garlic

Makes 4 servings

2 cups chicken broth
2 cups water
½ pound fresh pasta
1 tablespoon butter *or* margarine
2 cloves garlic, minced

¼ cup minced fresh parsley
1 teaspoon basil, marjoram, oregano, *or* thyme
Freshly grated Parmesan, Romano, *or* Sapsago cheese

Bring broth and water to a boil in a large pot. Add pasta and cook until tender but still firm, 4 to 6 minutes. Drain and transfer to a heated platter. Melt butter *or* margarine in a small saucepan and stir in garlic, parsley, and herbs. Heat gently. Pour parsley mixture over noodles and toss to coat well. Garnish with grated cheese.

Grilled Cheese and Walnut Salad with Mango Dressing

Makes 4 servings

1 head radicchio
1 head butter lettuce
1 head Arugula
4 to 6 ounces mild herbed goat cheese
½ cup walnut *or* hazelnut oil *or* vegetable oil

1 tablespoon mango chutney
1 tablespoon plain yogurt
2 teaspoons red wine vinegar
1 cup coarsely chopped walnuts

Discard any outer leaves, then wash and pat dry all greens. Refrigerate. Slice cheese into four chunks. Grill or broil briefly and set aside. Process or blend next 4 ingredients for dressing. Arrange lettuce leaves on a platter. Form a ring of Arugula over lettuce. Place cheese in center. Sprinkle with walnuts and drizzle on dressing.

Pork Chops with Brown Rice
Broiled Tomatoes
Suggested Accompaniment:
Mixed Green Salad
with Blue Cheese Dressing

Pork Chops with Brown Rice

Makes 4 servings

4 pork chops, about 1 pound
1 tablespoon cooking oil
1 4⁵/₈-ounce package quick-cooking brown and wild rice mix with mushrooms

1¹/₃ cup water
1 stalk celery, sliced
¹/₂ cup sour cream

In a skillet brown chops in hot oil over medium heat. Remove chops from the skillet; discard drippings. In the same skillet combine rice mix, water, and celery; place chops over rice mixture. Bring to a boil. Reduce heat and simmer, covered, for 30 minutes. Remove chops from the skillet; keep warm. Stir sour cream into rice mixture; heat through but do not boil. Serve with chops.

Broiled Tomatoes

Makes 4 servings

2 large ripe tomatoes
³/₄ cup soft bread crumbs
¹/₄ cup grated Parmesan cheese

2 tablespoons butter *or* margarine, melted
¹/₄ teaspoon dried crushed basil

Preheat broiler. Halve each tomato crosswise. Place cut side up in a shallow baking pan. Combine bread crumbs, Pamesan cheese, butter *or* margarine, and basil; sprinkle over tomatoes. Broil 3 to 4 inches from the heat source for about 4 minutes or until lightly browned.

Menus with Fish and Shellfish

Stuffed Pea Pods
Broiled Swordfish
Lemon-Dill Rice
Carrots in Lime Butter
Italian Tomato Cucumber Salad

Stuffed Pea Pods

Makes 4 servings

25 snow peas
4 ounces goat cheese
(Montrachet *or* Lezay)
¼ cup plain yogurt

1 teaspoon any flavored mustard
½ cup finely chopped Hot and
Spicy Pecans (below)

Cut stem ends of snow peas and pull down straight edge to remove any string. Blanch in boiling water for 30 seconds. Plunge peas into ice water. Using a sharp paring knife, slit open each pod along straight side. In bowl combine cheese, yogurt, mustard, and ¼ cup pecans. Pipe or stuff each pod with goat cheese mixture. Dip stuffing side of each pod into remaining chopped nuts to garnish.

Hot and Spicy Pecans

Makes 2 cups

2 cups pecan halves
Butter *or* margarine, melted
Cayenne
Cumin

Paprika
Cloves
Onion salt *or* chili powder

Roast pecans in 300° oven for 20 minutes. Sprinkle with remaining ingredients to taste. Use for Stuffed Pea Pods as directed; serve balance of pecans on the side.

Carrots in Lime Butter, Lemon-Dill Rice, page 36; Broiled Swordfish, Italian Tomato Cucumber Salad, page 37

Lemon-Dill Rice

Makes 4 servings

1 tablespoon safflower oil
 or vegetable oil
1 cup long-grain brown *or*
 white rice
1 cup finely chopped red onion
1 stalk finely chopped celery
1 large garlic clove, minced
1 13-ounce can chicken broth

1/3 cup water
1 to 2 tablespoons lemon juice
1/4 cup minced fresh dill *or*
 1 tablespoon dried dill
 Freshly ground pepper
 Fresh dill sprigs
 Lemon slices

Heat safflower oil over medium-high heat. Add rice, onion, celery, and garlic; sauté about 5 minutes. Add broth, water, and lemon juice. Bring to a boil; reduce heat and simmer, covered, 20 to 30 minutes. Stir in minced dill and pepper. Remove from heat. Cover and let stand 10 minutes. Garnish with dill sprigs and lemon slices.

Carrots in Lime Butter

Makes 4 servings

1 pound carrots
4 1/2 cups water
2 tablespoons sugar

1 to 2 tablespoons unsalted butter
2 tablespoons fresh lime juice

Cut carrots diagonally into 1/4-inch thick slices. In medium saucepan bring carrots and 4 cups cold water to a full boil. Boil for 3 to 5 minutes; drain. Return carrots to saucepan. Add 1/2 cup water and sugar. Bring to a boil over medium heat; cook until carrots are just tender and the liquid is reduced to 1 or 2 tablespoons, about 7 minutes. Stir in butter and lime juice.

Italian Tomato Cucumber Salad

Makes 4 servings

5 or 6 Italian-style plum tomatoes
  or 3 large ripe tomatoes
1 stalk celery, thinly sliced
1 cucumber, sliced
3 or 4 red onions, sliced
1 clove garlic, halved

Black peppercorn
Chopped fresh oregano
Minced fresh basil
2 tablespoons olive oil *or* vegetable oil
2 tablespoons red wine vinegar

Cut tomatoes into wedges and combine with celery, cucumber, and onion. Rub a glass serving bowl with cut side of garlic; add vegetables. Grind pepper over all and season generously with oregano and basil. Drizzle oil and vinegar evenly over salad; toss gently. Serve at room temperature.

Broiled Swordfish

Makes 4 servings

Freshly ground pepper
4 1¾-pound swordfish *or* halibut steaks, cut 1 inch thick
1 tablespoon butter
1 large red pepper, cut into julienne strips
1 large green pepper, cut into julienne strips

4 tablespoons lemon juice
¼ cup grated Parmesan cheese
2 tablespoons chopped fresh basil, optional
Lemon wedges

Preheat broiler to high. Grind pepper generously over swordfish. Heat butter over medium-high heat; add peppers and sauté until tender and well browned, about 10 minutes. Set aside. Broil swordfish 4 to 5 inches from heat source for 3 minutes. Sprinkle 2 tablespoons of lemon juice evenly over steaks. Turn fish, sprinkle remaining juice and broil for 5 minutes more or until fish flakes easily when tested with a fork. Spread peppers evenly over swordfish; sprinkle with Parmesan cheese and basil. Garnish with lemon wedges.

Menus with Fish and Shellfish

Cheese and Apple Wafers
Mexican Snapper
Steamed New Potatoes and Sesame Carrots
Green Salad with Mexican Dressing

Cheese and Apple Wafers

Makes 4 servings

1 cup flour
1¼ cup grated Cheddar cheese
¼ pound butter *or* margarine
1 teaspoon Worcestershire sauce

Minced chives, cilantro, *or* parsley
Poppy, caraway, *or* sesame seeds
Apple *or* pear wedges

Combine flour and cheese; cut in butter *or* margarine. Add sauce and blend well. Roll dough into long strips about ¾ inch in diameter. Freeze 15 minutes. Slice into thin wafers. Bake at 475° for 10 minutes on greased cookie sheet. Sprinkle wafers with different combinations of minced chives, cilantro, *or* parsley; poppy, caraway, *or* sesame seeds. Serve with apple wedges.

Mexican Snapper

Makes 4 servings

1½ pounds red snapper or cod fillets
½ cup chopped cilantro *or* parsley
½ cup finely chopped toasted almonds

¼ cup butter *or* margarine
Lime juice
Salt and pepper to taste
Diced avocados

Place fish fillets in a baking dish. Sprinkle with cilantro and almonds. Melt butter *or* margarine in saucepan; add lime juice and season to taste. Pour over fish. Cover and bake in a 350° oven for 30 minutes. Sprinkle with diced avocados and serve.

Mexican Snapper, Cod Variation, this page; Steamed New Potatoes and Sesame Carrots, Green Salad with Mexican Dressing, page 40

Steamed New Potatoes and Sesame Carrots

Makes 4 servings

10 to 12 small new potatoes
10 to 12 medium carrots
 1 teaspoon butter *or* margarine
 2 tablespoons sesame seeds
 2 tablespoons butter *or* margarine

1 tablespoon honey
1 tablespoon grated orange rind
1 teaspoon grated gingerroot
  Minced Parsley

Scrub potatoes but do not peel. Slice thinly and place in steamer. Peel and cut carrots into 3-inch sticks. Place in steamer above potatoes. Steam 15 minutes until tender. Melt 1 tablespoon butter *or* margarine in a medium skillet; add sesame seeds and toast until golden. Add the 2 tablespoons butter *or* margarine, honey, orange rind, and gingerroot; blend well. Remove carrots from steamer; toss in sesame glaze. Remove potatoes and sprinkle with parsley.

Green Salad with Mexican Dressing

Makes 4 servings

6 large radishes, sliced
1 large tomato, cut in wedges
4 to 6 large mushrooms, sliced
1 avocado, sliced
3 fresh peaches, sliced
¼ head iceberg lettuce, torn into
   bite-size pieces

¼ head romaine lettuce, torn into
   bite-size pieces
   Mexican Dressing (below)
   Shredded sharp Cheddar cheese

Arrange vegetables and fruit over lettuce in a large bowl. Add Mexican Dressing; toss and garnish with cheese. Serve immediately.

Mexican Dressing
Makes 1¼ cups

½ cup mild *or* hot taco sauce
¼ cup red wine vinegar
¼ cup olive oil
1 tablespoon minced parsley

1 tablespoon diced green chilies
1 teaspoon minced cilantro
1 teaspoon minced fresh oregano
  or ¼ teaspoon dried oregano

Combine all ingredients; mix thoroughly. Serve as directed.

Stir-Fry Pasta Primavera
Seafood Foil

Stir-Fry Pasta Primavera

Makes 4 servings

½ cup unsalted butter
1 medium onion, minced
2 large cloves garlic, minced
1 pound asparagus, cut diagonally in ¼-inch slices, tips intact
½ pound cauliflower, broken up
½ pound mushrooms, sliced
1 zucchini, cut in ¼-inch slices
1 small carrot, halved lengthwise and cut in ⅛-inch slices

½ cup chicken broth
¼ cup dry white wine
1 teaspoon dried basil leaves
½ teaspoon oregano leaves
1 cup frozen early peas, thawed
5 green onions, chopped
2 tablespoons minced parsley
Salt and pepper to taste
1 pound linguine, cooked and drained
½ cup grated Parmesan cheese

Heat wok or large, deep skillet over medium-high heat. Add butter, onion, and garlic; stir-fry until onion is tender, about 2 minutes. Stir in asparagus, cauliflower, mushrooms, zucchini, and carrot; stir-fry 2 minutes. Increase heat to high. Add broth, wine, basil, and oregano. Bring to a boil; boil until liquid is slightly reduced, about 3 minutes. Add peas and green onions; heat through, stirring gently, for 1 minute. Add parsley, salt, and pepper. Add pasta and cheese; toss until cheese is evenly distributed and pasta is heated through.

Seafood Foil

Makes 4 servings

4 1- to 1½-pound fish fillets (snapper, cod, or orange roughy)
½ cup thick salsa

8 large shrimp
Cilantro sprigs or parsley
1 lime, cut into wedges

Cut foil into 8 heart-shaped pieces 1 inch longer than fillets. Place a fillet on each heart; top with 2 tablespoons salsa, 2 shrimp, and 2 sprigs of cilantro. Cover with another foil heart; seal edges. Bake at 400° for 10 to 12 minutes. Transfer to dinner plates. Cut a large "X" in each foil packet; turn back foil to expose fish. Garnish with lime wedges and serve steaming hot.

Broiled Shrimp Kebabs
Pasta and Pea Pods

Broiled Shrimp Kebabs

Makes 4 servings

1 **pound fresh large shrimp in shells**
¼ **cup safflower oil**
4 **lemon slices**
4 **whole allspice**

3 **cloves garlic, minced**
1 **teaspoon crushed dried tarragon**
1 **teaspoon crushed dried oregano**
  Bay leaves, optional

Peel and devein shrimp, leaving tail intact. In a shallow dish combine oil, lemon, allspice, garlic, tarragon, and oregano. Add shrimp. Cover and marinate for 1 hour at room temperature, stirring occasionally. Preheat broiler. Drain shrimp, reserving marinade; discard lemon and allspice. Thread shrimp on short skewers alternately with bay leaves, if desired. Place on unheated rack of broiler pan. Broil 4 inches from heat source for 3 to 4 minutes or until shrimp turn pink. Turn and brush occasionally with reserved marinade.

Pasta and Pea Pods

Makes 4 servings

8 **ounces mostaccioli**
1 **6-ounce package frozen pea pods**
½ **cup butter *or* margarine**

  Salt and pepper to taste
¼ **cup grated Romano cheese**
  Julienned carrots, optional

Cook mostaccioli and pea pods according to package directions; drain and keep warm. In a skillet melt butter *or* margarine over medium heat until golden brown. Remove from heat; add mostaccioli and pea pods. Toss together. Season to taste with salt and pepper. Transfer to a serving bowl; sprinkle with Romano cheese. Garnish with julienned carrots, if desired.

Oven-Fried Fish
Crab-Stuffed Mushrooms
Suggested Accompaniment:
Coleslaw

Oven-Fried Fish

Makes 4 servings

1 **pound fresh fish fillets,**
thawed, cut ½-inch thick
1 **beaten egg**
2 **tablespoons milk**
¼ **cup fine dry seasoned**
bread crumbs

2 **tablespoons yellow cornmeal**
2 **tablespoons all-purpose flour**
¼ **teaspoon seasoned salt**
6 **tablespoons butter *or* margarine,**
melted
Lemon wedges

Rinse fish and pat dry. In a shallow dish combine egg and milk. In a second shallow dish combine crumbs, cornmeal, flour, and salt. Dip fish in egg mixture, then in crumb mixture. Place in a shallow baking pan. Drizzle fish with melted butter. Bake at 500° for 4 to 6 minutes or until fish flakes easily when tested with a fork. Serve with lemon wedges.

Crab-Stuffed Mushrooms

Makes 4 servings

3 **tablespoons butter *or***
margarine
12 **large mushroom caps**
2 **cloves garlic, minced**
½ **cup monterey Jack *or***
mozzarella cheese, shredded

1 **6-ounce can flaked crabmeat**
2 **tablespoons red *or* white wine**
1 **to 2 teaspoons Worcestershire sauce**
2 **tablespoons fine dry bread crumbs**
Freshly ground pepper
Shredded Monterey Jack cheese

Melt 1 tablespoon butter *or* margarine in sauté pan. Sauté mushroom caps, coating well with butter. Combine remaining butter *or* margarine and next 6 ingredients until blended. Place mushrooms on rimmed baking sheet. Evenly mound filling into each mushroom cavity, pressing lightly. Sprinkle with pepper and cheese. Broil about 6 inches from heat source 5 to 8 minutes. Serve immediately.

Steamed Vegetables
Chilled Fruit Soup
Crudités with Garlic Dip
Champagned Fish with Parsley Butter

Steamed Vegetables

Makes 4 servings

2 medium carrots, thinly sliced
¼ cup green beans, cut into thirds

1 cup cauliflower florets
1 tablespoon fresh lemon juice
1 teaspoon grated lemon peel

Steam vegetables over boiling water until tender-crisp, about 8 minutes. Toss in a serving bowl with lemon juice and peel.

Chilled Fruit Soup

Makes 4 servings

5 large ripe bananas, peeled and quartered *or* 1 bag frozen peaches *or* nectarines, thawed
2 tablespoons sugar
½ cup Neufchatel cheese
¼ cup plain yogurt

2 tablespoons orange juice concentrate, thawed
1 tablespoon lemon juice
2 to 3 tablespoons sweet *or* cream sherry
Kiwi fruit slices
Fresh mint sprigs

In a blender or food processor blend all ingredients, except kiwi and mint, until smooth. Taste and add additional lemon or sherry as desired. Pour into a serving bowl; cover and chill. Garnish with kiwi fruit slices and fresh mint sprigs.

Crudités with Garlic Dip

Makes 4 servings

4 medium cloves garlic
2 large egg yolks, at room
 temperature
1/8 teaspoon salt
1/4 teaspoon Dijon-style mustard
3/4 cup olive oil
1 teaspoon lemon juice

1/2 teaspoon cold water
1 cup cauliflower florets, steamed
1 cup broccoli florets, steamed
4 green onions, trimmed
1/2 cup fresh mushrooms
4 carrots, cut into 3-inch sticks
4 stalks celery, cut into 3-inch sticks

Crush garlic and reduce to a paste; place in a blender or food processor. Add egg yolks, salt, and mustard; blend briefly. Gradually stir in half the oil. Add lemon and water; add the remaining oil; blend slowly and steadily. Transfer to a glass serving bowl; cover and refrigerate. To serve, place dip in the center of a large platter and arrange vegetables around it.

Champagned Fish with Parsley Butter

Makes 4 servings

Freshly ground pepper
4 1 1/4-pound fish steaks, cut 1
 inch thick (halibut, swordfish,
 or salmon)

1/2 cup champagne
Parsley Butter (below)

Grind pepper generously over steaks. Pour champagne evenly over fish. Broil 4 inches from heat source for 3 to 5 minutes. Turn. Broil 4 minutes more or until fish flakes easily when tested with a fork. Top with a spoonful of Parsley Butter.

Parsley Butter
Makes 3/4 cup

1/2 cup butter, at room temperature
1/4 cup grated Parmesan cheese

1/2 cup chopped fresh parsley
1 to 2 cloves garlic, minced

Combine all ingredients; blend well. Serve as directed.

Champagned Fish with Garlic Butter, this page; Steamed Vegetables, Chilled Fruit Soup, Page 45

Chicken Puffs
Trout Meuniere
Asparagus with Blender Bearnaise
Herbed Squash and Mushrooms
Spinach Salad with
Lemon-Lime Vinaigrette

Chicken Puffs

Makes 1 dozen pastries

½ **package (10 ounces) puff
    pastry sheets**
1 **tablespoon butter**
1 **small red onion, minced**
2 **teaspoons curry**
1 **teaspoon chopped chutney**

1 **tablespoon chopped walnuts
    or almonds**
1 **tablespoon shredded coconut**
½ **cup half-and-half**
1 **cup chopped cooked chicken**

Roll out one sheet puff pastry. Cut out 1½-inch rounds with fluted cookie cutter. Bake in oven according to package directions. Melt butter in a large saucepan. Sauté onion until golden. Stir in curry, chutney, nuts, and coconut; cook 3 to 5 minutes. Add half-and-half and bring to a boil. Simmer 5 minutes. Add chicken and blend well. Serve warm or cold on puff pastry shells.

Herbed Squash and Mushrooms

Makes 4 servings

1 **pound (4 small) crookneck *or*
    zucchini squash, quartered**
½ **pound mushrooms, halved**

¼ **cup chicken broth**
½ **teaspoon dried basil or tarragon**
    Salt and pepper to taste

Place all ingredients in a skillet; cover and simmer until tender-crisp, 6 to 8 minutes.

Asparagus with Blender Bearnaise

Makes 4 servings

2 pounds asparagus	1 to 2 tablespoons butter
Boiling salted water	Blender Bernaise(below)

Wash asparagus and cut or snap off tough ends. In a wide frying pan with a little boiling water, lay spears parallel no more than three layers deep. Cook, uncovered, over high heat until stems are just tender when pierced with a fork, 6 to 8 minutes. Drain. Top with butter and serve with Blender Bearnaise.

Note: For lighter appetites, omit Blender Bearnaise and serve asparagus with Meuniere Sauce from Trout recipe.

Blender Bearnaise

Makes 1 cup

1/4 cup wine vinegar	6 black peppercorns
1/4 cup vermouth *or* white wine	6 parsley sprigs
1 shallot *or* green onion, minced	1 cup butter
1 teaspoon dried tarragon leaves	3 egg yolks
1 bay leaf	

In a small saucepan bring first 7 ingredients to a boil; reduce to 3 tablespoons. Melt butter in a separate saucepan. In blender whirl yolks until just blended. Add reduced wine mixture and blend briefly. Add melted butter, a droplet at a time, blending continuously on high speed. As mixture thickens, increase butter to a thin stream. Keep sauce warm by placing blender container in a pan of lukewarm water, if desired.

Note: For a faster Hollandaise version, simply omit first 7 ingredients and the first step. Proceed as directed. Makes 1/2 cup.

Curry Bearnaise Variation

Makes 1 cup

1 tablespoon vegetable oil	1 tablespoon curry powder
1/2 small onion, chopped	3/4 cup plain yogurt

Heat oil in skillet; sauté onion until tender. Stir in curry; cook 3 to 4 minutes, stirring constantly. Transfer to a blender or food processor. Add yogurt; blend until smooth.

Trout Meuniere

Makes 4 servings

4 medium trout	¼ cup butter
Lemon juice	¼ cup lemon juice *or* white wine
Freshly ground black pepper	¼ cup minced fresh parsley
2 tablespoons butter	Sliced kiwi, avocado, *or* mango
2 tablespoons oil	

Rub trout with lemon juice and pepper. Warm platter for fish in 200° oven. Heat butter and oil in a large frying pan over medium-high heat. Add trout and sauté until lightly browned on one side; when edges become opaque and curl slightly, 3 to 5 minutes, turn. Heat until fish flakes easily when tested with a fork in the thickest portion. Remove fish to warm platter.

Wipe out pan and melt butter. Add lemon juice and parsley all at once. Swirl and pour sauce over trout. Garnish with kiwi slices.

Spinach Salad with Lemon-Lime Vinaigrette

Makes 4 servings

1 bunch spinach, stems removed	1 cup bean sprouts, optional
3 green onions, sliced	6 to 8 cherry tomatoes, halved
½ cup sliced radishes	Lemon-Lime Vinaigrette (below)

Tear spinach into bite-size pieces. Arrange other vegetables in groups on top of spinach. Serve with Lemon-Lime Vinaigrette.

Lemon-Lime Vinaigrette
Makes 1 cup

¼ cup safflower oil	2 tablespoons lime juice
2 tablespoons lemon juice	2 tablespoons minced parsley

Combine all ingredients; mix well.

Trout Meuniere, Spinach Salad with Lemon-Lime Vinaigrette, this page; Herbed Squash and Mushrooms, page 48; Asparagus with Blender Bearnaise, page 49

Parmesan Pinwheels
Broiled Salmon with Linguine
and Watercress Sauce
Sliced Beefsteak Tomatoes

Sliced Beefsteak Tomatoes

Makes 4 servings

3 large beefsteak tomatoes
1/3 cup olive oil
1/4 cup lemon juice
1 tablespoon chopped fresh basil
   or 1/2 teaspoon dried basil

1 tablespoon freshly chopped rosemary
   or 1/2 teaspoon dried rosemary

Slice tomatoes. Whisk together remaining ingredients; pour over tomatoes. Let stand at room temperature until serving.

Broiled Salmon with Linguine and Watercress Sauce

Makes 4 servings

4 salmon steaks, 3/4 inch thick
1 tablespoon chopped fresh marjoram *or* 1 teaspoon dried marjoram

Salt and pepper to taste
Watercress Sauce(next page)
4 ounces thin linguine, cooked and well drained

Sprinkle both sides of fish with marjoram and salt and pepper to taste. On an oiled rack 4 inches from heat source broil steaks until first side is lightly browned, 5 to 8 minutes. Turn and broil 5 to 8 minutes more, until fish flakes easily when tested with a fork. Combine 3/4 cup of Watercress Sauce with prepared linguine. Serve balance of the Watercress Sauce over the salmon steaks.

Watercress Sauce

Makes 2 cups

1 cup tightly packed parsley
1 cup watercress leaves
6 large Boston lettuce leaves, centers removed
3 large shallots, quartered

1 small onion, cut into 1-inch chunks
3 tablespoons olive oil
1 tablespoon wine vinegar
1/3 cup unsalted tomato juice

Fit food processor with steel blade. Combine parsley, watercress, lettuce, shallots, and onions in work bowl; process with 3 on/off turns. Scrape down sides of bowl. Pour olive oil over mixture in a circular motion. Sprinkle with vinegar. Purée for 5 seconds. While machine is running, pour tomato juice through feed tube until well blended. Serve with salmon and linguine as directed.

Parmesan Pinwheels

Makes 4 servings

1 cup butter *or* margarine
1 cup flour
1/2 cup shredded sharp Meunster *or* sharp Brick cheese
1/2 cup sour cream
2/3 cup freshly grated Parmesan *or* Romano cheese

1/2 teaspoon cayenne pepper
1/2 teaspoon paprika
1/4 teaspoon salt
1/4 teaspoon Tabasco sauce
Fresh-cut vegetables *or* fruit, optional

Using a pastry blender, cut together butter *or* margarine and flour. Blend in Meunster cheese and sour cream. Divide dough into 4 parts; wrap and chill for 15 minutes. Combine Parmesan, pepper, paprika, salt, and Tabasco sauce; set aside. On a floured surface roll one part of pastry into a 12 x 6-inch rectangle. Sprinkle with 2 tablespoons of the Parmesan mixture. Fold in 6-inch sides to meet in center, forming a square. Sprinkle with 1 tablespoon of the Parmesan mixture. Fold lengthwise again. On folded edge make 1/4-inch cuts, 1 inch apart. Bring ends together, forming a wheel, and place on ungreased baking sheet. Repeat with remaining pastry sections. Bake 10 to 15 minutes at 450° or until golden brown. Serve with vegetables *or* fruit, if desired.

Menus with Lamb and Veal

Lamb Chops Persillade
Tomato Shells with Vegetable Purée
Suggested Accompaniment:
Long-Grain and Wild Rice with Mushrooms

Lamb Chops Persillade

Makes 4 servings

4 lamb loin chops,1 inch thick
2 cloves garlic, minced and stirred to paste
1 tablespoon butter
3 tablespoons minced shallots
⅓ cup fine bread crumbs
⅓ cup minced fresh parsley
1 teaspoon tarragon, basil, *or* thyme
Freshly ground pepper
Grated Parmesan cheese

Line broiler pan with foil to collect drippings. Rub chops with garlic paste. Broil 4 inches from heat source for 6 to 8 minutes on each side. Melt butter in a saucepan; sauté shallots and bread crumbs until golden brown. Remove from heat. Stir in parsley, herbs, and drippings from lamb chops. Add pepper and cheese to taste. Spread over one side of chops before serving.

Tomato Shells with Vegetable Purée

Makes 4 servings

1 pound broccoli, chopped
2 chayotes, peeled and sliced
2 large tomatoes, room temperature
¼ cup Neufchatel cheese
¼ cup ricotta cheese
Dash nutmeg *or* cayenne
Freshly ground pepper
Grated Romano cheese

Steam broccoli and chayote until tender, 12 minutes. Make deep zigzag cuts around the tomatoes; twist and pull gently apart. Scoop out pulp and seeds; set shells on a warm platter. In a blender process green vegetables, Neufchatel, ricotta, nutmeg, and pepper until smooth. Pour into tomato shells. Sprinkle with cheese. Broil until cheese is golden and tomato is hot.

Lamb Chops Persillade, Tomato Shells with Vegetable Purée, this page

Veal and Artichoke Sauté
Fresh Herbed Pasta
Sautéed Medley
Chilled Watercress Soup

Veal and Artichoke Sauté

Makes 4 servings

1 pound veal *or* turkey cutlets, cut to finger lengths
Flour
Salt and pepper
½ teaspoon sage
2 tablespoons butter *or* margarine

1 9-ounce package frozen artichoke hearts, thawed
½ cup dry white wine *or* vermouth
½ cup chicken broth
¼ cup half-and-half *or* whipping cream
Grated Parmesan cheese

Dust veal lightly with flour and seasonings. Sauté in butter over medium-high heat 4 to 6 minutes. Transfer to serving platter and keep warm. Add artichokes, wine, broth, and half-and-half to skillet. Cover and simmer until artichokes are tender. Pour over veal and dust with cheese.

Fresh Herbed Pasta

Makes 4 servings

2 quarts water
1 teaspoon salt
8 ounces wide fresh noodles
1 tablespoon oil

Freshly ground black pepper
2 tablespoons chopped fresh rosemary, thyme, *or* chives

Bring water and salt to a boil. Add noodles and oil; cook until tender but firm, 5 to 8 minutes. Drain. Toss with pepper and rosemary before serving.

Sautéed Medley

Makes 4 servings

¾ pound small new potatoes, quartered	2 tablespoons butter
Water	½ pound mushrooms, halved
1 teaspoon salt	1 teaspoon lemon juice
1 large carrot, cut in sticks	1 teaspoon dried basil
4 small white onions, halved	Grated Parmesan, Romano, *or* Sapsago cheese, optional

In a large kettle cover potatoes with water; add salt and boil until tender, about 10 minutes. After 5 minutes, add carrots and onions. Melt butter in a large skillet; sauté mushrooms. Drain boiled vegetables and sauté briefly with mushrooms. Add lemon juice and basil; toss to mix. Garnish with cheese, if desired.

Chilled Watercress Soup

Makes 4 servings

2 tablespoons butter	¼ teaspoon nutmeg
1 bunch green onions, chopped	2 teaspoons lemon juice
2 tablespoons all-purpose flour	Salt and pepper to taste
2 tablespoons nonfat dry milk	Yogurt
1 quart half-and-half, at room temperature	Lemon slices
2 bunches watercress, roughly chopped (reserve 4 sprigs for garnish)	

Melt butter in saucepan; sauté onion briefly. Stir in flour and dry milk; blend and cook until bubbly. Gradually add half-and-half. Cook, stirring continuously, until soup comes to a boil and thickens. Reduce heat; simmer. Add watercress, nutmeg, and lemon juice. Cover and simmer 3 minutes. Remove soup from heat and whirl in blender until smooth. Season to taste and chill. Garnish each serving with yogurt, a watercress sprig, and lemon slice.

Avocado Dip with Vegetables
Golden Cauliflower
Greek Stir-Fry
Pine Nut Pilaf

Avocado Dip with Vegetables

Makes approximately 1 cup

1 avocado, peeled and seeded
1/3 cup sour cream
2 tablespoons Italian salad
   dressing

1 teaspoon lemon juice
Dash garlic salt
1 to 2 tablespoons milk

In a bowl mash avocado, using a fork. Stir in sour cream, salad dressing, lemon juice, and garlic salt; add milk until of dipping consistency. Serve with crisp relishes.

Pine Nut Pilaf

Makes 4 servings

1 tablespoon olive oil *or*
   vegetable oil
1 medium red onion, minced
2 to 3 garlic cloves, minced
1¼ cups long-grain rice
1/3 cup pine nuts *or* slivered
   almonds

2¼ cup chicken broth
¼ cup lemon juice
1 to 2 tablespoons chopped fresh mint
Freshly grated rind of 1 lemon
Freshly ground pepper

Heat oil in a medium saucepan over medium-high heat. Add onion and garlic; sauté until soft, about 5 minutes. Add rice and nuts; stir until golden brown. Add broth and lemon juice; bring to a boil. Reduce heat; cover and simmer until liquid is absorbed, 20 to 25 minutes. Just before serving, add mint, lemon rind, and pepper; fluff with two forks.

Avocado Dip with Vegetables, this page

Greek Stir-Fry

Makes 4 servings

1 tablespoon olive oil *or* vegetable oil
1 pound lamb, cubed (leg, shoulder, or shank)
1 red onion, diced
2 to 3 cloves garlic, minced
1 cup red wine
1 cup beef broth

¼ cup minced fresh parsley
1 to 2 teaspoons chopped fresh mint *or* parsley
1 teaspoon oregano
1 small eggplant, diced
1 teaspoon arrowroot, optional
Sliced black olives
Parsley *or* mint

Heat oil in a wok or skillet. Add lamb, onion, and garlic; sauté until lamb is browned. Deglaze wok with wine. Add broth, parsley, mint, and oregano; simmer about 25 minutes. Add eggplant during the last 10 minutes of cooking time. Reduce liquid over high heat or thicken by stirring in arrowroot, if desired. Garnish with olives and sprinkle with parsley.

Golden Cauliflower

Makes 4 servings

2 tablespoons butter *or* margarine
4 cups thinly sliced cauliflower

⅓ cup water
1 cup shredded Cheddar cheese
1 teaspoon paprika

Melt butter *or* margarine in large skillet; add cauliflower and water. Cover and steam over high heat for 3 minutes. Sprinkle with cheese and paprika; cover and continue steaming until cheese melts and cauliflower is tender, about 2 minutes.

Menus Extras: Dessert

Layered Fruits with Citrus-Honey Ricotta

Makes 4 servings

1 cup ricotta cheese
1 cup cream cheese
  Grated rind of 1 lemon
  Grated rind of 1 orange
  Grated rind of 1 lime
1 to 2 tablespoons lemon juice
1 to 2 tablespoons orange juice

1 to 2 tablespoons lime juice
¼ cup honey
2 to 3 tablespoons fresh chopped mint, optional
  Sliced fresh fruits (berries, bananas, plums, peaches)
  Fresh mint leaves, optional

Combine cheeses, fruit zest, honey, and chopped mint, if desired; blend well. Layer mixture with sliced fruit in parfait glasses. Chill before serving. Garnish with fresh mint sprigs.

Bananas with Rum Cream

Makes 4 servings

1 egg, separated
¼ cup brown sugar
½ of a 4-ounce container frozen whipped dessert topping, thawed

1 tablespoon dark rum
4 small bananas, sliced
  Chocolate curls, optional

In a small mixer bowl beat egg white until soft peaks form; gradually add half of the brown sugar, beating until stiff peaks form. Transfer to a clean bowl. In the same mixer bowl, beat egg yolk until thick and lemon-colored; beat in remaining brown sugar and rum. Fold egg white and dessert topping into yolk mixture. Chill until serving time. To serve, place sliced bananas in 4 dessert dishes. Spoon rum cream over fruit. Garnish with choclate curls, if desired.

Hot Fruit Compote

Makes 4 servings

½ cup dry white wine, champagne, *or* sparkling cider
1 tablespoon brown sugar, optional
¼ teaspoon ginger
¼ teaspoon nutmeg
¼ teaspoon cinnamon
½ thinly sliced lemon *or* lime
4 small peaches, apples, *or* 2 fresh pears, sliced

Combine all ingredients except fruit in a saucepan and bring to a boil. Reduce heat. Add fruit; cook and stir occasionally until tender, about 10 minutes. Serve warm.

Fresh Fruit Gelati

Makes 1 quart

2 ripe bananas
2 ripe papayas
1 tablespoon orange juice
1 tablespoon lemon juice
1 tablespoon lime juice
1 tablespoon grated orange rind
1 tablespoon grated lemon rind
1 tablespoon grated lime rind
4 cups milk
½ cup sugar
1 teaspoon vanilla

Combine all ingredients in food processor. Process until blended. Transfer to shallow cake pan and freeze overnight. Process again until smooth. Transfer to bowl and freeze overnight again. Serve with cookies or fresh fruit slices.

Variations

Rhubarb-Strawberry Gelati: Replace bananas and papayas with 2½ cups *each* sliced rhubarb and trimmed strawberries. Add additional sugar to taste.

Pineapple-Kiwi Gelati: Replace bananas and papayas with 1 very ripe peeled and chopped pineapple plus 4 kiwi fruits, peeled and diced.

Fresh Fruit Gelati, this page

Book III Index

Book IV

All Holidays
Menus

By Barbara Grunes

ideals

Ideals Publishing Corp.
Nashville, Tennessee

Contents

A special thanks to Carole Janis for recipes and
food styling for the Gingerbread House.

ISBN 0-8249-3041-X

Published by Ideals Publishing Corporation
Nashville, Tennessee 37214
Published simultaneously in Canada

New Year's Eve Buffet

Menu for 10 to 12
Aloha Dip with Fresh Fruits • Eggnog
Spiced Mixed Nuts • Party Sandwich Loaf
Fisherman's Crab • Turkey French Toast
Teriyaki Kabobs • Hot Beef Sandwiches
Pasta Salad • Peach Oatmeal Bread
Apricot Squares • Chocolate Pound Cake

Aloha Dip

12 macaroons, crushed
¼ cup firmly packed light
 brown sugar
2 cups sour cream
 Pineapple chunks
 Assorted berries
 Peaches, sliced
 Melon chunks
 Kirsch *or* brandy, optional

In a bowl, stir together macaroons, sugar, and sour cream. Chill several hours to soften macaroon pieces. Do not stir again or macaroon pieces will break into small crumbs. Place chilled dip in center of a large platter. Arrange fruits of your choice in groups around dip. Sprinkle fruits with kirsch or brandy if desired.

Fisherman's Crab

½ cup margarine *or* vegetable oil
1½ cups sliced celery
1 pound mushrooms, sliced
½ cup chopped green onions
¼ cup chopped green pepper
4 cans (10¾ ounces *each*)
 cream of shrimp soup
1½ cups half-and-half
2 pounds crab meat, shell and
 cartilage removed
¼ cup diced pimiento
12 baked patty shells

In a large skillet or kettle, over low heat, melt margarine. Add celery; cook until celery is tender. Add mushrooms, green onions, and green pepper; cook until mushrooms are tender, stirring occasionally. Stir in soup, half-and-half, and crab meat. Heat until bubbly, stirring often. Fold in pimiento. Serve hot in patty shells.

Party Sandwich Loaf

1 unsliced sandwich loaf
   (1½ pounds)
Ham Salad
Egg Salad
Cream Cheese Frosting
Assorted vegetables and
   herbs for garnish

Remove crusts from sandwich loaf; slice into 7 layers lengthwise. Cover 3 layers with Ham Salad. Cover 3 layers with Egg Salad. Assemble loaf with alternate layers of ham and egg fillings. Wrap in plastic wrap; chill thoroughly. About 1 hour before serving, frost with Cream Cheese Frosting. Garnish as desired. Refrigerate until serving time.

Ham Salad

2 cups diced cooked ham
¼ cup chopped sweet pickle
2 tablespoons chopped onion
¼ cup mayonnaise, or as needed
   to bind
¼ teaspoon prepared mustard

In a small bowl, combine all ingredients.

Egg Salad

4 hard-cooked eggs, chopped
1 stalk celery, chopped
1 teaspoon grated onion
1 teaspoon prepared mustard
3 tablespoons mayonnaise
   Salt and pepper to taste
2 tablespoons chopped fresh
   parsley

In a small bowl, combine all ingredients.

Cream Cheese Frosting

11 ounces cream cheese,
   softened
2 tablespoons sour cream
2 teaspoons grated onion

In a small mixing bowl, beat together cream cheese, sour cream, and onion until smooth.

Note: Freeze juice or carbonated beverages in your ice cube tray for interesting additions to cold drinks. Or, add chunks of fruit or fresh mint leaves to water in ice cube trays before freezing.

New Year's Eve Buffet

Spiced Mixed Nuts

1 egg white
1 teaspoon cold water
1 pound mixed shelled walnuts, almonds, and pecans
½ cup sugar
½ teaspoon cinnamon
¼ teaspoon salt

Preheat oven to 225° F. Butter a cookie sheet. In a mixing bowl, beat egg white with cold water until bubbly. Add nuts; mix lightly until evenly coated. In a separate bowl, stir together sugar, cinnamon, and salt. Add nuts; toss until nuts are coated with sugar mixture. Arrange nuts evenly over prepared cookie sheet. Bake for 1 hour, stirring every 15 minutes.

Turkey French Toast

1 cup cooked minced turkey
1 tablespoon sweet pickle relish
¼ cup chopped celery
¼ cup mayonnaise
12 slices bread
3 eggs, lightly beaten
¾ cup milk
1 teaspoon sugar
4 to 6 tablespoons butter

In a mixing bowl, combine turkey, relish, celery, and mayonnaise. Spread on 6 slices of bread; top with remaining bread. In a shallow bowl, beat together eggs, milk, and sugar. In a large skillet, melt butter over medium heat. Dip both sides of one sandwich in egg mixture. Fry on both sides until golden brown. Repeat with remaining sandwiches. Cut on the diagonal into 24 triangles.

Pasta Salad with Pecans

1 pound spinach fettuccine, cooked according to package directions
¼ cup olive oil
3 cloves garlic, minced
1¼ cups chopped pecans
1 tablespoon basil
¼ cup chopped fresh parsley
½ teaspoon salt
½ teaspoon pepper
¼ cup freshly grated Parmesan cheese

In a serving bowl, toss pasta with olive oil. In a small bowl, combine garlic, pecans, and seasonings; mix well. Add pecan mixture to pasta; toss to coat. Stir in Parmesan cheese. Adjust seasoning. Chill until ready to serve.

New Year's Eve Buffet

Teriyaki Kabobs

¼ cup soy sauce
½ teaspoon chopped candied ginger
½ teaspoon sugar
1 small clove garlic, pressed
1 pound sirloin steak, 1 inch thick, cubed
1 pineapple, cut into 1-inch cubes
24 small stuffed green olives

In a bowl, stir together soy sauce, ginger, sugar, and garlic. Add steak cubes; stir to coat with marinade. Marinate, covered, overnight in refrigerator. The next day, drain steak. Skewer steak cubes and pineapple chunks on small picks. Broil 3 inches from heat for 5 minutes; turn. Broil 3 minutes longer. Add an olive to each pick; serve hot.

Hot Beef Sandwiches

½ cup butter, divided
5 pounds sirloin top roast
¾ cup sherry
1 large Bermuda onion, sliced
2 tablespoons Worcestershire sauce
3 tablespoons freshly squeezed lemon juice
½ teaspoon salt
1 pound mushrooms, sliced
3 beef bouillon cubes, dissolved in 1½ cups hot water
Crusty rolls

Preheat oven to 325° F. In a large skillet, melt ¼ cup butter. Brown roast on all sides. Place roast on a rack in a large shallow roasting pan. Roast for 2 hours. Pour sherry over roast and roast 1 hour longer. Remove from pan; set aside to cool. Reserve pan juices. In a large skillet, heat remaining ¼ cup butter. Sauté onion until tender. Stir in Worcestershire sauce, lemon juice, salt, mushrooms, bouillon, and juices from roast. Simmer 5 minutes. Slice roast very thin. Place slices in roasting pan. Pour bouillon-mushroom mixture over meat. Bake, covered, for 45 minutes. Serve on crusty rolls.

Peach Oatmeal Bread

2 cups whole wheat flour
1 cup quick-cooking rolled oats
¾ cup sugar
3 teaspoons baking powder
½ teaspoon salt
½ teaspoon baking soda
½ teaspoon cinnamon
2 cups chopped peaches
2 eggs, well beaten
1 cup milk
¼ cup vegetable oil

Preheat oven to 350° F. Butter a 9 x 5-inch loaf pan. In a mixing bowl, stir together flour, oats, sugar, baking powder, salt, soda, and cinnamon. Add peaches; stir to coat with dry ingredients. In a separate bowl, beat eggs with milk and oil. Add to flour mixture, stirring just until dry ingredients are moistened. Pour into prepared pan. Bake for 1 hour. Cool in pan for 10 minutes; transfer to a wire rack to cool completely. Wrap in aluminum foil.

Apricot Squares

1 cup butter, room temperature
½ cup sugar
½ teaspoon vanilla
2 cups all-purpose flour
1 jar (12 ounces) apricot jam
2 egg whites
½ teaspoon almond extract
1 cup confectioners' sugar
½ cup slivered almonds

Preheat oven to 350° F. In a mixing bowl, cream butter, sugar, and vanilla until fluffy. Stir in flour; blend well. Spread mixture into a 9 x 13-inch pan. Bake for 15 minutes. Cool. Spread the jam over the crust. Beat egg whites with almond extract until soft peaks form. Gradually beat confectioners' sugar into egg whites until stiff peaks form. Spread egg white mixture over the jam. Sprinkle with almonds. Bake for an additional 15 to 20 minutes. Cool. Slice into bars.

Chocolate Pound Cake

6 tablespoons butter, room temperature
1¼ cups sugar
3 eggs
1¾ cups all-purpose flour
½ cup cocoa
1½ teaspoons baking powder
½ teaspoon baking soda
¼ teaspoon salt
¾ cup sour cream
1 teaspoon vanilla
1 teaspoon chocolate extract
Confectioners' sugar

Preheat oven to 325° F. Grease a 9 x 5-inch loaf pan. In a mixing bowl, cream butter and sugar until fluffy. Beat in eggs. In a separate bowl, stir together dry ingredients. Add sour cream alternately with dry ingredients to creamed mixture; blend well. Blend in vanilla and chocolate extract. Pour batter into prepared pan. Bake for 1 hour and 15 minutes or until cake tests done. Cool cake in pan. When completely cool, turn out of pan and sprinkle with confectioners' sugar.

Eggnog

8 eggs
¾ cup sugar
½ teaspoon salt
½ cup rum
1 teaspoon vanilla
1 quart milk
2 cups heavy cream
Nutmeg

In large bowl of electric mixer, beat eggs at high speed until thick and foamy. At medium speed, gradually add sugar and salt. Add rum and vanilla. At low speed, gradually add milk. Chill. Before serving, whip cream; fold into egg mixture. Pour eggnog into punch bowl. Garnish with ground nutmeg.

Chinese New Year Dinner

Menu for 8

Wintermelon and Ham Soup • Pork with Vegetables
Spicy Chicken • Sautéed Fish with Hoisin Sauce
Lion's Head • Roast Pork
Almond Cookies • Fortune Cookies

Pork with Vegetables

4 tablespoons black bean sauce
2 tablespoons soy sauce
2 tablespoons dry sherry
4 tablespoons peanut oil
2 slices ginger root (¼-inch-thick *each*), peeled and minced
4 cloves garlic, minced
2 carrots, diagonally sliced
2 green peppers, cut in strips
1 pound lean pork, sliced into thin 1½-inch-long strips
1 cup sliced water chestnuts
1 cup chicken stock
4 teaspoons cornstarch mixed with 4 teaspoons cold water
Sliced almonds, optional

In a small bowl, mix bean sauce, soy, and sherry. In a wok or large skillet over high heat, heat oil. Add ginger and garlic; stir-fry 30 seconds. Add carrot and green pepper; stir-fry 1 minute. Add pork and bean sauce mixture; stir-fry 3 minutes. Add water chestnuts and stock; cover; cook 1 minute or until carrots are tender-crisp. Uncover. Stir cornstarch mixture until smooth; add to wok. Simmer, stirring constantly, until sauce thickens. Serve immediately. Garnish with almonds.

Sautéed Fish with Hoisin Sauce

6 tablespoons peanut oil
1¼ pounds flounder fillets
2 cloves garlic, minced
2 slices ginger root, peeled and minced
2 tablespoons light soy sauce
2 tablespoons Hoisin sauce
2 tablespoons white wine
Salt and pepper to taste

In a heavy skillet, heat 3 tablespoons of the oil. Sauté fillets 5 minutes on each side or until fish flakes easily when tested with a fork. Drain on paper toweling. Arrange fish on a serving plate. In the skillet, heat remaining oil. Add garlic and ginger; stir-fry for 10 seconds. Add remaining ingredients; heat 10 seconds. Drizzle sauce over fish. Serve with hot fluffy rice.

Chinese New Year Dinner

Wintermelon and Ham Soup _____

1 pound wintermelon, peeled,
  halved, seeds and pith
  removed
10 cups chicken stock
1 slice boiled ham, cut into
  julienne strips
  Salt and pepper to taste

Cut the wintermelon into 1 x 2-inch-long strips. In a saucepan, heat chicken stock. Add melon, ham, salt, and pepper. Simmer for 30 minutes or until the melon is tender.

Spicy Chicken on Shredded Lettuce _____

10 leaves Boston lettuce,
  shredded
1 teaspoon cornstarch
1 tablespoon water
2 teaspoons cornstarch
1 egg white
1 teaspoon white wine
½ teaspoon sugar
2 whole chicken breasts, boned
  and cut into ½-inch strips
4 tablespoons peanut oil
½ teaspoon hot pepper flakes
1 teaspoon minced ginger root
½ teaspoon salt

Arrange lettuce on serving platter. In a small bowl, mix cornstarch and water; set aside. In a separate bowl, stir together cornstarch, egg white, wine, and sugar. Add chicken; stir to coat. In a wok or heavy skillet, heat oil to very hot. Add hot pepper flakes and ginger; stir-fry 10 seconds. Add chicken pieces and salt; stir-fry until chicken turns white and is cooked through, about 3 minutes. Stir cornstarch mixture; add to wok. Heat and stir until mixture thickens slightly. Arrange chicken over lettuce.

Lion's Head _____

1 pound ground pork
4 Chinese mushrooms, soaked
  and shredded
¼ cup water chestnuts, minced
2 green onions, chopped
2 cloves garlic, minced
1 egg, lightly beaten
½ teaspoon salt
½ teaspoon pepper
2 teaspoons cornstarch
4 tablespoons peanut oil
½ head Chinese cabbage, thinly
  sliced
1 cup chicken stock
2 tablespoons light soy sauce
1 tablespoon cornstarch

In a medium bowl, stir together first nine ingredients. Form into 1-inch balls. In a wok or heavy skillet, heat oil. Brown pork balls in oil; set aside. In the same skillet, stir-fry cabbage 1 minute. Add stock and soy sauce. Arrange pork balls over cabbage in skillet. Reduce heat. Simmer, covered, over medium-low heat for 45 minutes. Arrange cabbage and pork balls on a serving dish. Whisk cornstarch into liquid in pan. Simmer, stirring constantly, until sauce thickens. Drizzle sauce over pork balls.

Chinese New Year Dinner

Roast Pork

2 cloves garlic, minced
3 slices ginger, minced and
  peeled
4 green onions, chopped
4 tablespoons sherry
2 tablespoons light soy sauce
3 tablespoons Hoisin sauce
  (available at oriental food
  stores)
3 tablespoons chili sauce
½ teaspoon salt
½ teaspoon pepper
1 pork tenderloin (2½ to 3
  pounds)
½ cup honey

Preheat oven to 325° F. In a large, shallow dish, combine garlic, ginger, onions, sherry, soy sauce, Hoisin sauce, chili sauce, salt, and pepper; blend well. Place pork tenderloin in marinade; turn to coat. Marinate 1 hour, turning once. Place tenderloin on a rack in a roasting pan. Roast for 1 hour, basting occasionally with honey. When pork is cool, cut thin slices. Serve with oriental noodles.

Almond Cookies

½ cup ground almonds
½ cup lard, room temperature
½ cup butter, room temperature
1 cup sugar
½ teaspoon salt
1 teaspoon almond extract
3 eggs
2¾ cups all-purpose flour

Preheat oven to 350° F. In a large mixing bowl, blend almonds, lard, butter, and sugar until fluffy. Mix in salt, almond extract, and eggs. Add flour; blend well. Cover batter; refrigerate 1 hour. Form into 1-inch balls. Place cookies on an ungreased baking sheet. Bake for 20 minutes. Transfer to a wire rack to cool. Makes 3 dozen cookies.

Fortune Cookies

2 egg whites
¼ cup sugar
½ teaspoon vanilla
5 tablespoons peanut oil
3 tablespoons cold water
1 cup flour
30 fortunes written on 3 x ¾-inch
  strips of paper

Preheat oven to 350° F. In a mixing bowl, stir together all ingredients, except fortunes, until blended. Drop batter by teaspoonfuls onto an ungreased cookie sheet, allowing 3 cookies per sheet. Bake for 5 minutes. Place fortunes in the center of each cookie. Fold cookie in half; pinch seam together. Fold corners down. Place each cookie in a cupcake tin to harden. Makes 30 cookies.

Oriental food stores are a pleasure to visit. Take advantage of their many kinds of soy sauce, noodles, dried mushrooms, and other seasonings, condiments, and snacks.

Valentine's Day Dinner

Menu for 2 to 4

Tuna Nuggets • Caponata
Tabouleh Stuffed Pork Chops
Herbed Cucumbers • Parsnips with Bacon
Chocolate Truffles • Strawberry Soufflé

Caponata

⅓ cup olive oil *or* vegetable oil
1 medium eggplant (about 1 pound), unpeeled, cubed
1 cup sliced onion
3 stalks celery cut into ½-inch pieces
1 can (15 ounces) tomato sauce with tomato bits
½ cup pitted ripe olives, halved
2 tablespoons capers
⅓ cup red wine vinegar
1½ tablespoons sugar
1 teaspoon salt
½ teaspoon pepper
Dark rye bread

In a large skillet over high heat, heat oil. Add eggplant, onion and celery. Sauté, stirring constantly for 10 minutes. Reduce heat to medium-low. Stir in remaining ingredients, except bread. Simmer, uncovered, stirring occasionally, until the mixture is thick and celery is still crisp. Spoon caponata into a bowl; cover. Chill at least 2 hours. Stir before serving. Serve with dark rye bread.

Tuna Nuggets

1 can (6½ ounces) tuna, drained and flaked
3 ounces cream cheese, room temperature
½ teaspoon lemon juice
1 teaspoon horseradish
Dash hot sauce
½ cup chopped fresh parsley

In a mixing bowl, stir together all ingredients, except parsley, until well mixed. Shape mixture into ½-inch balls. Roll tuna balls in parsley. Chill until serving time.

Strawberry Soufflé, 17

Tabouleh Stuffed Pork Chops _____

4 pork rib chops, cut 1¼ to 1½
   inches thick, trimmed of fat
¾ cup water
½ teaspoon salt
⅓ cup bulgur
½ cup shredded carrot
¼ cup chopped fresh parsley
2 green onions, chopped
1 teaspoon chopped fresh mint
   or ¼ teaspoon dried mint
1 tablespoon butter, melted
1½ teaspoons freshly squeezed
   lemon juice
¼ teaspoon salt
⅛ teaspoon ground allspice
   Freshly ground pepper
   to taste
2 tablespoons vegetable oil

With a sharp knife, cut an opening in the rib side of each chop, forming a pocket. Be careful not to cut through to the other side of chop. In a small saucepan, combine water and salt; bring to a boil. Stir in bulgur. Reduce heat, cover, and simmer over medium heat for 15 minutes. Add carrot; continue cooking, covered, for 10 minutes or until carrots are tender and water is absorbed. Remove from heat. Stir in parsley, green onions, mint, butter, lemon juice, and seasonings. Spoon about ½ cup stuffing mixture into each chop. In a large skillet, heat oil; brown chops on each side. Arrange chops in baking dish, cover and bake at 350° F. for 1 hour.

Parsnips with Bacon _____

4 slices bacon
1 pound parsnips, peeled and
   cut into julienne strips
1 small onion, minced
   Salt and pepper to taste
2 tablespoons chopped fresh
   parsley

In a large skillet, cook bacon until crisp. Transfer to paper towels to drain. Crumble bacon; set aside. To drippings in skillet, add parsnips and onion; toss to coat. Sprinkle with salt and pepper. Cook over low heat, covered, for 10 minutes or until vegetables are tender, stirring often. Add bacon and parsley to skillet. Stir well; serve.

Herbed Cucumbers _____

2 tablespoons salad oil
½ teaspoon salt
2 cucumbers, thinly sliced
1 large onion, sliced
2 tablespoons water
   Dash tabasco sauce
1 tablespoon crushed thyme

Heat oil with salt in a large skillet. Add cucumbers and onion. Cook over medium heat, stirring constantly, about 3 minutes. Add water, tabasco sauce, and thyme. Cover and cook, shaking skillet occasionally, for about 2 minutes or until onions are barely tender.

Chocolate Truffles

1 package (12 ounces) semisweet
  chocolate chips
¾ cup sweetened condensed
  milk
1 teaspoon vanilla
1½ cups vanilla wafer crumbs
2 tablespoons creme de café
  coffee liqueur
  Powdered cocoa

In top of double boiler over hot (not boiling) water, melt chocolate chips. Stir in condensed milk, vanilla, vanilla wafer crumbs, and liqueur. Beat until smooth. Refrigerate mixture about 45 minutes or until cool and easy to shape. With buttered hands, shape mixture into ¾-inch balls. Roll balls in cocoa.

Strawberry Soufflé

Butter
Granulated sugar
1 envelope unflavored gelatin
1 cup granulated sugar, divided
¾ cup cold water
3 cups fresh strawberries,
  hulled
4 eggs, separated
¼ teaspoon cream of tartar
  Red food coloring, optional
1 cup whipping cream, whipped

Butter bottom and sides of 1½-quart soufflé dish; sprinkle with sugar. Wrap a 4-inch band of aluminum foil, triple thickness, around the dish, overlapping 2 inches. Lightly butter inside of band and sprinkle with sugar. Fasten to soufflé dish so that collar extends 2 inches above rim of dish. In a medium saucepan, stir together gelatin and ¾ cup of the sugar. Stir in water; let stand 1 minute. Cook, stirring constantly, over low heat until gelatin dissolves completely, 5 to 8 minutes. Remove from heat. Mash strawberries; stir into gelatin. In a small bowl, beat egg yolks at high speed until thickened, about 5 minutes. Blend a little of the strawberry mixture into yolks. Add yolk mixture to strawberries; blend well. Chill, stirring occasionally, until mixture mounds slightly when dropped from a spoon, 30 to 45 minutes. Wash and dry beaters.

In a large bowl at high speed, beat egg whites and cream of tartar until foamy. Add remaining ¼ cup sugar, 1 tablespoon at a time, beating constantly until sugar is dissolved and whites stand in soft peaks. Beat in a few drops food coloring. Fold chilled gelatin mixture and whipped cream gently into egg whites. Pour into prepared dish. Chill until firm. Just before serving, carefully remove foil.

Easter Brunch

Menu for 6 to 8

Chili Dip for Shrimp
Potato Ham Boats
Eggs Benedict
Berry Mold
Orange Glazed Carrot Sticks
Banana Mocha Cake

Chili Dip for Shrimp _____

½ cup mayonnaise
½ cup sour cream *or* yogurt
2 tablespoons chopped sweet
   pickle
1 tablespoon chopped stuffed
   olives
2 teaspoons chili powder
1½ teaspoons grated or minced
   onion
1 hard-cooked egg, chopped

In a small bowl, combine all ingredients; mix well. Chill for several hours. Serve with shrimp.

Potato Ham Boats _____

8 large Russet potatoes
½ cup milk
4 tablespoons butter
2 eggs, well beaten
½ teaspoon salt
¼ teaspoon pepper
3 cups diced cooked ham
1 cup shredded sharp cheddar
   cheese, divided
½ cup minced green onion

Preheat oven to 400° F. Scrub potatoes; prick skins and bake for 50 to 60 minutes or until tender. Reduce oven temperature to 375° F. Cut potatoes in half lengthwise; scoop out pulp leaving a ¼-inch-thick shell. Mash pulp with milk, butter, egg, salt, and pepper. Stir in ham, ¾ cup cheese, and green onion. Spoon mixture into potato shells; bake at 375° F. for 20 minutes or until filling is lightly browned. Top with remaining cheese; return to oven and heat 5 minutes longer or until cheese melts.

Chili Dip for Shrimp
Peach Oatmeal Bread, 8

A GARDEN CLUB SUPPER
AT JOHN & LUCY'S

JULY 15
7:30 O'CLOCK

REGRETS ONLY
RSVP

Eggs Benedict

6 slices Canadian bacon (about
   6 ounces)
1 tablespoon vegetable oil
3 English muffins, split and
   toasted
1 tablespoon vinegar
6 eggs
   Blender Hollandaise Sauce
   Paprika
   Fresh watercress for garnish

In a heavy skillet, heat oil. Add Canadian bacon; sauté about 2 minutes on each side or until heated through. Place bacon on top of muffin halves; cover and keep warm. Add water to skillet to a depth of 1 inch. Stir in vinegar. Bring mixture to a boil; reduce heat. Break 1 egg into a shallow bowl; slip into water in skillet. Repeat with remaining eggs. Simmer, covered, for 3 to 5 minutes or until eggs are soft-cooked. Remove eggs with a slotted spoon and place over bacon; cover and keep warm. Prepare Blender Hollandaise Sauce. Spoon sauce over eggs. Sprinkle with paprika; garnish with watercress.

Blender Hollandaise Sauce

6 egg yolks
2 tablespoons freshly squeezed
   lemon juice
¼ teaspoon cayenne
1 cup butter

In a blender, place egg yolks, lemon juice, and cayenne. Process until smooth. In a small saucepan, heat butter until melted but not brown. With the blender running, pour butter into egg mixture in a slow, steady stream. Process a few seconds to thicken sauce.

Berry Mold

1 can (13½ ounces) crushed
   pineapple in syrup, drained,
   juice reserved
1 can (16 ounces) blueberries in
   water, drained, juice reserved
2 cups water
1 package (12 ounces) red
   raspberry-flavored gelatin
1½ cups sour cream
1 pint strawberries

In a saucepan, place reserved juice and 2 cups water. Bring mixture to a boil over medium heat. Remove from heat; stir in gelatin until dissolved. Set aside to cool. In a separate bowl, stir together pineapple, blueberries, and sour cream until sour cream is blended. Add fruit mixture to cooled gelatin; stir thoroughly. Pour into a lightly greased ring mold or heart mold. Chill until set, about 4 hours. Unmold; garnish with fresh strawberries.

Orange Glazed Carrot Sticks _____

1 pound carrots, pared and cut
   into julienne strips
3 tablespoons butter
¼ cup chopped onion
⅓ cup firmly packed light
   brown sugar
½ cup freshly squeezed orange
   juice
½ teaspoon salt

In a large skillet, cook the carrots, covered, in a small amount of water until tender. Remove carrots from skillet. In the same skillet, heat butter; add onion and cook until tender. Stir in brown sugar and orange juice; simmer 5 minutes. Add cooked carrots; sprinkle with salt. Simmer, spooning sauce over carrots until they are glazed and heated through.

Banana Mocha Cake _____

1 teaspoon instant coffee
   granules
1 cup mashed bananas (2 large
   bananas)
1¼ cups all-purpose flour
⅔ cup sugar
¼ cup cornstarch
3 tablespoons cocoa
1 teaspoon baking soda
½ teaspoon salt
1 egg, lightly beaten
⅓ cup vegetable oil
1 tablespoon vinegar
1 teaspoon vanilla
   Silky Mocha Frosting

Preheat oven to 350° F. In a small bowl, stir coffee into mashed bananas; blend well. In a 9-inch square baking pan, combine flour, sugar, cornstarch, cocoa, soda, and salt. Stir thoroughly with a fork. Make a well in the center of the dry ingredients. Place banana mixture, egg, oil, vinegar, and vanilla in the well. With a fork, stir dry ingredients into moist ingredients until well blended. Bake for 30 minutes. Cool completely before frosting with Silky Mocha Frosting.

Silky Mocha Frosting

3 tablespoons butter, softened
1½ cups confectioners' sugar
2 tablespoons cocoa
1 teaspoon instant coffee
   granules
2 tablespoons milk
½ teaspoon vanilla

In a small bowl, combine butter, sugar, cocoa, and coffee until well blended. Stir in milk and vanilla; beat until smooth.

Mother's Day Breakfast

Menu for 6

Blueberry Fruit Salad
Mom's Banana Breakfast Drink
Kids' Scrambled Eggs • Potato Waffles
Rhubarb Custard Kuchen • Brown Sugar Drops

Blueberry Fruit Salad

1 cup fresh blueberries
1 small banana, sliced
1 cup sliced strawberries
1 cup halved seedless grapes
2 cups cubed cantaloupe
4 tablespoons orange juice,
   divided
¼ cup mayonnaise
¼ cup plain yogurt
1 tablespoon honey
¼ teaspoon ground ginger

In a bowl, combine first 5 ingredients and 2 tablespoons of the orange juice; toss gently. In a separate bowl, stir together remaining orange juice, mayonnaise, yogurt, honey, and ginger. Chill. Arrange fruit on serving plates. Serve with honey yogurt dressing.

Kids' Scrambled Eggs

6 eggs
⅓ cup shredded Cheddar cheese
⅓ cup commercial sour cream
   Salt and pepper to taste
8 slices bacon, cooked, crumbled
2 tablespoons butter

Beat eggs with fork until well beaten. Blend in cheese, sour cream, seasonings, and bacon; set aside. In a large skillet over medium heat, heat butter. Pour in egg mixture. As it cooks, stir gently with a spoon. Continue until the eggs are set.

Mom's Banana Breakfast Drink

1 egg
1 cup milk
1 small ripe banana
1 tablespoon honey
1 scoop vanilla ice cream

In a blender, combine egg, milk, banana, and honey; process until smooth. Pour into a tall glass; top with ice cream.

Mother's Day Breakfast

Potato Waffles

2 cups all-purpose flour
⅔ cup potato flakes
4 teaspoons sugar
4 teaspoons baking powder
1 teaspoon salt
4 eggs
3 cups skim milk
2 tablespoons vegetable oil

In a large bowl, mix flour, potato flakes, sugar, baking powder, and salt. In a small bowl, beat together eggs, milk, and oil. Add to dry ingredients; mix well. Bake batter on waffle iron according to manufacturer's directions until waffles are golden brown.

Rhubarb Custard Kuchen

1¼ cups all-purpose flour
½ teaspoon salt
1 teaspoon sugar
1 teaspoon baking powder
½ cup butter, room temperature
1 egg yolk
2 tablespoons milk
4 heaping cups rhubarb, diced
1⅛ cups sugar
2 egg yolks
1 tablespoon all-purpose flour
3 egg whites, beaten stiff
½ cup sour cream
1 tablespoon grated orange
   peel
¼ teaspoon salt

Preheat oven to 350° F. In a mixing bowl, stir together flour, salt, sugar, and baking powder. Blend in butter, egg yolk, and milk. Pat dough into a 9 x 13-inch baking pan. In a bowl, mix together rhubarb and sugar; spread over crust. In a separate bowl, beat egg yolks with 1 tablespoon flour until well blended. Fold in stiffly beaten egg whites. Fold in sour cream, orange peel, and salt. Pour custard over rhubarb. Bake for 45 minutes.

Brown Sugar Drops

¼ cup packed light brown sugar
¼ cup butter
¼ cup dark corn syrup
½ cup all-purpose flour
1 teaspoon ground ginger
⅛ teaspoon salt

Preheat oven to 375° F. In a large saucepan, place brown sugar, butter, and corn syrup. Cook and stir mixture over low heat until butter melts; remove from heat. Stir in flour, ginger, and salt until ingredients are well blended. Drop batter by rounded teaspoonfuls about 4 inches apart onto a greased and floured cookie sheet. Bake for 5 minutes or until cookies are set. Cool 2 minutes; remove with a spatula. Makes 2 dozen.

Memorial Day Family Gathering

Menu for 12

Salmon Mousse with Avocado Sauce
Artichoke Dip • Potato Skins
Cheesy Chicken • Two Lettuce Salad
Strawberry Malakoff • Black Bottom Cupcakes

Salmon Mousse with Avocado Sauce

2 tablespoons unflavored
   gelatin
¼ cup cold water
½ cup boiling water
1 can (16 ounces) salmon, boned
3 tablespoons lime juice
3 shallots, minced
1 cup heavy cream, whipped
½ cup boiling water
½ cup mayonnaise
1 teaspoon basil
   Avocado Sauce

In a small bowl, sprinkle gelatin over cold water; stir. Add ½ cup boiling water, stirring until gelatin is dissolved. In a large mixing bowl, combine remaining ingredients. Stir in gelatin. Mound salmon mixture in a lightly greased 4-cup fish or ring mold. Cover loosely; chill until set. Loosen sides of mold with spatula. Unmold onto serving platter; garnish with cucumber slices, parsley, and tomatoes. Serve with Avocado Sauce.

Avocado Sauce

½ cup sour cream
½ cup mayonnaise
3 tablespoons chopped fresh
   parsley
1 tablespoon lemon juice
1 teaspoon prepared mustard
2 avocados

In a blender or food processor, blend all ingredients.

Cheesy Chicken

2 chickens, cut into serving
  pieces
¾ cup margarine
2 cups flour
1½ cups grated Romano *or*
  Parmesan cheese
1 teaspoon salt
1 teaspoon pepper
1 teaspoon basil *or* garlic
  powder
1½ teaspoons paprika
2 tablespoons onion flakes
4 eggs
13 ounces evaporated milk

Preheat oven to 350° F. In a small pan, melt margarine; set aside. In a shallow pan, mix flour, cheese, salt, pepper, basil, paprika, and onion flakes. In a separate bowl, beat eggs and milk until blended. Dip each chicken piece in egg-milk mixture; roll in flour and cheese mixture. Place on a baking sheet. Sprinkle chicken with remaining cheese mixture; drizzle with melted margarine. Bake 60 to 75 minutes.

Two Lettuce Salad

3 tablespoons tarragon vinegar
½ teaspoon salt
¼ teaspoon pepper
¼ teaspoon vegetable oil
1 head Boston lettuce, trimmed,
  rinsed, and dried
4 heads Bibb lettuce, trimmed,
  rinsed, and dried
1 Belgian endive, trimmed,
  rinsed, and dried
¼ pound snow peas, trimmed
¼ pound bean sprouts, blanched
  Salt and pepper to taste
½ teaspoon tarragon

In a jar with a tight-fitting lid, combine vinegar, salt, pepper, and oil; shake to blend. Tear salad greens into bite-sized pieces directly into a salad bowl. Add snow peas and bean sprouts; toss to mix. Season with salt, pepper, and tarragon. Just before serving, shake the dressing to blend; pour over salad. Toss salad to coat with dressing.

Potato Skins

8 large baking potatoes,
  scrubbed, pricked
6 tablespoons unsalted butter,
  melted
2 cups shredded Cheddar
  cheese
½ pound bacon, cooked and
  crumbled

Bake potatoes at 400° F. for 1 hour or until tender. Cool. Reduce oven temperature to 375° F. Cut potatoes in half lengthwise; scoop out insides, leaving a ¼-inch-thick shell. Brush the insides of the potato skins generously with melted butter. Sprinkle the insides with cheese and bacon. Arrange skins on a cookie sheet. Bake for 30 minutes. Cut into strips.

Memorial Day Family Gathering

Artichoke Dip

1 can (14 ounces) artichoke
  hearts, drained and chopped
1 package (8 ounces) mozzarella
  cheese, shredded
1 cup grated Parmesan cheese
1 cup mayonnaise
1 teaspoon garlic powder
  Chopped fresh parsley

Preheat oven to 350° F. In a mixing bowl, stir together artichoke hearts, mozzarella, Parmesan, mayonnaise, and garlic powder until well mixed. Mound mixture in a 1-quart casserole. Bake for 25 minutes or until mixture is bubbly and top is light brown. Top with parsley. Serve with crusty bread.

Strawberry Malakoff

6 ounces ladyfingers
1 cup plus 2 tablespoons butter,
  room temperature
½ cup sugar
1¼ cups ground almonds
1 cup heavy cream
1¼ pints fresh strawberries,
  sliced; divided

Butter a 5-cup charlotte mold or a bowl with a 5-cup capacity. Cut waxed paper to fit the mold bottom; butter the paper. Line bottom and sides of mold with ladyfingers, cutting the ladyfingers to give a tight fit. In a mixing bowl, cream butter and sugar until fluffy. Stir in almonds. Whip heavy cream until soft peaks form; stir cream into almond mixture. Fold in 1 pint strawberries. Mound mixture in prepared mold. Cover with plastic wrap and refrigerate overnight or until set. When ready to serve, run a knife around side of the mold; invert onto serving dish. Carefully remove mold and paper. Garnish with remaining strawberries. Serve immediately after unmolding.

Black Bottom Cupcakes

2 large ripe bananas
1½ cups all-purpose flour
1 cup sugar
¼ cup cocoa
1 teaspoon baking soda
½ teaspoon salt
⅓ cup vegetable oil
1 teaspoon vanilla
1 large firm banana
6 ounces cream cheese, room
  temperature
⅓ cup sugar
1 egg
6 ounces semisweet chocolate
  chips

Preheat oven to 350° F. Slice ripe bananas into blender. Blend until pureed. In a mixing bowl, stir together flour, 1 cup sugar, cocoa, soda, and salt. Stir in the pureed bananas, oil, and vanilla. Spoon equal amounts of the mixture into 18 paper-lined muffin cups. Slice 2 slices of firm banana into each cup. In a mixing bowl, beat cream cheese with ⅓ cup sugar until fluffy. Blend in egg. Stir in chocolate chips. Spoon equal amounts of chocolate chip mixture into the muffin cups. Bake for 30 minutes. Cool in the pan on racks.

Father's Day Dinner

Menu for 10

Citrus Punch
Seven Layer Salad
Shish Kabobs
Carrots with Mint
Chocolate Nut Drop Cookies

Citrus Punch

1 can (46 ounces) chilled
  pineapple juice
1 can (46 ounces) chilled orange
  or grapefruit juice
2 quarts chilled ginger ale
1 pint lemon or lime sherbet

In a punch bowl, stir together juices and ginger ale. Scoop sherbet into punch bowl. Serve immediately.

Seven Layer Salad

1 head lettuce, sliced
2 green peppers, chopped
4 stalks celery, chopped
¼ pound fresh mushrooms,
  sliced
1 sweet onion, chopped
2 cups frozen peas, thawed
2 cups mayonnaise
2 teaspoons sugar
1 teaspoon salt
½ teaspoon garlic powder
½ teaspoon marjoram
1 cup grated Cheddar cheese
4 strips bacon, cooked crisp,
  crumbled

In a glass serving bowl with straight sides, layer lettuce, green pepper, celery, mushrooms, onion, and peas. In a mixing bowl, combine mayonnaise, sugar, salt, garlic powder, and marjoram; blend well. Spread mayonnaise mixture evenly over the peas. Sprinkle with Cheddar cheese and bacon. Cover and refrigerate for at least 4 hours or overnight. When serving, be sure each portion contains some of each salad layer.

Shish Kabobs

1 cup vegetable oil
1 cup red wine
3 bay leaves, crumbled
2 tablespoons wine vinegar
3 cloves garlic, crushed
½ teaspoon pepper
6 pounds chuck steak, cut into
   1½-inch cubes
1 pound large fresh mushrooms
9 medium white onions, peeled
   and quartered
6 large green peppers, cut into
   sixths
1 pint cherry tomatoes

In a bowl, stir together first 6 ingredients to make marinade. Place steak cubes in a large, shallow pan. Pour marinade over steak; stir to coat. Cover and refrigerate for 8 hours; stir occasionally. Oil 12 long skewers. Skewer meat alternately with vegetables, beginning and ending with meat. Broil or grill for a total of 15 to 20 minutes, turning once. Brush with marinade while cooking.

Carrots with Mint

2 pounds carrots, pared,
   trimmed, and thinly sliced
¾ cup heavy cream
   Salt and pepper to taste
2 tablespoons chopped fresh
   mint leaves

In a large saucepan, bring 2 cups water to a boil. Add carrots. Simmer until tender, about 10 minutes; drain. Stir in cream, salt, and pepper; heat through. Sprinkle carrots with fresh chopped mint leaves.

Chocolate Nut Drop Cookies

¼ cup butter, room temperature
¼ cup peanut butter
½ cup sugar
1 extra large egg
¼ cup milk
½ teaspoon vanilla
½ cup all-purpose flour
¼ teaspoon baking powder
¼ teaspoon baking soda
½ teaspoon salt
½ cup rolled oats
3 ounces semisweet chocolate
   chips
⅓ cup chopped nuts

Preheat oven to 375° F. In a mixing bowl, blend butter and peanut butter. Add sugar, egg, milk, and vanilla; blend well. In a separate mixing bowl, stir together flour, baking powder, soda, salt, and oats. Blend dry ingredients into peanut butter mixture. Stir in chocolate chips and nuts. Drop by teaspoonfuls onto an ungreased baking sheet. Bake for 10 to 12 minutes or until cookies are golden brown. Makes about 35 cookies.

Seven Layer Salad, 29

Fourth of July Celebration

Menu for 10 to 12

Stuffed Edam Cheese • Garden Potato Salad
Salmon Steaks in Aspic • Charcoal Broiled Sirloin Steak
Deep Dish Apple Pie • Yankee Doodle Dandy Pie

Stuffed Edam Cheese

1 Edam cheese (1 pound)
4 tablespoons beer
1 tablespoon butter
½ teaspoon Worcestershire sauce
¼ teaspoon Tabasco sauce
¼ cup chopped pecans

With a knife or cookie cutter, cut a round of wax from top of cheese. Scoop out cheese, leaving a ½-inch-thick shell. In a mixing bowl, stir together cheese and remaining ingredients until creamy and well blended. Mound back into the cheese shell. Refrigerate for 1 hour before serving. Serve with crackers and crisp sliced vegetables.

Garden Potato Salad

5 hard boiled eggs, chopped
2½ pounds small potatoes, cooked, peeled, and sliced
1 medium onion, chopped
1 cucumber, peeled and chopped
1 cup chopped celery
1 cup chopped tomatoes
½ cup sliced radishes
1 teaspoon salt
½ teaspoon pepper
Seasoned salts to taste
1½ cups mayonnaise
½ cup milk
Paprika

Set aside ¼ cup of the chopped egg for garnish. In a mixing bowl, stir together remaining eggs, potatoes, vegetables, and seasonings. In a small bowl, blend mayonnaise and milk. Pour mayonnaise mixture over vegetables; mix well. Garnish with reserved egg and paprika.

Salmon Steaks in Aspic

6 salmon steaks, 1 inch thick
6 peppercorns, crushed
1 teaspoon salt
4 sprigs fresh dill
1 small onion, sliced
1 stalk celery, chopped
1 carrot, sliced
4 cups boiling water
2 envelopes unflavored gelatin
½ cup freshly squeezed lemon
juice
Cucumber slices, lemon slices,
and olives

Place fish in a large skillet. Add seasonings, vegetables, and boiling water. Cover and simmer for about 8 minutes or until fish flakes easily. Do not overcook. Cool fish in cooking liquid; transfer to a platter. Carefully remove skin and bones. Strain cooking liquid; return liquid to skillet. Soften gelatin in lemon juice; add to liquid in skillet. Heat, stirring constantly, until gelatin dissolves. Pour gelatin mixture into a bowl; refrigerate until just beginning to thicken.

Pour half of the gelatin mixture into a 13 x 9-inch baking dish. Arrange salmon steaks in the dish. Spoon remaining gelatin mixture over fish. Chill until firm. Cut around each salmon steak, leaving a border of gelatin. Arrange salmon on a lettuce-lined platter. Garnish with cucumber slices, lemon slices, and olives.

Charcoal Broiled Sirloin Steak

1 sirloin steak (5 pounds), 1½ to
2 inches thick, trimmed of fat
⅓ cup vegetable oil
⅓ cup red wine vinegar
2 cloves garlic, crushed
1 teaspoon basil
½ teaspoon salt
½ teaspoon pepper

Slash fatty edge of steak at 1-inch intervals. Place steak in a large pan. In a bowl, stir together remaining ingredients; pour over steak. Chill, covered, 2 to 3 hours, turning several times. Start charcoal fire 30 to 40 minutes before cooking time. Coals are ready when glowing and covered with gray ash. Rub hot grill with a bit of fat trimmed from steak. Grill 5 to 6 inches above coals on both sides, brushing occasionally with marinade. Allow about 25 minutes for rare, 30 minutes for medium on an open grill. To test for doneness, make a small slash in center of steak.

Fourth of July Celebration

Yankee Doodle Dandy Pie

1 package (3½ ounces) vanilla
   pudding mix
8 ounces cream cheese,
   softened
½ teaspoon vanilla
1 graham cracker piecrust
   (8 inches)
20 to 25 strawberries, hulled
1 pint blueberries
   Whipped cream or topping,
   optional

Prepare pudding mix according to package directions; remove from heat. Beat in cream cheese and vanilla until mixture is smooth. Pour filling into crust. Refrigerate 3 hours or overnight. Arrange strawberries in circle around outer edge of pie. Place 1 large strawberry in center of pie. Fill in remaining area with blueberries. Serve with whipped cream, if desired.

Deep Dish Apple Pie

1½ cups all-purpose flour
½ teaspoon salt
3 tablespoons butter, room
   temperature
2 tablespoons vegetable
   shortening, room temperature
1 egg yolk
4 to 6 tablespoons ice water

In a large mixing bowl, stir together flour and salt. Cut in butter and shortening until the mixture resembles coarse crumbs. Add egg and water; mix until mixture holds together. Gather dough into a ball; knead lightly. Cover with plastic wrap. Chill for 1 hour.

8 large firm cooking apples
½ cup granulated sugar
½ cup firmly packed light brown
   sugar
2 teaspoons grated lemon peel
1 teaspoon cinnamon
3 tablespoons butter, cut into
   ½-inch pieces

Preheat oven to 425° F. Butter a deep-dish 9-inch pie plate. Peel, core and slice apples. Place apples in a large mixing bowl. Toss with granulated sugar, brown sugar, and lemon peel. Place in buttered pie pan. Sprinkle with cinnamon; dot with butter.

3 tablespoons milk
3 tablespoons sugar
   Cheddar cheese

On a lightly floured board, roll crust to a 10-inch round. Fit crust over filling. Seal crust and flute edges. Make a ½ inch vent in center of crust. Brush crust with milk; sprinkle with sugar. Bake 15 minutes. Reduce heat to 350° F. Bake for 35 minutes or until crust is golden brown. Serve with Cheddar cheese.

Labor Day Dinner for the Family

Menu for 8

Anchovy Appetizer
Apple Date Salad
Stuffed Breast of Veal
Noodle Ring
Chocolate Acorns
Cream Puffs

Apple Date Salad

½ cup plain yogurt
3 tablespoons freshly squeezed
    lemon juice
1 tablespoon honey
24 whole pitted dates
3 stalks celery, sliced
2 firm, tart apples, cored
    and sliced
½ cup walnuts, halved
    Butter lettuce leaves

In a small bowl, stir together yogurt, lemon juice, and honey; chill. Quarter the dates and add to the dressing together with celery, apples, and walnuts. Spoon mixture onto a bed of lettuce and serve.

Anchovy Appetizer

1 can (2 ounces) anchovy fillets
1 clove garlic, minced
2 tablespoons olive oil
1 tablespoon red wine vinegar
1 tablespoon tomato paste
1 tablespoon finely minced ripe
    black olives
1 tablespoon grated onion
6 slices firm white bread

In a bowl, crush anchovies with a fork. Stir in all other ingredients, except bread, and mash to make a paste. Under the broiler, toast bread on one side only. Spread the untoasted side with the anchovy mixture, pressing down firmly. Place under the broiler; broil until light brown. Cut into quarters.

Stuffed Breast of Veal _____

1 breast of veal (about 5 pounds)
   boned, with pocket
   Salt and pepper to taste
4 tablespoons butter, divided
1 onion, minced
½ pound fresh mushrooms,
   sliced
¼ pound ground veal
1½ cups breadcrumbs
2 tablespoons fresh minced
   parsley
2 eggs, lightly beaten
¼ cup heavy cream
¼ teaspoon nutmeg
   Flour
1 medium onion, sliced
2 carrots, sliced
¼ teaspoon thyme
¼ teaspoon rosemary
2 bay leaves
1 cup chicken stock
1 cup dry wine

Season veal with salt and pepper. In a large skillet, heat 2 tablespoons of the butter. Add onion; sauté until tender. Add mushrooms; sauté until tender, stirring occasionally. Stir in ground veal; sauté 3 minutes, stirring often. Remove from heat; stir in breadcrumbs, parsley, eggs, cream, and nutmeg. Stuff breast with the mixture; close the opening with skewers or string.

Preheat oven to 350° F. Heat remaining butter in a roasting pan. Dredge veal lightly in flour. Brown in hot butter on all sides; remove from pan. In the roasting pan, place onion and carrots. Return meat to pan with remaining ingredients. Roast, covered, for about 1½ hours. Turn meat once or twice. Remove cover; add more broth if needed. Roast, basting often with pan juices, for another hour or until meat is tender and browned.

Note: In recipes calling for chicken stock, you may use homemade or canned broth, or use bouillon made with instant granules and boiling water.

Noodle Ring _____

¼ cup butter
½ cup firmly packed dark brown
   sugar
½ cup pecan halves
½ pound thin egg noodles,
   cooked according to package
   directions
2 eggs, lightly beaten
¼ cup butter, melted
1 teaspoon cinnamon
1 teaspoon nutmeg
½ cup sugar
½ teaspoon salt

Preheat oven to 350° F. In the bottom of a 6-cup mold, melt butter. Add brown sugar; press mixture into bottom of pan. Press pecans firmly into butter, flat side up, in an attractive pattern. Place noodles in a large mixing bowl. Add remaining ingredients; toss to mix. Place noodles over topping in mold. Bake for 1 hour. Unmold onto a serving platter.

Labor Day Dinner for the Family

Chocolate Acorns

3 egg whites
1 tablespoon vinegar
¼ teaspoon salt
1 cup sugar
1 teaspoon vanilla
½ pound blanched ground almonds
4 squares, 1 ounce each, unsweetened chocolate
1 cup semisweet chocolate chips, melted
½ cup finely chopped pistachios

Preheat oven to 250° F. In a large mixing bowl, beat egg whites until soft peaks form. Beat in vinegar and salt. Add sugar; continue beating until stiff peaks form. Fold in vanilla, almonds, and unsweetened chocolate. Drop by heaping teaspoonfuls 1 inch apart onto a greased cookie sheet. Bake for 25 to 30 minutes. When cookies are cool, dip halfway into melted chocolate, then roll in pistachios. Makes 5 dozen.

Cream Puffs

½ cup butter *or* margarine
1 cup water
1 cup all-purpose flour
¼ teaspoon salt
4 eggs
  Confectioners' sugar
  Chocolate syrup, if desired

Preheat oven to 400° F. In a saucepan, melt butter. Add water; bring to a boil. In a bowl, stir together flour and salt. Add to water all at once; stir vigorously. Cook, stirring constantly, until mixture forms a ball and leaves side of pan. Remove from heat; cool 5 minutes. Add eggs, 1 at a time, beating well after each addition. Drop batter by heaping tablespoonfuls 3 inches apart onto cookie sheets. Bake 30 minutes until golden brown and puffed. Remove from oven; split. Remove any uncooked dough. Fill with ice cream or whipped cream. Dust with confectioners' sugar. Drizzle with chocolate syrup.

Halloween Party for the Kids

Menu for 6 to 8

Witches' Brew Cider
Hot Dog Surprises
Skillet Sombrero Pie
Monster Cookies
Caramel Apples

Witches' Brew Cider

4 cups apple cider
2 cans (6 ounces *each*) frozen
　lemonade concentrate,
　thawed
2 cups water
8 cinnamon sticks
　Lemon slices

Into a large saucepan, pour cider, lemonade concentrate, and water; stir. Over medium heat, bring cider to a simmer. Pour into cups. Place a cinnamon stick and a lemon slice in each cup.

Hot Dog Surprises

8 hot dogs, minced
⅓ cup grated American cheese
2 hard-boiled eggs, peeled and
　chopped
3 tablespoons pickle relish
1 teaspoon prepared mustard
½ teaspoon garlic salt
8 hot dog buns

Preheat oven to 375° F. In a large mixing bowl, stir together all ingredients except buns. Partially hollow out centers of buns; fill with hot dog mixture. Wrap each bun in aluminum foil, sealing securely. Place on cookie sheets. Bake for 10 to 12 minutes.

Skillet Sombrero Pie

1 pound ground beef
1 package (10 ounces) frozen
  corn, thawed
1 can (8 ounces) tomato sauce
1 can (16 ounces) tomatoes
1 tablespoon instant minced
  onion
1 package (1¾ ounces) chili
  seasoning mix
1 package (6 ounces) corn chips
½ cup grated Cheddar cheese

In a large skillet over medium heat, sauté beef until browned. Stir in corn, tomato sauce, tomatoes, onion, and seasoning mix. Reduce heat. Simmer 10 minutes. Arrange chips in ring around edge of skillet. Sprinkle cheese over meat mixture; heat until cheese melts, 3 to 5 minutes. Serve pie directly from skillet.

Caramel Apples

1½ cups chopped peanuts
6 firm apples, washed and dried
1 teaspoon vanilla
1 teaspoon baking soda
¾ cup sugar
½ cup butter
⅛ cup white corn syrup

Place peanuts in a shallow bowl; set aside. Insert wooden skewers into the stem end of apples. In a small dish, stir together vanilla and baking soda; set aside. In a heavy saucepan, place sugar, butter, and corn syrup. Cook over medium heat, stirring to blend. Continue to cook until mixture reaches 300° F. on a candy thermometer. Stir in vanilla mixture. Dip and twist apples in hot caramel until coated. Roll apples in nuts. Place on waxed paper to harden.

Monster Cookies

2 eggs
½ cup butter *or* margarine,
  softened
½ cup packed light brown sugar
½ cup granulated sugar
½ cup peanut butter
1 teaspoon vanilla
1½ cups flour
½ cup quick-cooking rolled oats
1 teaspoon baking soda
1 package (7 ounces) candy-
  coated chocolate pieces *or*
  1 package (6 ounces)
  semisweet chocolate chips

Preheat oven to 350° F. In a mixing bowl, stir together eggs, butter, brown sugar, granulated sugar, peanut butter, and vanilla; blend well. Stir in remaining ingredients. For each cookie, drop 2 tablespoons dough 3 inches apart on baking sheet. Bake 10 to 12 minutes. Remove cookies from baking sheet to a wire rack to cool. Store in an airtight container.

Thanksgiving Brunch

Menu for 12

Clam Dip • Scallop Mousse
Baked Canadian Bacon • Cucumber and Onion Salad
Pumpkin Bread • Treasure Toffee Cake
Brie in a Coat • Apple Cider Punch

Clam Dip

16 ounces cream cheese
1 cup sour cream
2 cans (6½ ounces *each*) minced
  or chopped clams, drained
2 green onions, chopped
¼ cup finely chopped pimiento
2 teaspoons finely chopped
  jalapeno pepper
2 tablespoons lemon juice
2 teaspoons Worcestershire
  sauce

In a mixing bowl, beat cream cheese with sour cream until well blended. Stir in remaining ingredients. Cover and chill. Serve with corn or tortilla chips.

Scallop Mousse

5 tablespoons butter
4 tablespoons all-purpose flour
½ teaspoon salt
¼ teaspoon white pepper
¼ teaspoon nutmeg
1 cup heavy cream
2 cups milk
4 eggs
2 pounds scallops, pureed

Preheat oven to 350° F. Butter a 2-quart casserole. Place casserole in a slightly larger pan filled with water to a depth of 2 inches. In a large saucepan over medium heat, melt butter; whisk in flour until flour is absorbed. Add salt, pepper, and nutmeg. Blend in heavy cream and milk; heat and stir until mixture thickens. Remove from heat. Add eggs, 1 at a time, beating well after each addition. Stir in scallops. Pour into prepared casserole. Bake for 65 minutes.

Skillet Sombrero Pie, 41
Monster Cookies, 41
Witches' Brew Cider, 40

Thanksgiving Brunch

Baked Canadian Bacon

3 pounds Canadian bacon
1 orange, cut into thin slices
Whole cloves
½ cup molasses
¼ cup water
½ cup orange juice
¼ cup sugar
¼ teaspoon dry mustard

Preheat oven to 325° F. Remove casing from bacon and place, fat side up, in a baking pan. Bake for 2 hours. Attach orange slices to bacon with cloves. In a small bowl, mix together remaining ingredients. Pour over bacon. Bake, basting often, for 30 minutes.

Cucumber and Onion Salad

4 medium cucumbers, peeled and sliced thin
2 large Bermuda onions, sliced very thin
1 cup fresh chopped mint *or* parsley
½ cup red wine
1 cup salad oil
5 shallots *or* green onions, minced
Salt and pepper to taste

Arrange cucumbers in an overlapping circular pattern on a large salad plate. Scatter onions over cucumbers. In a jar with a tight-fitting lid, combine vinegar, oil, shallots, salt, and pepper. Shake to blend. Drizzle salad dressing over vegetables. Sprinkle with chopped mint.

Pumpkin Bread

1 cup firmly packed light brown sugar
½ cup granulated sugar
1 cup cooked *or* canned pumpkin
½ cup vegetable oil
2 eggs, beaten
2 cups all-purpose flour
1 teaspoon baking soda
½ teaspoon salt
½ teaspoon nutmeg
½ teaspoon cinnamon
½ teaspoon ginger
1 cup golden raisins
½ cup chopped walnuts
¼ cup water

Preheat oven to 350° F. Oil a 9 x 5-inch loaf pan. In a mixing bowl, stir together brown sugar, granulated sugar, pumpkin, oil, and eggs. Beat until blended. In a separate bowl, stir together flour, soda, salt, and spices. Add to pumpkin mixture; blend well. Stir in raisins, nuts, and water. Spoon into prepared loaf pan. Bake for 65 to 75 minutes or until a wooden pick inserted near the center comes out clean. Cool in the pan for 10 minutes. Turn out on a wire rack to cool completely.

Apple Cider Punch

2 quarts apple cider
4 cups cranberry juice
2 cups orange juice
2 cans (12 ounces) apricot
  nectar
2 cups sugar
4 sticks cinnamon
  Orange slices studded with
  whole cloves

In a large kettle, combine all ingredients except orange slices. Simmer for 15 to 20 minutes. Garnish punch with floating clove-studded orange slices. Serve hot.

Treasure Toffee Cake

¼ cup sugar
1 teaspoon cinnamon
¼ teaspoon nutmeg
2 cups flour
1 cup sugar
1½ teaspoons baking powder
1 teaspoon baking soda
¼ teaspoon salt
1 teaspoon vanilla
1 cup sour cream
½ cup butter, softened
2 eggs
¼ cup chopped nuts
3 chocolate toffee bars
  (1⅛ ounces *each*), coarsely
  crushed
¼ cup melted butter
  Confectioners' sugar

Preheat oven to 325° F. Butter and flour a 10-inch bundt pan. In a small bowl, stir together cinnamon and sugar. In a mixing bowl, combine remaining ingredients except nuts, candy bars, and melted butter. Beat until all ingredients are well blended and the batter is light. Spoon half of the batter into prepared pan. Sprinkle with 2 tablespoons cinnamon-sugar mixture. Spoon remaining mixture into pan. Top with remaining cinnamon-sugar mixture. Top with nuts and chopped candy. Pour melted butter over all. Bake 45 to 50 minutes. Cool in pan 5 minutes. Remove from pan; dust with confectioners' sugar.

Brie in a Coat

12-inch round of Brie, paper
  wrapping removed
½ cup confectioners' sugar
½ cup sliced almonds

Place brie on a cookie sheet. Sprinkle sugar evenly over the cheese. Arrange the sliced almonds in an attractive pattern over sugar. Preheat the broiler to 450° F. Place cheese under the broiler for 1½ minutes or just until the sugar melts and starts to bubble. Serve with sliced fresh fruit.

Thanksgiving Dinner

Menu for 10 to 12

Cranberry Pineapple Salad
Carrot Curls and Radish Fans
Zucchini Custard Casserole
Roast Turkey with Wild Rice Stuffing
Brussels Sprouts • Sweet Potato Bake
Braided Filled Onion Loaf
Pecan Pie
Lace Cookies
Cranberry Jelly Candy

Cranberry Pineapple Salad

1 can (8 ounces) crushed
  pineapple, packed in juice,
  drained; reserve juice
2 tablespoons lemon juice
1 package (3 ounces) raspberry-
  flavored gelatin
1 can (14 ounces) cranberry
  sauce
¾ cup chopped celery

In a saucepan, mix together reserved juice, ½ cup water, and lemon juice; bring to a boil. Remove from heat; add gelatin; stir until gelatin dissolves. Add cranberry sauce; stir thoroughly. Refrigerate until mixture begins to set. Stir in pineapple and celery. Refrigerate until firm.

Brussels Sprouts

2½-3 pounds small brussels
  sprouts, ends trimmed and cut
  with an "X"
¼ cup butter
1 tablespoon prepared mustard
  Salt and pepper to taste

In a saucepan, cook brussels sprouts in boiling salted water until barely tender, about 10 minutes; drain. In a large skillet, heat butter. Stir in mustard and simmer until blended, stirring constantly. Add brussels sprouts; toss to coat. Season with salt and pepper.

Treasure Toffee Cake, 45

Sweet Potato Bake

1 can (8 ounces) pineapple
    chunks packed in juice,
    undrained
5 cups mashed sweet potatoes
    or yams
½ teaspoon salt
2 tablespoons butter
1 small package miniature
    marshmallows
⅓ cup pecan halves

Preheat oven to 350° F. Cut pineapple chunks in half. In a bowl, stir together pineapple chunks and juice, potatoes, salt, and butter. Place half of the potato mixture in a buttered casserole. Top with half the marshmallows. Add remaining potato mixture. Arrange pecans on top. Cover and bake for 30 minutes. Remove cover for last 10 minutes of baking. Add remaining marshmallows. This can be made the night before and refrigerated. Add the nuts and remaining marshmallows just before baking.

Zucchini Custard Casserole

1 pound zucchini
1 teaspoon salt
¼ cup chopped onion
6 eggs
1 cup milk
½ teaspoon basil
½ teaspoon oregano
2 tablespoons all-purpose flour
2 cups shredded Cheddar
    cheese, divided

Preheat oven to 350° F. Cut zucchini crosswise into ¼-inch slices, then into quarter slices. Place zucchini in colander; set colander in a bowl or in the sink. Sprinkle zucchini with salt; stir thoroughly. Let stand for 10 minutes. In a medium saucepan, bring 1 cup water to a boil. Add zucchini and onion. Simmer, covered, over medium heat until zucchini is tender-crisp, about 5 to 7 minutes; drain. Turn into a 9 x 9-inch baking dish or shallow 1½-quart casserole. Beat eggs, milk, and seasonings with fork until blended. Sprinkle flour over zucchini and toss lightly. Pour in egg mixture, then add 1½ cups of the cheese. Bake about 30 minutes, or until knife inserted near center comes out clean. Sprinkle remaining cheese over top of casserole.

Carrot Curls and Radish Fans

1 pound carrots
2 packages radishes

With a vegetable parer, cut carrots into thin lengthwise strips. Roll up slices; secure with wooden picks. In a bowl filled with ice cubes and water, place carrot curls. Slice radishes with parallel cuts reaching almost to stem end; do not cut through. Place radishes in the ice water with carrot curls. When ready to serve, drain vegetables; remove picks.

Thanksgiving Dinner

Braided Filled Onion Loaf

1 package active dry yeast
¼ cup lukewarm water
4 cups all-purpose flour
¼ cup sugar
1½ teaspoons salt
½ cup hot water
½ cup milk
¼ cup butter, room temperature
1 egg
¼ cup butter, melted
¾ cup finely chopped onion
1 tablespoon freshly grated
   Parmesan cheese
1 tablespoon sesame seed
1 teaspoon garlic salt

In a large mixing bowl, dissolve yeast in water. Add 2 cups of the flour, sugar, salt, water, milk, ¼ cup butter, and egg. Stir until all ingredients are blended. Gradually stir in remaining flour until dough leaves sides of bowl. Place dough in an oiled bowl; turn to oil dough. Cover loosely and place in a warm area to rise until doubled in bulk, about 1¼ hours. Preheat oven to 350° F. In a bowl, mix together melted butter, onion, Parmesan cheese, sesame seed, and garlic salt. Punch down dough. On a lightly floured board, knead dough until smooth and elastic. Roll dough to a 12 x 18-inch rectangle. Spread filling on dough. Cut dough lengthwise into three 4 x 18-inch strips. Roll up each strip lengthwise; seal edges. On a buttered cookie sheet, braid strips, keeping seam sides down. Set bread aside to rise in a draft free area for 1 hour. Bake for 45 to 50 minutes. Cool on a wire rack.

Roast Turkey

1 turkey (10 to 12 pounds)
   Wild Rice Stuffing
1 cup melted butter *or*
   margarine

Preheat oven to 325° F. Stuff neck and body cavities of turkey with Wild Rice Stuffing. Truss bird and place on a rack in a shallow roasting pan. Roast, uncovered, 4 hours or to an internal temperature of 190° F. When turkey begins to brown, cover lightly with a tent of aluminum foil. Baste occasionally with butter during roasting.

Wild Rice Stuffing

3 cups chicken broth *or* bouillon
1 cup raw wild rice
½ cup butter
1 cup diced celery
1 can (4 ounces) mushrooms
¼ cup minced onion
   Salt and pepper to taste
½ teaspoon sage

In a saucepan, bring broth to a boil; add rice. Simmer, covered, 30 to 45 minutes or until broth is absorbed. In a skillet, melt butter; sauté celery, mushrooms, and onion for 3 minutes. Stir in seasonings. Stir vegetable mixture into cooked rice.

Thanksgiving Dinner

Pecan Pie

¼ cup butter, room temperature
½ cup sugar
1 cup light corn syrup
¼ teaspoon salt
3 eggs
1 cup pecan halves
1 9-inch unbaked pastry shell
  Sweetened whipped cream

Preheat oven to 350° F. In a mixing bowl, cream butter with sugar until fluffy. Add corn syrup and salt; blend well. Add eggs, 1 at a time, beating well after each addition. Stir in pecans. Pour into pie shell and bake for 50 minutes or until a knife inserted in the center of the filling comes out clean. Cool and serve with whipped cream.

Cranberry Jelly Candy

1 can (16 ounces) jellied
  cranberry sauce
3 packages (3 ounces *each*)
  cherry, raspberry or orange-
  flavored gelatin
1 cup sugar
½ bottle (3 ounces) liquid fruit
  pectin
1 cup chopped nuts
  Additional sugar *or* flaked
  coconut

Place cranberry sauce in a saucepan; beat until smooth. Bring to a boil over medium heat. Stir in gelatin and sugar; simmer 10 minutes, stirring frequently until gelatin is dissolved. Remove from heat. Stir in fruit pectin. Add nuts and stir 10 minutes to keep nuts from floating. Pour into buttered 9-inch square pan. Chill until firm, about 2 hours. Sprinkle sugar or flaked coconut on a sheet of waxed paper. Turn candy out onto paper; cut into ¾-inch squares with spatula dipped in warm water. Roll each square in sugar. After about an hour, roll in sugar again to prevent stickiness.

Lace Cookies

¼ cup butter
¼ cup vegetable shortening
½ cup light corn syrup
¾ cup packed light brown sugar
1 cup unsifted all-purpose flour
¾ cup ground pecans
1 cup semisweet chocolate
  pieces

Combine butter, vegetable shortening, corn syrup, and sugar in a medium saucepan; bring to a boil. Remove from heat. Mix in flour and nuts. Drop batter by rounded teaspoons onto a greased and floured cookie sheet, 3 inches apart. Bake at 325° F. for 8 to 10 minutes. Cool 1 minute, remove from cookie sheet with a spatula. Melt chocolate in the top of a double boiler over hot (not boiling) water, stirring until smooth. Brush each cookie with chocolate.

Christmas Open House

Strawberry Punch

½ gallon vanilla ice cream,
   softened
2 quarts strawberry soda
2 quarts ginger ale
1 quart strawberries, hulled

In a punch bowl, place ice cream, strawberry soda, and ginger ale. Stir to blend. Add strawberries. Let stand for 1½ hours. Stir before serving.

Spiced Wine

3 quarts claret
   Grated peel of 3 oranges
   Grated peel of 3 lemons
12 cinnamon sticks
1½ teaspoons nutmeg
12 whole cloves, tied in a
   cheesecloth bag
6 tablespoons sugar

In a large kettle, simmer all ingredients for 10 minutes. Remove cloves before serving.

Turkey Quiche

1 frozen deep dish pie shell
4 cups cubed cooked turkey
½ cup chopped onion
1 tomato, chopped
4 ounces Monterey Jack cheese
4 ounces Cheddar cheese
1 cup sour cream
1 teaspoon tarragon
¼ teaspoon garlic powder
5 eggs, lightly beaten

Preheat oven to 350° F. In frozen pie shell place turkey, onion, and tomato. In a small bowl, stir together Monterey Jack and Cheddar. Sprinkle ½ of the cheese mixture over ingredients in pie shell. Add sour cream and seasonings to eggs. Pour egg mixture into pie shell. Top with remaining cheese. Bake for 45 minutes or until set.

Lamb Ring with Potato Puffs

2 pounds lean ground lamb
3 eggs, divided
½ cup chopped green pepper
2 tablespoons minced onion
1 tablespoon fresh chopped
   parsley
1 teaspoon salt
¼ teaspoon pepper
3 cups mashed potatoes

Preheat oven to 350° F. In a large bowl, combine lamb, 2 eggs, green pepper, onion, parsley, salt, and pepper; blend well. Press mixture into an 8-inch ring mold. Bake at 350° F. for 1 hour. Spoon off any accumulated fat. Unmold onto a shallow non-stick baking pan. Beat remaining egg into mashed potatoes. Mound potatoes around lamb ring. Raise oven temperature to 425° F. Bake for 10 minutes or until potatoes are lightly browned.

Holiday Slaw

1 head cabbage, shredded
1 onion, minced
1 red bell pepper, chopped
1 green pepper, chopped
1 cup mayonnaise
4 tablespoons red wine vinegar
3 tablespoons sugar
   Salt and pepper to taste

In a deep bowl, toss cabbage, onion, and peppers. In a bowl, stir together remaining ingredients. Stir mayonnaise mixture into vegetables. Cover and chill until ready to serve.

Anchovies and Pimientos

3 jars (6 ounces *each*) sweet
   roasted peppers, drained and
   cut into strips
3 cans (2 ounces *each*) anchovies
2 tablespoons olive oil
3 cloves garlic, minced
1 teaspoon oregano

Arrange peppers attractively on a serving platter. Drain anchovies; arrange over peppers. Sprinkle with olive oil, minced garlic, and oregano. Cover loosely and chill until ready to serve.

Seafood Crepes

8 tablespoons butter
6 tablespoons flour
2 cups half-and-half
1 cup milk
½ cup sherry
2 cups lightly packed shredded brick cheese, divided
1½ pounds small shrimp
12 ounces scallops, sliced
1 pound mushrooms, sliced
2 tablespoons chopped pimiento
2 tablespoons chopped green pepper
1 teaspoon Worcestershire sauce
2 teaspoons salt
Dash Tabasco sauce
28 Crepes

Prepare Crepes; set aside. Preheat oven to 350° F. In a 2-quart saucepan over medium heat, melt 6 tablespoons butter. Stir in flour. Cook, stirring constantly, until smooth and bubbly. Add half-and-half and milk; bring to a boil, stirring constantly. Boil 1 minute. Add sherry and 1 cup cheese. Heat and stir over low heat until cheese melts. Set aside. In a large skillet, melt remaining butter; sauté shrimp, scallops, and mushrooms until mushrooms are tender. Remove from heat. Stir in remaining ingredients and 1½ cups cream sauce. Place about ¼ cup seafood mixture down center of each of 28 Crepes; fold sides over to enclose filling. Spread ½ cup cream sauce evenly over the bottom of two 9 x 13-inch baking pans. Place Crepes seam sides down in pans. Pour remaining sauce over center of Crepes. Bake, covered, 25 minutes. Uncover; sprinkle cheese evenly over center of each Crepe. Bake for 2 minutes or until cheese melts. Sprinkle with paprika.

Crepes

2 eggs
1 cup plus 2 tablespoons milk
1 cup flour
1 tablespoon vegetable oil
⅛ teaspoon salt
2 tablespoons melted butter

In a medium bowl, beat eggs. Add milk, flour, oil, and salt. Beat again until batter is smooth. Cover and refrigerate 2 hours. Preheat a 6 or 8-inch omelet pan. Brush with a little of the butter. Pour about 3 tablespoons batter into pan and cook 2 to 3 minutes, rotating pan as batter is poured. Cook until lightly browned on bottom. Loosen edges with spatula and gently lift crepe. Stack between pieces of waxed paper. Keep covered. Makes 14.

Orange Madeleines

3 eggs
1 tablespoon freshly squeezed
  orange juice
1 cup sugar
2 tablespoons grated orange
  peel
1⅓ cups cake flour
  ½ teaspoon baking powder
  ¼ teaspoon salt
  ½ cup butter, melted and cooled
  Confectioners' sugar

Preheat oven to 350° F. Butter and flour madeleine pan (available in gourmet shops). Beat eggs, orange juice, and sugar in a large mixing bowl. Continue beating until light and fluffy. Mix in orange peel. Sift together flour, baking powder, and salt. Stir in butter. Fill molds half-full with batter. Bake 12 minutes. Unmold cookies onto a serving plate. Refill mold and repeat until all batter is used. Sprinkle madeleines with confectioners' sugar.

Chocolate Kirsch Cake

8 eggs, separated, room
  temperature
1 cup sugar
1 teaspoon vanilla
8 tablespoons kirsch, divided
3 ounces semisweet chocolate,
  melted
1 cup cake flour
1 semisweet chocolate bar
  (8 ounces)
3 cups heavy cream
½ cup confectioners' sugar
1 can (16 ounces) sour pitted
  cherries, drained
10 whole maraschino cherries
  with stems

Preheat oven to 350° F. Butter and flour two 8-inch layer cake pans. In a small mixing bowl, combine egg yolks, sugar, vanilla, and 4 tablespoons kirsch. Beat until mixture doubles in volume. Add chocolate in a slow steady stream, mixing until blended. Sprinkle flour over mixture; blend well. Beat egg whites into chocolate batter. Pour batter into prepared cake pans. Bake for 15 to 20 minutes, or until cake tests done. Invert cakes on a rack; cool. Over waxed paper, scrape chocolate bar with a vegetable peeler to make chocolate curls. Freeze chocolate curls until ready to use. Whip cream until it begins to thicken. Gradually sprinkle sugar, 4 tablespoons at a time, over cream, beating until all the sugar has been added and soft peaks form. Cut each cake layer into 2 layers with a serrated knife. Place 1 layer on a serving platter. Sprinkle 1 tablespoon of kirsch over cake. Spread layer with whipped cream. Arrange ⅓ of the sour cherries over cream. Repeat layers twice. Top with remaining cake layer. Spread remaining whipped cream around sides and top of cake. Gently arrange chocolate curls on sides of cake. Decorate top of the cake with stemmed cherries. Chill cake until ready to serve.

Gingerbread House

Gingerbread Dough

5 cups shortening
5 cups brown sugar, packed
5 tablespoons cinnamon
6 tablespoons ginger
10 eggs
5 cups dark corn syrup
8 teaspoons baking soda
28 cups flour

Cream shortening, sugar, and spices in a large mixing bowl. Beat in eggs. Add corn syrup; blend well. Mix baking soda and flour together in separate bowl. Add ½ of the flour mixture to creamed ingredients; beat well. Stir in remaining flour mixture; beat until smooth. Wrap airtight. Chill at least 5 hours or overnight. Makes enough dough for house, trees, reindeer, and fence in photo.

Decorator Icing

4 pounds confectioners' sugar
12 egg whites
2 teaspoons cream of tartar

In a large mixing bowl, beat all ingredients together for about 10 minutes or until stiff peaks form. Cover with damp towel; take out only as needed, as this frosting hardens quickly. Note: Icing may be stored for several days in refrigerator. Beat again before using.

Christmas Wreath Candy

⅓ cup butter or margarine
20 marshmallows
   Green food coloring
2¼ cups cornflakes

Prepare this candy just before you plan to use it, as it hardens quickly. In microwave or top of double boiler, melt butter and marshmallows. Add food coloring as desired. Remove from heat. Add cornflakes and stir until well coated.

For assembly and decorating instructions, see page 59.

Christmas Open House

To cut out house:

Draw pattern pieces on cardboard or paper according to sizes indicated below, or as desired. Cut out pattern. On lightly greased, *inverted* cookie sheet, roll out dough to ³/₁₆″ thickness. Dust pattern pieces with flour. Place patterns on dough. Cut through dough with sharp knife. Without moving cut-out pieces, remove patterns and excess dough. Bake in place on *inverted* cookie sheet at 375° F. until lightly browned. Check cookie edges once during baking, straightening edges with a knife, if necessary. When dough is baked and still warm, loosen pieces with spatula. Do not remove from cookie sheets until completely cool. Use same dough and same procedure to make trees, reindeer, and fence, rolling dough somewhat thinner for smaller pieces. Cut tree cookies using pattern pictured. Shape reindeer using cookie cutters. For fence, cut strips of dough in varying lengths. Let baked dough sit 5-6 hours before assembling house.

To assemble house:

Use pastry bag with number 4 or 5 tip throughout assembly process. Mortar house with decorator icing, beginning with sides, front and back of house. Wherever seams meet, mortar with icing and press together gently. Prop pieces up with cans until icing sets. Wait overnight before putting on roof. Then thickly mortar with icing where front and back and side pieces meet roof. Press pieces together carefully. Mortar along seam at peak of roof. Assemble chimney pieces and mortar to roof. Let set 1 to 2 hours before decorating.

To decorate house:

Using same decorator icing and pastry bag, ice 12 vanilla wafers and dust with red sprinkles. Secure wafers with decorator icing, as pictured. Loop shingles of icing on roof. Thickly squiggle icing unevenly on edges of roof to simulate snow. Ice life savers to side of house. Line silver beads along roof top.

Decorate front of house with jelly rings, life savers, gumdrops, and red hots as pictured. Outline door with icing; attach gumdrop door knob; set aside.

With Christmas Wreath Candy, form wreath around door. Accent with red candy or icing to resemble holly. Mortar or set door in place, leaving slightly ajar.

Outline path with decorator icing and peppermint candy. Mortar gingerbread fence pieces together; place where desired. Sprinkle trees and reindeer lightly with sifted confectioners' sugar. Sprinkle confectioners' sugar around house to simulate snow. Fluff cotton to simulate chimney smoke.

Pattern Specifications:

> walls (2 pieces): 4″ x 12″
> roof (2 pieces): 14″ x 11″
> front and back: 12″ x 12″, cutting to form
>   roof peak, window, and door

Christmas Dinner

Menu for 10

Hot Crabmeat Appetizer
Ham Balls
Citrus Salad
Sour Cream Scalloped Potatoes with Ham
Broccoli Casserole
Glazed Cornish Game Hens
Sicilian Cake

Hot Crabmeat Appetizer

2 tablespoons milk
16 ounces cream cheese, softened
2 cans (6½ ounces *each*) flaked crabmeat
¼ cup instant chopped onion
1 teaspoon cream-style horseradish
1 teaspoon salt
White pepper to taste

Preheat oven to 375° F. In a small bowl, combine milk and cream cheese; blend well. Blend in remaining ingredients. Mound in a baking dish. Bake for 15 minutes. Serve hot with crackers.

Ham Balls

1 pound ground beef
1 pound ground ham
2 eggs
1½ cups cracker crumbs
1 cup firmly packed light brown sugar
1 teaspoon prepared mustard
½ cup water
½ cup vinegar

Preheat oven to 350° F. In a large bowl, mix together beef, ham, eggs, and cracker crumbs until well blended. Shape into balls; place on a large, rimmed baking sheet. In a separate bowl, stir together remaining ingredients until well blended. Pour over ham balls. Bake 1½ hours. Makes about 60.

Citrus Salad

8 large oranges, peeled and
   thinly sliced
2 medium Bermuda onions,
   thinly sliced
¼ cup olive oil
¼ cup red wine vinegar
½ teaspoon salt
½ teaspoon white pepper
1 head Boston lettuce

In a mixing bowl, mix oranges and onions. In a jar with a tight-fitting lid, combine oil, vinegar, salt, and pepper. Shake until blended. Pour over oranges and onions; toss lightly to mix. Arrange lettuce on chilled salad plates. Arrange tossed oranges and onions on lettuce.

Sour Cream Scalloped Potatoes with Ham

2 slices (½-inch thick *each*)
   smoked ham
8 medium potatoes, sliced thick
1 can (10¾ ounces) condensed
   cream of mushroom soup
1 cup sour cream
1 teaspoon salt
1 cup sliced onions
½ teaspoon white pepper
1 cup shredded Cheddar cheese

Preheat oven to 325° F. Butter a 3-quart casserole. Cut ham into 8 serving pieces. Slice potatoes. Combine soup, sour cream, salt, and pepper. In prepared casserole, alternate layers of ham, potatoes, and onions with sour cream mixture, ending with sour cream. Top with shredded cheese. Cover casserole loosely with aluminum foil. Bake for 2½ hours.

Broccoli Casserole

2 packages (10 ounces *each*)
   frozen cut broccoli
2 eggs, well beaten
1 can condensed Cheddar
   cheese soup
½ teaspoon crushed oregano
1 can (8 ounces) stewed
   tomatoes, cut up
3 tablespoons freshly grated
   Parmesan cheese

Cook frozen broccoli in unsalted water 5 minutes or until broccoli is tender. Drain well. In a mixing bowl, combine beaten eggs, soup, and oregano; stir in stewed tomatoes and broccoli. Pour mixture into a 10 x 6-inch baking dish. Sprinkle with Parmesan cheese. Bake uncovered at 350° F. for 30 minutes or until heated through.

Glazed Cornish Game Hens —————————

10 Cornish game hens
  Salt and pepper to taste
  Butter
  Garlic powder
  Paprika
½ teaspoon melted butter
1 jar (12 ounces) currant jelly

Preheat oven to 350° F. Sprinkle inside of hens with salt and pepper. Tie legs together with string. Rub hens with softened butter; season to taste with garlic powder and paprika.

Place hens on a rack in a shallow pan. Brush with melted butter. Roast for 1 hour, basting once with melted butter. In a saucepan, heat currant jelly. Spoon over hens. Return hens to oven; roast, basting occasionally, an additional 30 minutes or until hens are tender and browned. Transfer hens to a serving platter. Remove strings. Spoon remaining warm jelly over hens.

Sicilian Cake —————————

1 baked pound cake
⅓ cup dark rum
1 pound creamed ricotta cheese
⅓ cup sugar
¾ cup semisweet chocolate bits, chopped
⅓ cup candied cherries
⅓ cup candied orange peel
2 tablespoons all-purpose flour
  Chocolate Frosting

Cut cake into 4 horizontal layers with a serrated knife. Sprinkle rum over cake layers; set aside. In a mixing bowl, beat cheese and sugar until fluffy. Stir in chocolate. In a small bowl, toss cherries and orange peel with flour. Place fruit on a breadboard or in a food processor; chop coarsely. Add chopped fruit to cheese mixture; stir thoroughly. Place one layer of cake on a serving platter. Spread with ⅓ cheese mixture. Repeat until all 4 cake layers are stacked. Do not cover top of cake with cheese mixture. Cover cake with plastic wrap; refrigerate for 1 hour. Frost top and sides of cake with Chocolate Frosting. To serve, cut into very thin slices.

Chocolate Frosting

3 cups confectioners' sugar
3 ounces unsweetened chocolate, melted and cooled
¼ cup butter
1 egg yolk

Sift sugar into a large mixing bowl. Stir in chocolate, butter, and egg yolk. Beat until smooth.

Book IV Index